EMOTION:

Bodily Change

An Enduring Problem in Psychology

SELECTED READINGS

Edited by

DOUGLAS K. CANDLAND

Bucknell University

AN INSIGHT BOOK

D. VAN NOSTRAND COMPANY, INC.

PRINCETON, NEW JERSEY

TORONTO   LONDON

NEW YORK

D. VAN NOSTRAND COMPANY, INC.
120 Alexander St., Princeton, New Jersey
(*Principal Office*)
24 West 40 Street, New York 18, New York

D. VAN NOSTRAND COMPANY, LTD.
358, Kensington High Street, London, W.14, England

D. VAN NOSTRAND COMPANY (Canada), LTD.
25 Hollinger Road, Toronto 16, Canada

PRINTED IN THE UNITED STATES OF AMERICA

Foreword

By the Editors of the Series

In the field of psychology we believe that the student ought to get the "feel" of experimentation by reading original source materials. In this way he can acquire a better understanding of the discipline by seeing scientific ideas grow and change. However, one of the main problems in teaching is the limited availability of these sources, which communicate most effectively the personality of the author and the excitement of ongoing research.

For these reasons we have decided to edit several books,* each devoted to a particular problem in psychology. In every case we attempt to select problems that have been and are controversial—that have been and still are alive. We intend to present these problems as a set of selected original articles, arranged in historical order and in order of progress in the field. We believe that it is important for the student to see that theories and researches build on what has gone before; that one study leads to another, that theory leads to research and then to revision of theory. We believe that *telling* the student this does not make the same kind of impression as letting him see it happen in actuality. The idea is for the student to read and build ideas for himself.

Suggestions for Use—These readings books can be used by the student in either of two ways. They are organized so that, with the help of the instructor (or of the students if used in seminars), a topic can be covered at length and in depth. This would necessitate lectures or discussions on articles not covered in the series to fill in the gaps. On the other hand, each book taken alone will give a student a good idea of the problem being covered and its historical background as well as its present state and the direction it seems to be taking.

* (Pub. note: a sub-series within the Insight Book Series.)

110493

Preface

That the concept of "emotion" admits to a variety of definitions, theories, and methods of investigation is ample evidence that the concept qualifies as an enduring problem in psychology. Traditionally, the term "emotion" has included a variety of behaviors, some of which are readily observed (as the cry of a hurt child) while others are merely inferred from behavior (as the idea of love). It would seem that the availability of emotional phenomena for investigation would have encouraged research and resulted in the findings of satisfactory answers to the many problems concerned with emotion; however, as is true with so many other "obvious" phenomena, just the reverse has been true.

It has been argued (and is argued by some authors represented in this book) that emotion is such a large and ill-defined construct that it hampers both theory and research. Other authors argue that the problems of emotion are semantic problems. Other authors point out that emotion is merely a name for loosely related patterns of behavior. Whichever argument may eventually hold true, emotion has survived as the arrogant child of psychology: the more it is ignored and relegated to a place in the corner as "merely a semantic problem," the more arrogant and brutish it becomes to theory.

Perhaps the prognosis of, and certainly the difficulty with, emotion was aptly expressed by M. F. Meyer, who thirty years ago remarked:

> The whale has a twofold distinction among the fishes: first, when seen from a distance, it looms large among them; and second, on close examination, it is found to be no fish at all. Something like that I predict for the theory of emotions among the theories in psychological textbooks and periodicals (Meyer, M. F. That whale among the fishes—the theory of emotions. *Psychol. Rev.*, 1933, 40, p. 192).

*   *   *

In keeping with the ideal of this subseries as set forth in the foreword by the general editors of the series, this book was edited with the idea of giving the student "a good idea of the problem being covered and its historical background as well as its present state and the direction it seems to be taking." These readings were selected with the realization that it would not be possible to present all of the approaches to the study of emotion. Accordingly, this book has been edited with the idea of indicating the directions which research and theory on emotion have moved. Unhappily, this approach has required the elimination of many techniques and approaches which may very well prove to be better methods for the study of emotion as research continues.

Since the compiling of a book of readings requires that some selections be removed from the context in which they were written or with disregard of the purpose for which they were written, this work can serve only to indicate some of the "highlights" in the study of emotion. The references which comprise Part IV of this book are recommended for those readers who wish to continue with the study of emotion.

*   *   *

The editor is grateful for the advice of the general editors of this series, as well as to aid from Professor P. L. Harriman and the authors whose works are represented in this book. Professors Robert Leeper, Harold Schlosberg and Paul Thomas Young were especially generous with their time. Mrs. Mary Candland designed the cover and adapted some of the drawings and J. L. Culbertson, Mrs. Emily Foust, Z. M. Nagy, Mrs. Elizabeth Veening, D. W. Bloomquist, and Miss Clara Stoner assisted with the technical problems of preparing this book.

D. K. C.

Lewisburg, Pennsylvania
February 1962

Contents

PREFACE · v

PART I
PROBLEMS AND THEORY

1. EMOTIONAL BEHAVIOR · · · · · · · · · · · · · · · · · · · 3
   by M. A. Wenger, F. N. Jones, and M. H. Jones

2. WILLIAM JAMES ON EMOTION · · · · · · · · · · · · 11
   by William James

3. THE FEARS OF CHILDREN · · · · · · · · · · · · · · · 17
   by John B. Watson

4. AN EXPLANATION OF "EMOTIONAL" PHENOMENA WITHOUT THE USE OF THE CONCEPT "EMOTION" · 22
   by Elizabeth Duffy

5. MOTIVES AND EMOTION · · · · · · · · · · · · · · · · 35
   by Robert Ward Leeper and Peter Madison

PART II
METHODS AND TECHNIQUES

6. METHODS FOR THE STUDY OF FEELING AND EMOTION · 57
   by Paul Thomas Young

PART III
EXPERIMENTAL FINDINGS AND OBSERVATIONS

7. A LABORATORY STUDY OF FEAR: THE CASE OF PETER · 91
   by Mary Cover Jones

8. EMOTIONAL DEVELOPMENT IN EARLY IN-
   FANCY   100
      by Katharine M. Banham Bridges

9. EMOTIONAL BEHAVIOR OF THE RAT   126
      by Norman L. Munn

10. ON THE NATURE OF FEAR   139
      by D. O. Hebb

11. USE OF CONDITIONED AUTONOMIC RESPONSES
    IN THE STUDY OF ANXIETY   170
      by John I. Lacey, Robert L. Smith and
      Arnold Green

12. THE ALARM REACTION   187
      by P. C. Constantinides and Niall Carey

13. ULCERS IN "EXECUTIVE" MONKEYS   198
      by Joseph V. Brady

14. THE PHYSIOLOGY OF FEAR AND ANGER   208
      by Daniel H. Funkenstein

15. THE DESCRIPTION OF FACIAL EXPRESSIONS IN
    TERMS OF TWO DIMENSIONS   220
      by Harold Schlosberg

16. AN EXPERIMENTAL APPROACH TO THE ANAL-
    YSIS OF EMOTIONAL BEHAVIOR   235
      by Joseph V. Brady and Howard F. Hunt

PART IV

ADDITIONAL READINGS   253

INDEX   261

Part I
Problems and Theory

1

Emotional Behavior

M. A. WENGER, F. N. JONES, M. H. JONES
University of California, Los Angeles

The term "emotion" has been subjected to a variety of definitions, a fact which may very well account for the variety of theories which have been created to account for emotional processes. The following selection, which discusses some of the different approaches which have been made to the study of emotion, is by Professor M. A. Wenger and is taken from his chapter on "emotional behavior" which appears in his book with Professors F. N. Jones and M. H. Jones, Physiological Psychology (New York: Holt and Company, 1956) and is reprinted with permission of the authors and publisher. (The book is copyrighted by Holt, Rinehart and Winston, Inc.)

The reader interested in evaluating Professor Wenger's analysis of emotion more fully may wish to consult the original source.

Emotion is a peculiar word. Almost everyone thinks he understands what it means, until he attempts to define it. Then practically no one claims to understand it. Scientists who investigate it disagree. Philosophers, novelists, and others who write about it disagree. But, in the meantime, we all go about our individual ways, sometimes enjoying our "emotions," sometimes bemoaning them.

Emotion is many things for different people. For some it is a mental experience; for some it is a way of acting; for some it is a series of events occurring within our bodies; while for some it is a form of motivation. Many regard most emotion as "bad;" while others regard much emotion as "good." The Greeks wrote about emotion in much the same terms we use today, and sometimes it seems we have not learned very much about this subject during the last 20 to 25 centuries. Most of us still consider emotion important in life, however, regardless of how we define it or how well we think we understand it. But it is considered important for various reasons.

Those who consider most emotion as bad would hold that it should be understood so that we may better be able to minimize the disruptions in our lives that are attributed to it. They might speak of the nonutilitarian significance of emotion, cite evidence of the irrational judgments reached during fear or rage as compared with the rational judgments of unemotional contemplation, and emphasize the value of emotional control. We certainly should have to agree with them that sometimes emotion may do us harm; and, therefore, sometimes we should attempt to control it.

Those who consider much emotion as good would hold it important in enriching our lives, in removing the apathy of dullness. They might emphasize the value of emotion in learning, the value of anxiety in the construction of the codes of ethics and laws that make civilization possible, the impetus it affords to all thought and action. Here, too, we should have to agree in part. We all consider the unemotional person as either dull, or "cold-blooded" and calculating. We know that we remember well those situations which caused strong emotion in us. We know that anxieties for the future lead us to plan our lives; and we know that excitement, fear, or rage gives us strength for acts which ordinarily we would not be able to accomplish.

Recently another reason for considering emotion as important has pressed itself on us. It is the growing realization that many of our diseases—whether called "mental" or "physical"—are intimately related to emotion. It has long been common to regard the *neuroses* and *psychoses* as associated with preceding extreme emotion. More recently we have discovered that a host of *psychosomatic disorders*—for example, asthma, ulcers, high blood pressure, and various skin ailments—also are associated with emotion. All in all, regardless of whether we consider most emotion as good or bad, we cannot escape the conclusion that emotional behavior is important in everyday life. [A paragraph of the original is omitted at this point.]

EMOTION AS VISCERAL ACTION

The point of view that action of the internal or visceral parts of our bodies is the salient feature of emotion is both old and new. It is old in the sense that part of it was well described by Plato and Aristotle. It is new in the sense that much of it has been ignored or forgotten until recently, and in that the whole story has not yet been told.

Plato thought of emotion in terms of pleasure and pain and, with the early cynics, for him there could be no pleasure without prior pain. Aristotle gave us our first extensive classification of emotion and he used many terms which have followed us to this day. He emphasized the striving for pleasure and the attempted aversion of pain; thus, he might be referred to as the first dynamic psychologist. But he, Plato, and most of the early Greek writers emphasized that emotion primarily is an affair of the heart, the bowels, or the womb.

Such a theme runs through most descriptions of emotion (or passion, as it then was called) until the 18th century. By this time man had become convinced that the brain was important. Soon the brain came to be regarded as the "seat" of the passions (which by now usually were called emotions) and the subservient body was largely forgotten. Of course, the new breed of physicians never forgot it entirely but they were few and far between in a philosophical age. Gradually another breed appeared, who might be called "psychophysiologists"; and gradually we have witnessed a reinstatement of the importance of the affairs of the body in emotion. In short, there is a growing tendency to think about emotion in terms of patterns of psychophysiological response, particularly with respect to the functions mediated by the autonomic nervous system.

For some contemporary writers, emotion is a behavior pattern that occurs in the viscera and other bodily parts;

but any emotional experience that occurs in the cortex is secondary. For others, emotion is a cortical event which depends upon response patterns that have occurred elsewhere—in the viscera, in the skeletal muscles, in the hypothalamus, or in some combination of these three. For some of both groups, the bodily pattern must be preceded by a psychological event if it, or subsequent mental events, are to be called emotion.

There are two entirely different points of view represented here, of course, and each is qualified. Let us restate them more specifically.

Class I. Emotion is a noncortical bodily event; consciousness of emotion is a mental event which depends upon the prior bodily event.

Class II. Emotion is a mental event which depends in part upon other bodily events.

Although these two statements seem to be similar they actually are quite different. For example, substitute the term "motion" for "emotion" and read them again. If we were to accept this second definition of "motion" then it would follow that we could know little about motion in a newborn human infant or in an animal other than man. Yet statement II is precisely the way emotion is defined by many people (both scientists and laymen); although often they find it easy to infer emotion in infants and subhuman animals from what they then call "emotional expression." If such "expression" occurs in a decorticate animal (who, presumably, cannot really be experiencing emotion) it then is said to indicate "sham emotion." Such circumlocutions serve only to muddle further an important area of behavior. They are unnecessary if we employ definition I.

Let us now consider three subclasses of these two points of view:

Ia. Emotion is vasomotor disturbance. (This was the view of Lange (1), whose name often is erroneously combined with that of James.)

IIa. Emotion is a mental event. It is the feeling of changes occurring in the viscera and the skeletal muscles, which changes have been initiated directly by perception of an appropriate stimulus. (This is the view of James (2), who referred to "perception of the exciting fact.")

IIb. Emotion is a mental event. It depends upon changes in the hypothalamus which have been initiated by an appropriate stimulus. (This is the "thalamic theory" of Cannon and Bard (3)).

These last two points of view have dominated psychology throughout its recent development, but both leave much to be desired. Perhaps most to be regretted is the fact that both claim that some bodily events (be they visceral or skeletal as in IIa, or hypothalamic as in IIb) do not produce emotion; but neither specifies the nature of the appropriate stimuli for those changes that will produce emotion. Some writers attempt to resolve this problem by claiming that emotion occurs only when *learned* motives are involved; thus, suffocation or hunger would not be emotion or produce emotion, unless the threat to life was perceived and reacted to. Although such a view is commonly held and may appeal to you since you are used to it, we do not find it convincing. It would have to deny emotions to newborn organisms; and it would have to hold that identical patterns of bodily events sometimes are emotional, but other times are nonemotional.

Such problems are resolved, however, if one adopts a class I definition and rigorously defines the bodily event that shall be called emotion. Let us see how this works out in some statements concerning emotion as visceral action.

(1) Altered activity of the autonomic nervous system and the tissues or organs that it innervates is the sole factor common to the majority of stated or implied definitions of emotion or emotional behavior in man or other animals, whether described by scientist or layman.

The logical reduction of such a proposition becomes,

(2) Altered activity of the autonomic nervous system and the tissues or organs that it innervates is a sufficient and necessary criterion of emotion or emotional behavior.

This appears to be a straightforward statement except

for the term "altered activity." Presumably, each such alteration is measurable, and one might modify the definition by stating the units of change required to satisfy the designation, "emotion." Such an approach to the problem would be comparable to defining the number of inches a child must grow before it may be considered "tall," or the amount of air that must be forced into a balloon before it can be considered "big." Let us utilize, instead, a continuum such as length or volume.

Let us assume the bottom limit of our continuum for organismic emotional behavior as "death," a state in which there is no activity or reactivity of the *autonomic nervous system* (ANS). A next step on the continuum might be that demonstrable in deep anesthesia, when the ANS is active but relatively unreactive to new stimuli.

Now let us delimit the term "emotion" as a noun indicative of a state of internal (visceral) motion or action, then add permissive statements concerning skeletal muscle activity and mental activity, and then reword our proposition.

(3) Emotion is activity and reactivity of the tissues and organs innervated by the autonomic nervous system. It may involve, but does not necessarily involve, skeletal muscular response or mental activity.

In living organisms equipped with autonomic nervous systems, emotional behavior would thus be continuous and the task of investigation would be to measure the degree of behavior in different situations in terms of (a) activity and (b) reactivity. Techniques would have to be devised for valid measurements of many of the organs involved: for some they are available, for others considerable work already has been done.

Extensive research has been reported, for example, on measurements of electrical conductance of the skin and of the *galvanic skin response* (GSR): the first, a rough measure of level of activity; and the second, a fairly precise measure of reactivity of sweat glands, which are known to be innervated by fibers of the sympathetic branch of the ANS. By our definition, both measures would be expressions of emotional behavior and any change in either measure would indicate a change in emotional behavior.

Work with these measures, however, forces two additional considerations to our attention. In the first place, the autonomic fibers that innervate the sweat glands are cholinergic in nature and are not reactive to adrenalin as are the adrenergic fibers. We find, then, a pattern of increased *sympathetic nervous system* (SNS) activity following injection of adrenalin, but no marked change in sweating. Furthermore, different patterns of sweating are well known, and many researchers have demonstrated change in conductance level and GSR without finding changes in other sympathetically innervated organs. These considerations may be stated as two corollaries:

(A) Change in emotional behavior may be detectable in one autonomically innervated tissue or organ and be undetectable in others.

(B) Change in emotional behavior may be detectable in a part of one autonomically innervated tissue or organ and be undetectable in other parts.

With these corollaries in mind, we may state an extension of proposition (3):

(4) Change in emotional behavior is altered activity or reactivity in a part of one, or more, tissue or organ innervated by the autonomic nervous system.

The investigator who accepts propositions (3) and (4) must devise techniques for simultaneous measurement of level of activity and degree of reactivity of many autonomically innervated functions before he can describe, predict, and control emotional patterns. Concerning some such functions there already exists much suggestive evidence, some of it quite specific, which may be employed in the formulation of initial hypotheses. Within our own observations of emotional behavior in ourselves and others, and within the observations of many others as recorded in the history and literature of all mankind, we have at the moment certain insights into differential physiological patterning of which we have made little use. At the very least, they furnish us certain tentative hypotheses around which to design more decisive laboratory experiments.

REFERENCES

1. LANGE, C. *The Emotions*. Translation appears in Dunlap, K. (ed.), *The Emotions*, Baltimore: Williams and Wilkins Co., 1922.
2. JAMES, W. *Psychol. Rev.*, 1894, **1**, 516-529.
3. BARD, P., Chap. 6 in Murchison, C. (ed.) *Handbook of General Experimental Psychology*. Worcester, Mass.: Clark Univ. Press, 1934.

2

William James on Emotion

WILLIAM JAMES

Although William James wrote with clarity and depth on a large number of topics of psychological interest, his comments on emotion resulted in a theory of emotion which bears his name. The following selection is taken from James' chapter on emotion in Principles of Psychology *(Vol. II, New York: Holt and Company, 1890), and is reprinted with the permission of the publisher. (The book is copyrighted by Holt, Rinehart, and Winston, Inc.)*

The selection is taken from the middle of the chapter. Prior to the place where this selection begins, James has discussed the work of the Danish psychologist, C. Lange. Although there are differences between James' theory and that of Lange, the general theory that emotion is the product of physiological changes, rather than the reverse, is commonly called the James-Lange theory. Following the selection reprinted here, James considers objections to his theory and to that of Lange.

James later clarified his viewpoint in a paper which appeared in Psychol. Rev., *1894, 1, 516-529.*

Our natural way of thinking about these coarser emotions is that the mental perception of some fact excites the mental affection called the emotion, and that this latter state of mind gives rise to the bodily expression. My theory, on the contrary, is that *the bodily changes follow directly the perception of the exciting fact, and that our feeling of the same changes as they occur is the emotion.* Common-sense says, we lose our fortune, are sorry and weep; we meet a bear, are frightened and run; we are insulted by a rival, are angry and strike. The

hypothesis here to be defended says that this order of
sequence is incorrect, that the one mental state is not
immediately induced by the other, that the bodily manifestations must first be interposed between, and that the
more rational statement is that we feel sorry because we
cry, angry because we strike, afraid because we tremble,
and not that we cry, strike, or tremble, because we are
sorry, angry, or fearful, as the case may be. Without
the bodily states following on the perception, the latter
would be purely cognitive in form, pale, colorless, desti-
tute of emotional warmth. We might then see the bear,
and judge it best to run, receive the insult and deem it
right to strike, but we should not actually *feel* afraid or
angry.

Stated in this crude way, the hypothesis is pretty sure
to meet with immediate disbelief. And yet neither many
nor far-fetched considerations are required to mitigate
its paradoxical character, and possibly to produce con-
viction of its truth.

To begin with, no reader of the last two chapters will
be inclined to doubt the fact that *objects do excite bodily
changes* by a preorganized mechanism, or the farther
fact that *the changes are so indefinitely numerous and
subtle that the entire organism may be called a sounding-
board*, which every change of consciousness, however
slight, may make reverberate. The various permutations
and combinations of which these organic activities are
susceptible make it abstractly possible that no shade of
emotion, however slight, should be without a bodily
reverberation as unique, when taken in its totality, as
is the mental mood itself. The immense number of parts
modified in each emotion is what makes it so difficult
for us to reproduce in cold blood the total and integral
expression of any one of them. We may catch the trick
with the voluntary muscles, but fail with the skin, glands,
heart, and other viscera. Just as an artificially imitated
sneeze lacks something of the reality, so the attempt to
imitate an emotion in the absence of its normal instigat-
ing cause is apt to be rather 'hollow.'

The next thing to be noticed is this, that *every one of
the bodily changes, whatsoever it be, is* FELT, *acutely or
obscurely, the moment it occurs.* If the reader has never

paid attention to this matter, he will be both interested
and astonished to learn how many different local bodily
feelings he can detect in himself as characteristic of his
various emotional moods. It would be perhaps too much
to expect him to arrest the tide of any strong gust of
passion for the sake of any such curious analysis as this;
but he can observe more tranquil states, and that may be
assumed here to be true of the greater which is shown
to be true of the less. Our whole cubic capacity is
sensibly alive; and each morsel of it contributes its
pulsations of feeling, dim or sharp, pleasant, painful, or
dubious, to that sense of personality that every one of
us unfailingly carries with him. It is surprising what little
items give accent to these complexes of sensibility. When
worried by any slight trouble, one may find that the
focus of one's bodily consciousness is the contraction,
often quite inconsiderable, of the eyes and brows. When
momentarily embarrassed, it is something in the pharynx
that compels either a swallow, a clearing of the throat,
or a slight cough; and so on for as many more instances
as might be named. Our concern here being with the
general view rather than with the details, I will not
linger to discuss these, but, assuming the point admitted
that every change that occurs must be felt, I will pass on.

I now proceed to urge the vital point of my whole
theory, which is this: *If we fancy some strong emotion,
and then try to abstract from our consciousness of it all
the feelings of its bodily symptoms, we find we have
nothing left behind,* no 'mind-stuff' out of which the
emotion can be constituted, and that a cold and neutral
state of intellectual perception is all that remains. It is
true that, although most people when asked say that their
introspection verifies this statement, some persist in
saying theirs does not. Many cannot be made to understand the question. When you beg them to imagine
away every feeling of laughter and of tendency to laugh
from their consciousness of the ludicrousness of an
object, and then to tell you what the feeling of its ludicrousness would be like, whether it be anything more
than the perception that the object belongs to the class
'funny,' they persist in replying that the thing proposed
is a physical impossibility, and that they always *must*

laugh if they see a funny object. Of course the task proposed is not the practical one of seeing a ludicrous object and annihilating one's tendency to laugh. It is the purely speculative one of subtracting certain elements of feeling from an emotional state supposed to exist in its fulness, and saying what the residual elements are. I cannot help thinking that all who rightly apprehend this problem will agree with the proposition above laid down. What kind of an emotion of fear would be left if the feeling neither of quickened heart-beats nor of shallow breathing, neither of trembling lips nor of weakened limbs, neither of goose-flesh nor of visceral stirrings, were present, it is quite impossible for me to think. Can one fancy the state of rage and picture no ebullition in the chest, no flushing of the face, no dilatation of the nostrils, no clenching of the teeth, no impulse to vigorous action, but in their stead limp muscles, calm breathing, and a placid face? The present writer, for one, certainly cannot. The rage is as completely evaporated as the sensation of its so-called manifestations, and the only thing that can possibly be supposed to take its place is some cold-blooded and dispassionate judicial sentence, confined entirely to the intellectual realm, to the effect that a certain person or persons merit chastisement for their sins. In like manner of grief: what would it be without its tears, its sobs, its suffocation of the heart, its pang in the breastbone? A feelingless cognition that certain circumstances are deplorable, and nothing more. Every passion in turn tells the same story. A purely disembodied human emotion is a nonentity. I do not say that it is a contradiction in the nature of things, or that pure spirits are necessarily condemned to cold intellectual lives; but I say that for *us*, emotion disassociated from all bodily feeling is inconceivable. The more closely I scrutinize my states, the more persuaded I become that whatever moods, affections, and passions I have are in very truth constituted by, and made up of, those bodily changes which we ordinarily call their expression or consequence; and the more it seems to me that if I were to become corporeally anæsthetic, I should be excluded from the life of the affections, harsh and tender alike, and drag out an existence of merely cognitive or intellectual form. Such an

existence, although it seems to have been the ideal of
ancient sages, is too apathetic to be keenly sought after
by those born after the revival of the worship of sensibility, a few generations ago.

Let not this view be called materialistic. It is neither
more nor less materialistic than any other view which
says that our emotions are conditioned by nervous processes. No reader of this book is likely to rebel against
such a saying so long as it is expressed in general terms;
and if any one still finds materialism in the thesis now
defended, that must be because of the special processes
invoked. They are *sensational* processes, processes due
to inward currents set up by physical happenings. Such
processes have, it is true, always been regarded by the
platonizers in psychology as having something peculiarly
base about them. But our emotions must always be
inwardly what they are whatever be the physiological
ground of their apparition. If they are deep, pure,
worthy, spiritual facts on any conceivable theory of their
physiological source, they remain no less deep, pure,
spiritual, and worthy of regard on this present sensational theory. They carry their own inner measure of
worth with them; and it is just as logical to use the
present theory of the emotions for proving that sensational processes need not be vile and material, as to use
their vileness and materiality as a proof that such a theory
cannot be true.

If such a theory is true, then each emotion is the
resultant of a sum of elements, and each element is
caused by a physiological process of a sort already well
known. The elements are all organic changes, and
each of them is the reflex effect of the exciting object.
Definite questions now immediately arise—questions
very different from those which were the only possible
ones without this view. Those were questions of classification: "Which are the proper genera of emotion, and
which the species under each?" or of description: "By
what expression is each emotion characterized?" The
questions now are *causal:* Just what changes does this
object and what changes does that object excite?" and
"How come they to excite these particular changes and
not others?" We step from a superficial to a deep order

of inquiry. Classification and description are the lowest stage of science. They sink into the background the moment questions of genesis are formulated, and remain important only so far as they facilitate our answering these. Now the moment the genesis of an emotion is accounted for, as the arousal by an object of a lot of reflex acts which are forthwith felt, *we immediately see why there is no limit to the number of possible different emotions which may exist, and why the emotions of different individuals may vary indefinitely*, both as to their constitution and as to objects which call them forth. For there is nothing sacramental or eternally fixed in reflex action. Any sort of reflex effect is possible, and reflexes actually vary indefinitely, as we know.

We have all seen men dumb, instead of talkative, with joy; we have seen fright drive the blood into the head of its victim, instead of making him pale; we have seen grief run restlessly about lamenting, instead of sitting bowed down and mute; etc., etc., and this naturally enough, for one and the same cause can work differently on different men's blood-vessels (since these do not always react alike), whilst moreover the impulse on its way through the brain to the vaso-motor centre is differently influenced by different earlier impressions in the form of recollections or associations of ideas.[1]

In short, *any classification of the emotions is seen to be as true and as 'natural' as any other*, if it only serves some purpose; and such a question as "What is the 'real' or 'typical' expression of anger, or fear?" is seen to have no objective meaning at all. Instead of it we now have the question as to how any given 'expression' of anger or fear may have come to exist; and that is a real question of physiological mechanics on the one hand, and of history on the other, which (like all real questions) is in essence answerable, although the answer may be hard to find.

[1] Lange, C. Ueber *Gemüthsbewegungen*, uebersetzt von H. Kurella. Leipzig: 1887, p. 75.

3

The Fears of Children

JOHN B. WATSON

John B. Watson was one of a group of psychologists which was instrumental in changing the study of psychology from inferred mental processes toward the study of overt and measurable behavior. Concurrent with the emphasis on observable behavior was a change in the way in which emotion was studied: emphasis was placed on the observable aspects of emotion, rather than on subjective evaluation of emotional experiences.

The work from which the following selection was taken was written primarily to show how the assumptions and findings of behaviorism apply to the rearing of children. The selection presents a portion of Watson's comments regarding how fear is developed in children: an experimental report on the same topic is included in this book of readings in the article by Mary Cover Jones.

This selection is from Psychological Care of Infant and Child (New York: Norton, 1928, pages 45-56) and is reprinted with the permission of the publisher.

Children's fears are home grown just like their loves and temper outbursts. The parents do the emotional planting and the cultivating. At three years of age the child's whole emotional life plan has been laid down, his emotional disposition set. At that age the parents have already determined for him whether he is to grow into a happy person, wholesome and good-natured, whether he is to be a whining, complaining neurotic, an anger driven, vindictive, over-bearing slave driver, or one whose every move in life is definitely controlled by fear.

17

BUT HOW DO PARENTS BUILD IN FEARS?

In the preceding chapter I brought out the fact that all we have to start with in building a human being is a lively squirming bit of flesh, capable of making a few simple responses such as movements of the hands and arms and fingers and toes, crying and smiling, making certain sounds with its throat. I said there that parents take this raw material and begin to fashion it in ways to suit themselves. This means that parents, whether they know it or not, start intensive training of the child at birth.

It is especially easy to shape the emotional life at this early age. I might make this simple comparison: The fabricator of metal takes his heated mass, places it upon the anvil and begins to shape it according to patterns of his own. Sometimes he uses a heavy hammer, sometimes a light one; sometimes he strikes the yielding mass a mighty blow, sometimes he gives it just a touch. So inevitably do we begin at birth to shape the emotional life of our children. The blacksmith has all the advantage. If his strokes have been heavy and awkward and he spoils his work, he can put the metal back on the fire and start the process over. There is no way of starting over again with the child. Every stroke, be it true or false, has its effect. The best we can do is to conceal, skillfully as we may, the defects of our shaping. We can still make a useful instrument, an instrument that will work, but how few human instruments have ever been perfectly shaped to fit the environments in which they must function!

I think I can take you into the laboratory and give you a clear picture of the kinds of sledge hammers you are using in fashioning the fear life of your child.

Our laboratory work shows the fear life of the newborn infant is simplicity itself. From birth the child will show fear whenever a sudden loud sound is made close to its head and whenever it is thrown off its balance, as for example, when its blanket is quickly jerked. No other fears are natural; all other fears are built in.

And yet, think how complicated is the fear life of the three-year-old, the adolescent, the timid adult. Study the fears of the adults around you. I have seen a grown man cower and cringe and literally blanch with fear at the sight of a gun. I have seen a man stay all night in a hotel rather than enter his dark home when family and servants are away. I have seen a woman go into hysterics when a bat flew into a room. I have seen a child so torn by fear of moving animal toys that his whole organized life was in danger. Think of our fear of lightning, wind, railway trains, automobile accidents, ocean travel, burglars, fire, electricity and the thousands of other things that literally torture us even in this modern, supposedly secure life we lead. Think how peaceful, how calm, how efficient our lives would be if we were no more fearful than the newborn baby.

WHAT CAN THE LABORATORY SAY
ABOUT THE WAY FEARS GROW UP?

Suppose I put before you a beautiful, healthy, well-formed baby nine months of age. On his mattress I place a rabbit. I know this baby's history; I know he has never seen a rabbit before. He reaches for the rabbit first with one hand, then the other the moment his eyes light upon it. I replace the rabbit with a dog. He behaves the same way. I next show him a cat, then a pigeon. Each new object is gleefully welcomed and equally gleefully handled. Afraid of furry objects? Not at all. But how about slimy objects? Surely he is afraid of cold, clammy, squirmy animals. Surely he is afraid of fish and frogs. I hand him a gold fish, alive and squirming. I put a green frog in front of him. Something new, again for the first time. Yes, a new world to work at. Immediately he goes after it as vigorously as after the other members of the animal kingdom. But surely all ancient history tells us that man instinctively avoids the snake. Literature is full of references to the fact that man's natural enemy is the snake. Not so with our lusty nine months infant. The boa constrictor I put in front of him —when young the most harmless of snakes—calls out the most vigorous of all those favorable friendly responses.

But won't our infant cry out in fear when I put him in the total darkness of a lightproof room? Not at all.

But won't flame, that most terrifying of all physical agents, when seen for the first time at this tender age throw him almost into a fit? Let us take an iron pan and make a little bonfire of newspapers, being careful to keep it far enough away to keep the child from harm.

This infant must be phlegmatic, without emotional life. Not at all. I can convince you easily otherwise. In my hands I have a steel bar about an inch in diameter and about four feet long, and a carpenter's hammer. The child is sitting up looking at the attendant. I hold the steel bar about a foot behind his head where he can't see me. I rap the steel bar sharply with the hammer. The picture changes immediately. First a whimper, a sudden catching of the breath, a stiffening of the whole body, a pulling of the hands to the side, then a cry, then tears. I bang it again. The reaction becomes still more pronounced. He cries out loud, rolls over to his side and begins to crawl away as rapidly as possible.

Suppose I let him sit quietly on a blanket over his mattress. He may be very still, just dozing, or he may be playing eagerly with a toy. Suddenly I jerk the blanket, pull his support from under him. This sudden loss of support produces almost the same reaction as the loud sound. I haven't hurt him by pulling the blanket, he falls over from his sitting position fifty times a day and never whimpers. Your training has nothing to do with the fear he shows at loud sounds and loss of support, nor will any training ever completely remove the potency of these things to call out fears. I have seen the most seasoned hunter when dozing, jump violently when his comrade strikes a match to kindle the camp fire. You have seen the most intrepid of women show terror in crossing a perfectly safe foot bridge that sways with her weight.

Fear of all other objects is home-made. Now to prove it. Again I put in front of you the nine months old infant. I have my assistant take his old playmate, the rabbit, out of its pasteboard box and hand it to him. He starts to reach for it. But just as his hands touch it I bang the steel bar behind his head. He whimpers and cries and shows fear. Then I wait awhile. I give him his blocks to play with. He quiets down and soon becomes busy with them. Again my assistant shows him the rabbit. This time he reacts to it quite slowly. He doesn't plunge his hands out as quickly and eagerly as before. Finally he does touch it gingerly. Again I strike the steel bar behind his head. Again I get a pronounced fear response. Then I let him quiet down. He plays with his blocks. Again the assistant brings in the rabbit. This time something new develops. No longer do I have to rap the steel bar behind his head to bring out fear. *He shows fear at the sight of the rabbit.* He makes the same reaction to it that he makes to the sound of the steel bar. He begins to cry and turn away the moment he sees it.

I have started the process of fear building. And this fear of the rabbit persists. If you show the rabbit to him one month later, you get the same reaction. There is good evidence to show that such early built in fears last throughout the lifetime of the individual.

We have a name in the laboratory for fears built up in this experimental way. We call them *conditioned* fears and we mean by that "home-made fears." By this method we can, so far as we know, make any object in the world call out a *conditioned* fear response. All we have to do is to show the infant any object and make a loud sound at the same moment.

But this fear of the rabbit is not the only building stone we have laid in the child's life of fear. After this one experience, and with no further contact with animals, all furry animals such as the dog, the cat, the rat, the guinea pig, may one and all call out fear. He becomes afraid even of a fur coat, a rug or a Santa Claus mask. He does not have to touch them; just seeing them will call out fear. This simple experiment gives us a startling insight into the ways in which our early home surroundings can build up fears. You may think that such experiments are cruel, but they are not cruel if they help us to understand the fear life of the millions of people around us and give us practical help in bringing up our children more nearly free from fears than we ourselves have been brought up. They will be worth all they cost if through them we can find a method which will help us remove fear.

4

An Explanation of "Emotional" Phenomena Without the Use of the Concept "Emotion"

ELIZABETH DUFFY

Women's College, University of North Carolina

Professor Duffy has been the protagonist of the belief that the use of the concept emotion is misleading in that it groups disparate behaviors under the simple, and confusing, label "emotion." In this paper Professor Duffy points out why she believes psychologists have felt it necessary to retain the concept and suggests an alternative method for viewing emotion.

The article is reprinted from the Journal of General Psychology, *1941, 25, 283-293, by permission of the author and the journal.*

For many years the writer has been of the opinion that "emotion," as a scientific concept, is worse than useless. In 1934, in an article published in the *Psychological Review*, she examined the various types of definition of emotion offered by psychologists and reached the conclusion that no one of these types of definition succeeded in describing a state or response pattern of the organism different in *kind* from other states or response patterns (3). "Emotion" apparently did not represent a separate and distinguishable condition. Each definition purporting to describe such a distinguishable condition succeeded in describing, not a difference in *kind* of response, but merely a difference in the *degree* to which certain characteristics of response were manifest. Nor was there any criterion by which to determine *what particular degree* of a certain characteristic should be called "emotion" and what degree should be called "non-emotion." Instead, the phenomena described appeared to occur in a continuum, or rather in a number of continua, since more than one aspect of behavior was involved in the description of "emotion," and there was no indication as to what points on the continua represented the transition from "non-emotion" to "emotion." The concept "emotion" apparently referred to the extremes of certain continua of response, but it implied, not continuous variation in these phenomena, but a sharp break between "emotion" and "non-emotion." In fact, "emotion" was supposed to follow different principles of action from "non-emotion." The writer contended that the concept "emotion" should be abandoned and the phenomena loosely referred to by this term should be studied in their own right as separate aspects of response occurring in continua rather than in discrete categories.

But, alas, the concept "emotion" has not been abandoned. Psychologists remain convinced that the term refers to a distinguishable category of response, and they persevere in the attempt to give this category more adequate definition. The descriptions of "emotion" which have appeared since 1934 differ in no significant respects from those which had appeared prior to that time. The reading of these definitions has left the writer with a sentiment similar to that expressed by William James in regard to the classificatory descriptions of the separate emotions—that he "should as lief read verbal descriptions of the shapes of the rocks on a New Hampshire farm as toil through them again." Yet if psychologists continue to believe that "emotion" exists there must be some reason for their belief. And the reason must be one which is not affected by the demonstration of the inadequacy of our present definitions of "emotion." That inadequacy merely spurs them to renewed efforts to describe in a satisfactory manner a category of response whose existence they do not question.

One reason for the well nigh universal belief in "emotion" is that every man has experienced a vivid, unforgettable condition which is different from the ordinary condition in which he finds himself. It may be more pleasant or more unpleasant, but it appears to have a unique quality which differentiates it from the general run of his experience. To this condition he gives the name "emotion," and it would take more than the arguments of a misguided psychologist to convince him that he does not experience that which he knows so well he does experience. Hence, if a psychologist wishes to question the concept "emotion," it is not sufficient that he show the inadequacies of the concept; he must offer in addition some explanation of the experiences which have been called "emotion." He must show that these experiences, which appear to be unique, are in fact merely manifestations in extreme degree of phenomena which are of very general occurrence, and which follow the same principles of action throughout the continua of their occurrence, rather than different principles of action during the condition called "emotion." To that task I now address myself.

The experience which is labelled "emotion" is the conscious aspect of a response, or group of responses, which the individual makes to a stimulating situation which he interprets as having marked significance for himself, favorable or unfavorable. I think it will be agreed that the individual does not experience "emotion" except in situations which are of significance to him. He is "afraid" or "angry" when he is threatened, or when his progress toward an important goal is blocked. He is "joyful" or "elated" when his progress toward an important goal is facilitated. Hence, "emotion" is the individual's response to situations which promise well or ill for the attainment of his goals. The term refers to how the individual *feels* and how he *acts* when his *expectations* in regard to a situation are that it will, or it will not, permit him to reach some rather strongly desired goal. The strength or intensity of the "emotion" is roughly proportional to the degree of importance of the particular goal to the individual, and to the degree of threat or of promise which the present situation bears with reference to that goal. However, it must be emphasized that the response of the individual, or the "emotion" he manifests, is that which is appropriate to the situation as *he interprets it*, not that which would be appropriate to the situation in the opinion of other individuals. The "emotional" response of the neurotic or the psychotic, for example, is frequently too much or too little for the situation as it is generally interpreted, but it is no doubt appropriate to the situation as it is viewed by the individual making the response. It follows, then, that the "emotion" experienced in a given situation depends upon the nature of the individual's goals and upon the background of experience and quality of insight which he brings to bear upon the interpretation of the situation. Older children, for example, fear situations which younger children do not fear (6). Their expectations in regard to these situations are different.

Starting from the proposition that "emotion" represents an adjustment of the individual, or a response to the stimulating situation as the individual interprets it, we may ask what are the characteristics of the response or adjustment which is called "emotion." In the first place, emotion represents a change in the *energy level*, or degree of reactivity, of the individual. The excited individual has an energy level which is higher, and the depressed individual an energy level which is lower, than that which he ordinarily experiences. By "energy level" I refer to the degree of mobilization of energy within the organism, which Cannon (1) found to be very high during the excited "emotions"; or to what Freeman (5, p. 326) has defined as "the general organic background (neuro-glandular-muscular) which operates to sustain and energize overt phasic response." Change in energy level appears to be the most characteristic feature of the condition called "emotion." It occurs as an adjustment to the stimulating situation. Situations which are interpreted as threatening or thwarting are characteristically responded to with increased energy, for by means of this increased vigor of response the individual may, in spite of difficulties, be able to reach his goal. Such vigorous response is frequently observed in "fear" or "anger." Increase in the energy level of response is observed also, though perhaps to a lesser degree, in "joy," for "joy" is the response made when the situation suddenly changes, or is interpreted to change, in such a way that progress toward the goal is facilitated. Under these circumstances the individual either actually or imaginatively moves quickly forward to the attainment of his goal. The phenomenon is similar to that observed when the rat in the maze moves more quickly through the alleys at the end of his route and nearest to the food box, or when the human subject works most rapidly on the last of a group of problems which he must solve. The *energy level* of the individual's responses *increases*, then, both when progress toward his goal is blocked and when barriers to his progress are suddenly removed.

Under what circumstances do we find, not an increase, but a decrease in *energy level?* Characteristically, I believe, when the individual is making no attempt, or almost no attempt, to reach a goal. Such is the situation found in depression. When an individual's progress toward a goal is completely blocked by some circumstance which he interprets as an insuperable obstacle, he ceases to be active in relation to that goal. We say that he has "given up," or that he is "resigned," or that he is in a "depressive stupor," depending upon the degree of departure of his activity level from that which is usual. This lack of responsiveness, this low energy level, may persist for a considerable length of time and may affect the individual's responses to other goals which are not in themselves unattainable. Because the individual has given up hope of reaching some highly desired goal, other goals have lost their appeal. There is no longer sufficient "motivation" for normally vigorous action.

But we do not always find clear-cut instances of either striving with great effort to reach a goal or sinking into almost complete inactivity in relation to all goals. Sometimes the picture is confused. In agitated despair, for example, the individual has given up all hope of reaching a particular highly desired goal, but he has not become inactive. His energy level is high. In this case the blocking of progress toward a goal of primary importance has resulted, not in lack of interest in all other goals, but in great compensatory activity, as seen, for example, in attempts at revenge or suicide. This example and the others which we have cited illustrate the principle that the energy level of the individual will be high or low depending on whether he is or is not attempting to reach goals of great importance to him, or, in other words, according to the degree to which he is motivated.

But *all* behavior is motivated. Without motivation there is *no activity*. The conditions to which we give the name "emotion" represent merely unusually high or unusually low degrees of motivation and consequently unusually high or unusually low levels of energy. We have no criterion, however, by which to determine whether a given energy level is high enough or low enough to be called "emotion," and it would not be useful to employ such a criterion if we had it unless it could be shown that energy levels high enough or low enough to be called "emotion" result in behavior different in *kind*, and not merely in *degree*, from that resulting from levels of energy intermediate between these extremes. The responses called "emotional" do not appear to follow different principles of action from other adjustive responses of the individual. Changes in internal or external conditions, or in the interpretation of those conditions, always result in internal accommodations. The responses made are specifically adjustive to the situation and are not subject to classification into such categories as "emotional" and "non-emotional." An example of this fact may be seen in some studies of the maintenance of the blood sugar level made by Silvette and Britton (8). It was demonstrated that changes which occur in the blood stream may be induced by any of a number of factors which affect the essential equilibria of the organism—by "emotion," by intense physical activity, or by a change in temperature. There is no reason to conclude that the blood sugar changes occurring when the organic equilibrium was disturbed by so-called "emotional" stimuli were any different from those occurring when the same degree of disequilibrium was produced by physical activity or exposure to cold.[1] All responses—not merely "emotional"

---

[1] Silvette and Britton (8, p. 691) make the following observation: "It is pertinent to emphasize that the influences of emotion on important chemical constituents of the body are essentially similar to those which are brought about by severe muscular exertion. Both motion and emotion result in release to the blood stream and degradation in the tissues of energy-supplying substances, and concurrent accumulation of the products of tissue oxidation or metabolites."

responses—are adjustive reactions attempting to adapt the organism to the demands of the situation. The energy level of response varies with the requirements of the situation as interpreted by the individual. Diffuse internal changes (especially in the viscera) are involved in the production of these changes in energy level. But continuous visceral activity, with accompanying changes in energy level, is a function of life itself, not merely a function of a particular condition called "emotion." We have in fact a continuum of response which has been artificially broken into the categories, "emotional" and "non-emotional."

A second characteristic of "emotional" responses is that they are frequently, if not usually, disorganized. The angry or fearful individual often fumbles in his movements and is confused in his thinking. His speech is frequently incoherent. The depressed individual, too, may manifest incoördination in speech, thought, and movement. However, disorganization of response is a function, I believe, not of a unique state or condition called "emotion," but a function, though not an invariable one, of any behavior which occurs at a very high or a very low energy level. Since the term "emotion" is applied to much of the behavior which occurs at high or low levels of energy, disorganization of response has appeared to be a distinguishing feature of "emotion." We have on record, however, a number of instances in which "emotion" has been accompanied by no disorganization of response, and a number of instances in which disorganized responses have occurred under conditions not ordinarily called "emotional." Stratton (9), for example, has reported a case in which the "emotion" aroused in a man by the sight of the flaming bathrobe of his niece caused him to think and to move with extraordinary speed and effectiveness. The heightened energy level produced by the situation resulted in this instance, not in disorganization, but in increased speed and force of action, with no loss in coördination. Some degree of disorganization of response has been found, on the other hand, in most situations where the adjustive response is not a well-established habit. It occurs frequently during the learning of a new motor skill or during the attempt to solve a difficult "mental" problem. It is likely to occur in any type of situation in which the individual is too highly motivated, i.e., has too high an energy level. The over-eager golfer, teeing off, makes a poor shot. The enthusiastic child, speaking of something which interests him intensely, begins to stammer. Disorganized responses occur also when the individual is drowsy or fatigued. Under these conditions the energy level is usually too low for effective behavior. And, finally, disorganization of response occurs as a result of the physiological condition by glandular dysfunction or by the administration of drugs. It is apparent, then, that disorganized response is not peculiar to "emotion;" nor is there any particular degree of disorganization of response which is called *always* by "emotional" stimuli. But most "emotional" conditions, involving as they do unusually high or unusually low levels of energy, usually involve also disorganization of response, but the disorganization appears to be a function, not of "emotion" *per se*, but of the *energy level* of the response, since disorganization is found at high and at low levels of energy which are not ordinarily called "emotional." [2]

A third characteristic attributed to "emotion," and one which is generally considered most indisputable, is that "emotion" involves a unique kind of sensation or quality of consciousness. Whatever may be said about the lack of uniqueness of "emotional" *responses*, the individual is likely to feel that the *conscious* quality of "emotion" is different from that which he experiences under any other circumstances. He describes "a lump in the throat," or "a turning of the stomach," or the heart's "skipping a beat." These sensations appear to him to be not merely different in *degree* but actually different in *kind* from those which he experiences on ordinary occasions. Sometimes, when he is "emotional," he feels unusually helpless and confused. At other times he feels unusually powerful. So different are these feelings from his usual experiences that he may report that he feels "beside himself" with anger or with joy. Is it possible that a conscious state of this kind, one of the most vivid

[2] For a fuller discussion of *energy level* and of *disorganization of response*, see E. Duffy (4).

ever experienced by the individual, differs merely in degree, and not in unique quality, from the states of consciousness which make up most of our experience in everyday life? I think it is.

The subjective qualities of "emotion" appear to derive from two sources: (a) awareness of the bodily changes which occur in the process of adjusting the energy level of the individual to the demands of the situation, and (b) awareness of the stimulus situation and of the set for response to that situation. "Emotional" experience is merely the conscious counterpart of the adjustments which the individual makes to stimulating conditions which are of sufficient significance to cause a marked change in his energy level and his set for response.

Sudden and extreme changes occur in the viscera and in the skeletal muscles when the individual attempts to make a quick and extensive readjustment for which he is not "set" or prepared. The *sudden* change in the situation demands a *sudden* change both in overt movement and in the processes supplying the energy for that movement. These sudden changes in physiological functioning are experienced by the individual as strange and vivid sensations which are described in such picturesque terms as those of the stomach's "taking a flop" or the heart's "being in the throat." Such sensations occur only when the "emotional" stimulus appears unexpectedly or when the *interpretation* of the situation abruptly changes. Situations which demand, not sudden readjustments, but more gradual readjustments, such, for example, as the change in energy level and in overt behavior which occur as the individual gradually comes to believe that he is exposed to danger, also produce changes in conscious experience which correspond to the changes in adjustive activity, but in these situations the individual is not conscious of sudden, violent changes in the viscera, for no such changes occur, since no sudden change in the stimulus situation requires them. When the energy level of the individual increases or decreases in marked degree, the individual "feels" different from the way he does under ordinary circumstances; he experiences different sensations. If this change in energy level takes place gradually, is not too extreme, and persists for some time, he experiences a "mood;" if it takes place in extreme degree or occurs suddenly, he is likely to experience an "emotion."

But the awareness of "how the body feels" does not make up the whole of the conscious quality of "emotion." The bodily sensations have an external reference. They are viewed by the individual as having been *caused* by a certain situation. They are part of a more comprehensive whole which includes the *interpretation* of the *stimulus situation*, *expectations* of future developments in the situation, and the *set* of the individual for response to that situation. Without this characteristic context for the visceral sensations the individual who experiences visceral changes is likely to be uncertain as to whether or not he is experiencing "emotion." Experiments by Cantril and Hunt (2) and by Landis and Hunt (7) offer support for this point of view. Subjects to whom adrenalin was administered (which, of course, produced visceral changes similar to those occurring during the excited emotions) reported in some instances that they experienced "emotion," in other instances that they did not experience "emotion," and in a number of cases that they felt *"as if"* they were angry or *"as if"* they were afraid.

The conscious experience of "emotion" appears, then, to be a complex which includes awareness of the stimulus situation and its significance, awareness of the set for response, and awareness of certain physiological changes which are occurring in the individual. But what "non-emotional" state of consciousness is devoid of any one of these factors? And what characteristic quality of any one of these factors has been found to be present in "emotional" states alone? The consciousness of these various aspects of the situation may be somewhat "blurred" during "emotion," especially during the *strong* "emotions"; but disorganization is to be expected in both experience and behavior which occur at a very high or a very low energy level.

The "unique" conscious quality attributed to "emotion" appears to refer either to the pleasantness-unpleasantness aspect of *all* experience, and not merely of "emotional" experience, or else to the vivid and unusual sensations experienced when sudden and extreme physiological readjustments occur, as they do when a sudden change in energy level is demanded. If it refers to the former, it may be said to represent a characteristic of consciousness itself and not a distinguishing feature of "emotion." If it refers to the latter, it may be said to represent the conscious counterpart of adjustive responses which differ from other responses in *degree* rather than in *kind;* hence the conscious experience must itself differ from other conscious states in degree rather than in unique quality. Changes in energy level, in degree of organization of responses, and in conscious state occur in a continuum. There is no point on this continuum where a "non-emotional" energy level changes suddenly to an "emotional" energy level; there is no point at which a "non-emotional" degree of disorganization of response changes suddenly to an "emotional" degree of disorganization; and there is no point at which a "non-emotional" conscious state changes suddenly to an "emotional" one. These characteristics of experience and behavior show continuous variation rather than separation into hard and fast categories. Extremes of the continuum are readily identified as "emotion;" intermediate points offer difficulty in identification. For example, slight changes in energy level such as occur during "interest" or "boredom" usually leave the individual uncertain as to whether he is experiencing "emotion;" extreme changes, such as occur in "anger," are unequivocally identified as "emotion." The conscious quality of "emotion," like other aspects of "emotion," represents a variation in *degree* rather than a difference in *kind.*

I am aware of no evidence for the existence of a special condition called "emotion" which follows different principles of action from other conditions of the organism. I can therefore see no reason for a psychological study of "emotion" as such. "Emotion" has no distinguishing characteristics. It represents merely an *extreme* manifestation of characteristics found in some degree in all responses. If there is any particular point at which a difference in *degree* becomes a difference in *kind* this fact has not been demonstrated. Yet in psychological description we deem it necessary to state that "emotional" processes *also* follow laws already laid down for other kinds of behavior. For example, when we have shown that behavior in general shows the phenomenon of "conditioning," we find it necessary to state that "emotional" behavior *also* may be conditioned. When we have shown that motives affect the level of activity of the individual, we find it necessary to state that "emotions" also may have this result. It would be more in accord with the facts to state instead that the energy level of an organism depends upon the degree and suddenness of the disturbance of its equilibrium by both internal and external factors, and that the responses made are specifically adjustive to the situation. Since situations show endless variation in their details, adjustments to those situations must show corresponding variation. They will not be readily classifiable, therefore, into "emotion" or "non-emotion," or into any of the categories represented by our names for the specific "emotions."

All responses, not merely "emotional" responses, occur as adjustments to stimulating conditions. *All* responses, not merely "emotional" responses, occur at some particular *energy level*. *All* responses, like "emotional" responses, show *direction* toward a goal; and *all* responses manifest *discrimination*, or response to relationships. "Emotion" is an adjustment made to a stimulating condition of such a kind that the adjustment involves a marked change in energy level. It involves, like other behavior, interpretation of the situation, or response to relationships. And from the goal-direction of the overt behavior, or of the set for response, are derived the classificatory divisions into the particular "emotions," such as "fear" or "rage." Its characteristics—its principles of action—are those of behavior in general. It has no laws or qualities of its own. It is futile, therefore, to look for an "indicator" of "emotion." It is futile to inquire, "What *are the effects produced by* 'emotion'?" For a so-called "emotional" condition will *vary* in its effects, depending upon the *energy level* at which the behavior occurs, upon the adequacy with which *direction* toward the goal is maintained (or disorganization or response avoided), and upon the nature of the *response to the relationships* in the situation. Behavior not classified as "emotional" also varies with variations in these three aspects of response. Instead of investigating "emotion" *per se*, we could more usefully study variations in these three fundamental dimensions of behavior, determining the conditions under which such variations occur and the effects produced by their occurrence. Perhaps, when we formulate our questions better, Nature will be more obliging in her replies.

REFERENCES

1. Cannon, W. B. *Bodily Changes in Pain, Hunger, Fear, and Rage* (2nd ed.). New York and London: Appleton, 1929.
2. Cantril, H., and Hunt, W. A., Emotional effects produced by the injection of adrenalin, *Amer. J. Psychol.*, 1932, **44**, 300-307.
3. Duffy, E., Emotion: an example of the need for reorientation in psychology, *Psychol. Rev.*, 1934, **41**, 184-198.
4. ———, The conceptual categories of psychology: a suggestion for revision, *Psychol. Rev.*, 1941, **44**, 177-203.
5. Freeman, G. L., The postural substrate, *Psychol. Rev.*, 1938, **45**, 324-334.
6. Jones, H. E., and Jones, M. C., Fear, *Child. Educ.*, 1928, **5**, 136-143.
7. Landis, C., and Hunt, W. A., Adrenalin and emotion, *J. Exper. Psychol.*, 1932, **39**, 467-485.
8. Silvette, H., and Britton, S. W., The comparative effects on carbohydrate metabolism of exhausting motive and emotive responses and exposure to cold, *Amer. J. Physiol.*, 1932, **100**, 685-692.
9. Stratton, G. M., The functions of emotion as shown particularly in excitement, *Psychol. Rev.*, 1928, **35**, 351-366.

5

Motives and Emotions

ROBERT WARD LEEPER AND PETER MADISON

University of Oregon and Swarthmore College

The distinction between what qualifies as an emotion and what qualifies as a motive is often unclear. It is for this reason that it is not unusual to find emotion and motivation treated as a single group of phenomena by many theorists.

The following selection by Professors Robert Leeper and Peter Madison is taken from their book Toward Understanding Human Personalities *(New York: Appleton-Century-Crofts, Inc., copyright © 1959) and serves to indicate the theoretical position which Professor Leeper has developed. The reader who is interested in this viewpoint, and in the arguments that have been made against it, will find the additional references to the "Leeper-Young" and "Leeper-Duffy" controversies listed in Part IV of this book of readings.*

The selection is condensed and slightly modified from the original with the permission of the publisher and Professor Leeper.

Let us begin by taking an example of the influence of hunger, which all psychologists accept as a clear-cut instance of motivation. In the following paragraphs from his book, *The Heart of the Antarctic*, Sir Ernest Shackleton[1] is speaking of the final part of a trip that he and three other men made in 1908-09 in an effort to reach the South Pole. On this trip, they traveled over 1700 miles from their base camp. At first they had the aid of four

[1] Sir Ernest Shackleton, *The Heart of the Antarctic*, Philadelphia (J. B. Lippincott Co., 1909), Vol. 2, pp. 2-9. Reprinted with permission.

Siberian ponies; later, after the ponies gave out, they had to haul their sleds by hand. The terrain was often very rough, and the weather intensely cold.

We would make the biscuits last as long as possible. . . . If one of us dropped a crumb, the others would point it out, and the owner would wet his finger in his mouth and pick up the morsel. Not the smallest fragment was allowed to escape.

We used to "turn backs" in order to ensure equitable division of the food. The cook would pour the hoosh into the pannikins and arrange the biscuits in four heaps. Perhaps someone would suggest that one pannikin had rather less in it than another, and if this view was endorsed by the others there would be a readjustment. Then when we were all satisfied that the food had been divided as fairly as possible, one man would turn his back, and another, pointing at one pannikin or group of biscuits, would say, "Whose?" The man who had his back turned, and therefore could not see the food, would give a name, and so the distribution would proceed, each of us always feeling sure that the smallest share had fallen to his lot. . . .

During the last weeks of the journey outwards, and the long march back, . . . we really thought of little but food. The glory of the great mountains that towered high on either side, the majesty of the enormous glacier up which we travelled so painfully, did not appeal to our emotions to any great extent. . . . We could not joke about food, in in the way that is possible for the man who is hungry in the ordinary sense. We thought about it most of the time, and on the way back we used to talk about it, but always in the most serious manner possible. . . .

On the outward march we . . . had to keep some distance apart in case one man fell into a crevasse, . . . and the blizzard . . . from the south made unnecessary conversation out of question. . . . It was on the march back that we talked freely of food. . . . The wind was behind us, . . . and . . . we were able to keep close together. We . . . could take turns in describing the things we would eat in the good days to come. . . .

It is with strange feelings that I look back over our notes, and see the wonderful meals that we were going to have. . . .

On a typical day we would be beginning to march with some degree of comfort, and one of us would remark, "Well, boys, what are we going to have for breakfast today?"

We had just finished our breakfast as a matter of fact, but the question would receive our most serious and careful consideration at once, and we would proceed to weave from our hungry imaginations a tale of a day spent in eating. . . .

We did not smile at ourselves or at each other as we planned wonderful feats of over-eating. We were perfectly serious about the matter, and we noted down in the back pages of our diaries details of the meals we had decided to have as soon as we got back. . . . All the morning we would allow our imaginations to run riot in this fashion. Then would come one o'clock. . . . We would drop the harness from our tired bodies. . . . An hour later we would be on the march again, once more thinking and talking of food, and this would go until the camp in the evening. We would have another scanty meal, and turn into the sleeping-bags, to dream wildly of food that somehow we could never manage to eat.

The experiences of these men show some concrete ways in which hunger operates as a regulating mechanism in our lives. We need to rephrase these effects in more abstract language, though, so that we can use this example to help us see whether other processes exert essentially similar influences. We note the following effects:

1. Hunger modifies perceptual processes, particularly in the direction of making relevant things stand out focally. Thus, as was said, the men's attention would pounce on tiny crumbs of biscuit that got dropped. There has been a great deal of research work in psychology in recent years exploring the hypothesis that motivation tends to distort our perceptions, making important things look bigger to us. This is a minor influence, if a real one at all. Hunger did not make the crumbs look bigger to Shackleton's men; it merely made the crumbs stand out vividly.

2. Hunger tends to determine the content not merely of direct sensory processes, but also of the thought processes or associations. Even between meals, when no food was present in the sense of stimuli, it was still a case of "Well, boys, what will we have when we get back to civilization and can have anything we want?" Even in their sleep, they dreamed about food.

3. Hunger tends to make men learn new ways of trying to satisfy their motives. All their ritual of dividing

up equal portions of food, for example, was a new tactic that they learned because they were so strongly motivated, as were all the magnificent culinary inventions they jotted down on back pages of their diaries.

4. After men have learned new ways of trying to satisfy hunger, the hunger motive tends to guarantee that they will *use* these new habits.

5. Hunger tends to determine the choice of positive goals. Shackleton's group was traveling through a country of magnificent beauty. They were men who, under other circumstances, would have gotten great aesthetic enjoyment from the landscape. But even though they knew that all of their talk about food could not increase by one crumb the amount of food available among all these snow-swept valleys, they focused their attention on everything connected with food rather than on enjoyment of the scenery.

6. Hunger makes men willing to endure hardship and undergo penalties. It was not easy for Shackleton's men to haul the sleds that carried their food. They were so near exhaustion that, sometimes, when they tried to lift their arms to set up their tents, their hands would start to become frostbitten because the circulation in their arms became less with raising them. But none of them would have dreamed of leaving their food behind so that they could lighten their loads. They might have been glad to have a chance to haul ten times as much!

In short, we see that hunger serves as an energizing and directing influence in our lives. It arouses, sustains, and directs activity—not just any activity, but activity directed toward the goal of serving that particular motive. Or, somewhat more specifically, we may say that hunger (1) modifies perception, (2) influences thinking, (3) leads to learning new ways of motive-satisfaction, (4) leads to the use of new habits, (5) affects goal-choices, (6) and compels work and the acceptance of penalties to satisfy the motive. These six influences of hunger illustrate our chief means of knowing whether or not a person or an animal is motivated. We do not need to depend on the person's introspective report that he is intensely motivated (though this is often an im-

portant and reliable guide). We can watch the individual's activity and, from his behavior, determine whether
or not he is motivated.

HOW THE SAME CRITERIA APPLY TO
EMOTIONAL PROCESSES

It has been relatively easy for us to see, both in technical psychological discussions and in everyday life, that
hunger operates in a manner fairly analogous to the way
a thermostat operates in controlling a furnace. For even
though extra food is on the table, a person tends not to
eat after his hunger is satisfied. And, on the other hand,
it does not take the sight or smell of food to stir him into
food-seeking behavior. He may not be able to get food
through his goal-seeking activity, just as was the case with
Shackleton's men, but his behavior is concerned with a
goal of eating, nevertheless. And this behavior is
obviously related to some definite physiological processes
and mechanisms within the body. We do not have much
difficulty in getting the idea that hunger, thirst, and
similar physiologically-based motives are directing, organizing, steering processes.

But it has been more difficult to see that perhaps we
need to think of emotional processes as motives. A few
psychologists have even proposed that emotional responses are just the opposite of motives—that, whereas
motives are organizing in their influence, emotional
processes are intrinsically disorganizing.

Let us examine emotions, however, in the light of the
six influences that we enumerated above. If, indeed, we
grant that these influences identify a process as a motive, and if their operation in the case of emotional
processes is also evident, then it would follow that emotional processes must be included within the larger class
of motives. They might be motives somewhat different in
character from physiologically-based motives like hunger,
but still belong within the large, important category.

Before proceeding farther we need to have a concrete
instance of emotion before us, like the following ac-

count of the behavior of one family during a fire-bug
scare in their community:

When we returned from a trip, we heard much neighborhood talk about a fire bug. There had been such a scare
several years ago when arsonists burned up over $500,000
worth of barns in the surrounding countryside.

Sunday evening I was putting the children to bed. They
too had heard all the neighborhood talk of the fire bug's
weekly burnings, as well as our own family conversation over
the newspaper accounts. Just then the fire siren sounded.

"Would he burn our house, Daddy?" asked one child
fearfully, as the shrieking siren died away in the distance.

I reassured the children that it was unlikely, since only
uninhabited buildings, barns, and cars had so far been
burned.

"Did he burn the building across the street, Daddy?"
asked another, referring to a recent dramatic fire of unknown
origin that the children had seen the previous Sunday.

"No one knows," I replied, "but there weren't any people in that building, so we're sure he wouldn't burn houses
with people in them."

My wife and I talked about the children's fears. We
were uneasy too. We talked about the need for an escape
ladder from the second floor and about the pattern of recent fires, drawing comparisons with the arsonist burnings
of the previous year.

To reduce our fear, we bought several fire whistles that
would go off automatically when heated, and distributed
these around the house. A neighbor bought a ladder partly
as a fire-protection measure and showed us where he stored
it in the garage if we needed to reach the second floor, so
we gave up the idea of a rope ladder. We also arranged
with our neighbor to leave an upstairs door into the adjoining apartment unlocked as a fire exit, and told the children
about this.

I remember my thoughts as I locked up the house one
night: "He hasn't burned inhabited houses, but fire setting
is a crazy impulse, what is to stop him from burning homes?
Our basement door is unlocked at night. How easy it would
be to come in and set a fire! It would be an inferno before
we even awoke, two floors above." Images of leaping flames
surrounding the children flashed through my mind. I could
see us struggling to reach them, cut off in the end room
as they were!

I decided to lock the cellar door and did so every night
until the fire bug was finally caught.

Here are "emotional" responses. Do they show the properties our analysis of hunger in the Shackleton case revealed?

1. Fear affected the perceptual processes of the parents in making relevant things stand out in a focal way (they saw the firetrap nature of the children's room; the father saw the unlocked basement door in a different light).

2. Their thought processes were strongly influenced by the fear (the family and the whole town talked about the fires).

3. The parents learned new routes of expression for the motives now active (they pored over catalogues and discovered that they could buy fire sirens that heat would trigger and so warn of a fire in the basement or attic).

4. They used the new habits (by actually buying and installing the sirens).

5. They used old habits in service of the motive (as by locking doors and leaving exit passageways unlocked).

6. The fear led them to choose between goals (they spent much time in the evenings discussing this problem rather than on more pleasant things, and they gave up buying some needed household things to get the warning sirens; a neighbor spent over fifty dollars for a ladder; the father took pains to go down every night to lock the basement door).

What differences can be found between the hunger motive and the emotion of fear? Apparently both hunger and fear operate to arouse, sustain, and direct activities in these six important ways that are the mark of motivation!

Or, for that matter, it seems that emotional processes sometimes exert these influences so strongly that they countermand the influences of physiologically-based motives. Look again at the behavior of Shackleton's men. Suppose we ask whether their behavior was more powerfully directed by the motive of hunger than by any other process.

When we raise this question, immediately we can see that some other motive must have been involved. These men were "intensely, fiercely hungry." But what they did through the first half of their trip was steadily to work their way into a barren region where they knew they could find no food and where they were getting farther and farther away from the food stored at their base. And yet they kept moving on. Why?

We examine their behavior in the light of the six criteria analyzed above. All of these criteria indicate that they were motivated by more than just hunger. When they came to a fork in some valley they were traversing, they did not choose their route at random, or on the basis of the easiest travel or the most beautiful scenery. Each day, they were bent on putting the maximum distance between themselves and their well-stocked home base. They willingly endured the discomfort of intense hunger in the interests of another goal. Their behavior does not become understandable until we realize how desperately they wanted to reach the South Pole, with all the glory and other fruits of being the first men to do so. (They failed by only 97 miles!)

What were these other values or other goals? One could not say for sure without knowing the men individually. Perhaps in one case the main goal was professional prestige. In another case a highly personal curiosity or love of adventure, regardless of whether the trip later would ever be discussed with others. In another case perhaps a love of meeting and overcoming obstacles or of surpassing others. Perhaps an interest in geographical exploration from many other trips elsewhere in the world. We could decide between such alternatives only with extensive further observations of what choices these men made, what situations produced new learning in them, what choices they made of perceptual content, and so on.

In any case, we may be certain that the motivation would not have originated in tissue-states within their bodies; also that the motives that led them on toward the South Pole must have been stronger than their intense hunger, stronger than the need to terminate their exertions, stronger than any other motive springing from a bodily condition.

Or suppose we look at two other aspects of their behavior. We might ask, "Why didn't they eat more heartily? Actually, at each meal, they had more food with them than they prepared and consumed. If they were so hungry, why didn't they 'dig in'? Or, if they were so hungry, why didn't they try to steal food from one another?"

There apparently were regulating factors that controlled the men on both of these scores. Fear in the one case, perhaps; sense of honor or sense of comradeship, perhaps, in the other. From a behavioral point of view, we are compelled to recognize that apparently there were either some emotional processes in these men, or some representational processes, or some thought processes, that exerted effects characteristic of motives. Not only that, but when hunger pulled in one direction and these other processes pulled in another, these men acted more in accordance with these other processes than in accordance with their fierce hunger.

There is one difficulty. "What about the fact," you might say, "that the men talked and thought incessantly about food? It was only at intervals, at the most, that they thought about the fact that they were trying to reach the South Pole or that they needed to conserve their food. But they seem almost perpetually to have been conscious of their hunger."

Our answer to this question depends on how much we want to restrict the idea of motivation to the field of *conscious* mental activity. It is only in that sense that hunger was a more omnipresent motive than the desire to reach the South Pole. For if we deal with this matter *behaviorally*, rather than just in terms of conscious experience, we see that wherever food-seeking behavior competed with Pole-seeking behavior, Pole-seeking behavior won. Only at the last heartbreaking spot, where they estimated they were only about a hundred miles from the Pole, but where they had to admit that their resources of strength and food were so depleted that they could not extend their journey except at the certain cost of their lives, did they subordinate the Pole-seeking to anything else. Indeed, in most of their journey, even though they were not consciously thinking "We must struggle toward the Pole," there must have been some long-sustained processes within them that made them take one weary step after another in a direction dictated by this goal. And when the exigencies of the situation demanded especially careful choice of routes, they would then momentarily turn their attention consciously to topographical matters rather than to the allurements of food.

EMOTIONS, THEREFORE, ARE MOTIVES, THOUGH DIFFERENT IN SOME RESPECTS FROM PHYSIOLOGICALLY-BASED MOTIVES

The conclusion of this first step in our analysis, therefore, is that emotions or emotional processes *are* motives. There are other things that can be said about emotions, too, as some psychologists have pointed out, such as that they can add color and vividness to life. But the main point to be understood about emotional processes is that they arouse, sustain, and direct activity in basically the same ways that hunger and thirst do.

To say this does not say that all motives are emotions, any more than we could say that because all typewriters are machines, therefore all machines are typewriters. Instead, emotions are merely one subclass of the larger category. The other main subclass, contrasted with emotions, is composed of physiologically-based motives. Some of these are cyclical, such as hunger, thirst, and fatigue, which depend on a gradual development of conditions that finally produce such motives in a strong form. Some other physiologically-based motives rest on specific stimulation that need not be cyclical at all, as in cases of pain aroused by a burn, an electric shock, or a toothache. In the case of all physiologically-based motives, however, the motive exists only as long as some rather definite physiological condition continues to affect the central nervous system. Thus a toothache persists so long as certain sensory stimuli arouse nerve impulses that proceed from the tooth to the brain. When the dentist injects novocaine into the nerve and thus blocks the passage of nervous impulses, the toothache-motive stops.

Emotional processes, on the other hand, are matters of relatively long-sustained representational processes. They are matters of the individual's perception of his situation. Perceptual processes can continue without steady support from external stimuli. Thus, suppose a person who is very fearful of dentists has finally been driven to the dentist's office by a bad toothache. Suppose that the dentist has anesthetized the nerve and yet the person is still pale and trembling. The dentist might say to him, "Now, look—the toothache is gone, isn't it?" "Yes." "Well, why not relax? If you don't like the sight of my instruments or me, close your eyes and shut us out. I'll turn on the radio and all you will hear will be music. At least while I'm studying these x-rays, you ought to feel comfortable."

No dentist would try any such argument, of course, because he knows better. But if one did, the patient might well reply: "My toothache is gone, and I'll admit that I can shut out all the external stimuli that would make me feel afraid. But that doesn't matter. I can't kid myself. I *know* that I'm in your office and that you're going to start drilling pretty soon, and I hate it. You might as well turn your music off, unless you want it, and I might as well keep my eyes open and watch what you do." Emotions don't depend just on what stimuli are being received at the moment; they generally are representations or "perceptions" which started from stimuli of minutes or even hours before.

Emotional processes, in other words, are like processes of mental set for multiplying or adding—they are processes that can be aroused by rather slight cues, but that can guide other aspects of psychological activity in significant ways, and that can continue to operate over long periods of time even if the person does not continue consciously to hold the same mental set that was aroused in the first place.

THE BIOLOGICAL ADVANTAGES OF
EMOTIONAL MOTIVES

Ever since Charles Darwin published his book, *Expression of the Emotions in Man and Animals*, in 1872, psychologists have granted that emotional responses have certain limited biological advantages. Many animals respond in ways that make them look more dangerous when they are attacked, just as house-cats snarl and make their hair stand on end and so look bigger and stronger. The internal physiological effects of anger, rage, and fear frequently have biological value. A man or animal running away from an enemy can run faster and longer because certain of his emotional processes accelerate his heart beat, drive the blood supply from his digestive organs to the large muscles of the body, and release extra blood sugar, which is a source of energy, from the liver. Physiologists and psychologists have long recognized the advantages in these so-called emergency responses.

This is an instance, however, of the point that people develop an understanding of relatively tangible matters long before they come to understand other more subtle relationships. Thus, in the present instance, the physiological by-products that appear with such emotional processes are much less important in the whole economy of the organism than is the fact that emotional processes are motives—that they influence the other parts of the *psychological* functioning of the individual in ways that also are characteristic of physiologically-based motives.

Emotional motives have the following four special advantages as compared with physiologically-based motives:

1. *There are advantages in the fact that the emotional motives do not possess the strongly cyclical characteristic so typical of many, though not all, physiologically-based motives*. This cyclical character is appropriate for many physiologically-based motives. Thus, after hunger has been satisfied, it is appropriate that the organism should pass through a period of quiescence before becoming hungry again. In the case of the sex motive, a period of quiescence permits replenishment of the glandular products involved in a renewal of sex activity.

But in matters related to emotional activity, there is typically no such advantage in this cyclical phenomenon. Thus, if a hen has frightened away one cat that threatened her chicks, this does not mean that she can safely abandon, even for a short period, her readiness to respond in the same way to any other prowling cat. The hen is dealing with needs created by *environmental* factors rather than by any developments within her own body. Consequently, a kind of motivation that may operate continuously for long periods is needed, one that also may remain latent during other long periods merely because, under other environmental conditions, this motivation is not needed.

2. *Emotional motives can be touched off by much more delicate stimuli, and by much more precisely differentiated stimuli, than are required for the arousal of physiologically-based motives.* This is obviously true with regard to situations that are emotionally significant because of past learning. In these cases, it is easy to see that emotional processes can be excited by stimuli as slight as anything that the organism can differentiate perceptually, as in cases where deer have learned to respond with fear to the scent of cougars. But this principle is also seen in cases of unlearned emotional responses. If animals did not have such unlearned emotional responses, they would have to start their learning from some experience in which they actually received physical injuries from an enemy. But with unlearned emotional responses, much slighter cues can operate. Thus, Tinbergen has shown that young goslings will hide when they see a cardboard model with the silhouette of a hawk soaring overhead, but are not disturbed when something with the silhouette of a goose soars above them. Anyone who has observed quail knows that the warning cry of the mother bird causes her young to scatter and "freeze" and remain so quiet that, with their protective coloration, it is almost impossible to find them in the dried leaves and grass, even right at your feet.

3. *Emotional motives constitute the sort of motives that are developed by learning, and they are the ones, consequently, that can be elaborated for the particular circumstances of the given individual's life.* It is important, particularly in the case of the more complex organisms, and outstandingly in the case of man, that motivation should be highly variable from one individual to another. Thus, in a highly specialized civilization, there would be a lot of discontent if it were not possible for different persons to take delight in quite different sorts of vocational activity. It is because of this that the surgeon, the coal miner, and the political leader may each

love his own work, despite the enormous differences of activity. Because of their susceptibility to learned modification, emotional motives also get shaped to suit slightly different situations, so that a beekeeper, for instance, can work comfortably with bees under conditions where it is sensible for him to open up the hive, though he stays adequately motivated *not* to disturb the bees at other times when they would really "give him the works."

4. *Emotional motives have the advantages of operating as positive feedback mechanisms.* Perhaps you have encountered the phenomenon of *positive feedback* that is heard when the loud-speaker of a public-address system is too close to the microphone. The person speaks into the microphone, and the loudspeaker amplifies his voice; the increased sound comes back to the microphone, and is intensified still further. Once such a vicious spiral is started, the howl can get worse and worse, right to the upper limit of sound-production by the system.

The occurrence of such a phenomenon is a nuisance in most physical systems. Therefore, when engineers build complex systems that are intended to operate in self-regulating ways, they build them with a *negative feedback* or *reverse feedback,* instead. Thus, when the load on a steam engine gets lighter, and the engine starts to work more rapidly than it should, a governor reduces the amount of steam going to the pistons instead of increasing it (as would be the case with a positive-feedback system).

In these physical devices, however, there is some supply of energy already present in more or less optimal amount. The only thing that needs to be done is to increase or decrease the utilization of this energy to suit the changing conditions. But an organism is not like that. The organism does not have its different motivational energies already mobilized and pressing for expression. There isn't one "head of steam" that corresponds to "aggressive energy" and another "head of steam" that corresponds to "sex energy." Within the organism, instead, although there are potentialities for arousing any number of emotional processes in very strong form, these potentialities remain latent most of the time. At most moments, the potentially-intense emotional processes are like smouldering fires that have been carefully banked.

It would be wasteful for an organism to function otherwise. Energies would be unnecessarily squandered to maintain a considerable number of different emotional processes at full strength when only one or two were appropriate to the immediate situation. But at the same time it is true that an organism needs to be able to mobilize quickly any one of these energies when it really is relevant. When a deer approaches a water hole, it may be fairly quiet and unfearful at the moment (though probably, as a wild animal, never entirely devoid of some active fear). But when a sound is heard that indicates possible danger, there is a quick focusing of the eyes and of the perceptual processes generally on the spot from which the sound came, rather than on the water ahead. By this focusing the deer sees a cougar or hunter that otherwise would not have been perceived. And this perception will arouse an even more intense emotional response than that stirred up by the original sound.

In such situations we have the essentials of a positive-feedback system. Emotional processes seem to do the very sort of thing that engineers try to avoid in their mechanical devices. Emotional processes are a means—through such successively clarified representational processes, and through the working of reintegrative mechanisms—of quickly developing a strong motive out of what was merely a latent potentiality a moment before.

In each of these four respects, then, we see that emotional processes are not luxuries or frills from the standpoint of the fundamental life-needs of the organism. They sometimes create problems, of course, just as it is true that a person's struggles to obtain the air he needs may cause him to drown, whereas had it not been for this motive, he could have reached the surface before his need for air became too desperate. However, we ought not to derive our general picture of emotional processes only from situations in which emotions work disadvantageously, any more than we should regard fire or winds or rainfall as basically harmful because of the damage they can do. We need to see that, on the contrary, emotional processes are efficient mechanisms for the energizing and regulating of activity with reference to long-range objectives. They are indispensable in complex organisms. Human beings have survived, in the long course of evolution, partly because they are such emotionally sensitive and responsive creatures.

EMOTIONAL MOTIVES AS PERCEPTUAL PROCESSES

In the preceding discussion, there is one difficulty that may have been cropping out repeatedly in your thinking. You may have been saying to yourself: "True enough, the examples of emotion cited in this chapter have been instances of guiding, directing, organizing processes. The family worried about the arsonist, for example, certainly showed some well-organized thought and action. But what was described about that family was primarily their *perceptions* and *thinking*, and not their *emotional* processes as such. So, I am not sure that this chapter has been talking about emotions; it has been talking about perceptual processes for the most part."

If you have been bothered in some such way, you have been sharing much the same view that has prevailed rather extensively among psychologists regarding emotional processes. The most common views have drawn quite a contrast between emotional responses, on the one hand, and perceptual and conceptual processes on the other. Thus, some psychologists have hardly conceived of emotional responses as psychological processes at all, but have described them as primarily reactions of the visceral organs (of organs in the main body cavity and of the circulatory system more generally). Many other psychologists have tended to view emotions in somewhat the same way we do in everyday thought when we think of emotions merely as feelings, or affect. Thus, this way of thinking about emotions finds expression in statements about conflicts between intellectual processes and emotional processes (such as, "I knew what I should have done, but my emotions got the better of me").

Our ordinary language encourages this kind of view.

It includes a host of terms such as *fear, hatred,* and *delight* that refer to emotional processes as if they were merely generalized, diffuse processes. And we often use the names of emotions in this way. Thus, we say that it is fear that makes an elderly man pick his way carefully down an icy street, it is fear that makes a man run from a bull, it is fear that makes an inexperienced person afraid to speak before a group of people.

But before we decide to follow this everyday tradition, we ought to look more closely at such examples. We ought to check (either by introspective reports or by extensive behavioral observations) to see whether the "fear" that makes the elderly man move slowly down the street is the same "fear" that operates in the other cases. We find, of course, that it is not. The fear that operates in the elderly man is a specific, definitely-structured thing. It is a process that pictures his situation and its possibilities in quite particular terms. The fears that motivate the man being chased by a bull and the man who gets weak knees when he tries to speak to a group are different fears, and they too picture the situations of these men in precise ways. What follows from this, therefore, is that *emotional processes,* rather than being something outside of and distinct from perceptual processes, *are one type of perceptual process.* They are processes that represent realities, just as other sorts of perceptual processes do, but they are perceptual processes that are motivationally significant.

To clarify this interpretation of emotional processes, we might use this analogy: we may say that perceptual processes are like motion pictures. That is, they are processes that have some detail and fullness as representations of objective realities. Some of these motion pictures are merely in black and white. These might be compared to the perceptual processes that have no motivational character. But other motion pictures are in color. We might compare these latter movies to emotional processes. The fact that color (or motivational significance) is present in these perceptual processes does not mean that they are any less detailed, any less "perceptual" than those neutral perceptual processes usually employed in perceptual experiments. They do not have any less detail or less ideational content about them than the motivationally neutral perceptions; the difference is only that something has been added. (In the case of movies, of course, the pictures are either definitely black and white or definitely colored. A closer analogy with emotional processes would be suggested if we imagined that the movies virtually always have some color in them, but that the color varies from a virtually-absent shading in some perceptions to intense and vivid coloring at the other extreme.)

When we say all this, one objection has to be met. Both in clinical work and in everyday life, we see many examples of emotional responses where there is little that can be observed introspectively except some vague state of feeling. For example, people speak of having moods: "I don't know why I feel so gloomy—there isn't anything in particular that I'm gloomy about, but I just can't shake off the feeling." Or "I don't know why I'm feeling so happy today, but it's just that I seem on top of the world." Clinicians describe states of worry that they sometimes see in patients and speak about them as matters of "free-floating anxiety." The intimation in this phrase is that there is affect or feeling that is devoid of ideational content.

We have already met this same problem with regard to other processes, however. When subjects were asked to find a solution for Maier's problem of connecting nine dots by four straight, connected lines, these subjects did not realize that they had made any assumptions that limited their mode of attack on the problem. But Maier's research showed that people in problem-solving situations *do* have "directions" in their thinking that they are not conscious of. In these other areas, therefore, we know that we cannot take the introspective observation of the person as necessarily indicating the full nature of his psychological processes.

In the same way, when moods or "free-floating affects" are studied carefully enough, as in long therapeutic work, it becomes very clear that in the unconscious parts of the responses of these persons, there is actually a lot of specific perceptual detail. For instance, the so-called "free-floating anxiety" shows up with a given person only in certain sorts of situations, or it is related only to certain ways of acting on his part. Therefore, the full emotional process of the person or full perceptual process of the person is *not* one merely of affect, but has the larger character that perceptual processes have.

THE PROBLEM OF WHETHER EMOTIONS ARE
BASICALLY DISORGANIZING

There is one further difficulty that we should mention, but that we will not consider in detail. A number of psychologists have interpreted emotional processes as being basically different from motivational processes because they have portrayed emotional processes as being basically disorganizing. They have cited examples like this: when a boxer gets angry he starts to box more wildly and lays himself open to attack; when a person is in love it is hard for him to think about his work; when a person is worried about a sick child at home it is almost useless for him to try to enjoy a concert that, at another time, would please him very much; and when a person is afraid that he will be criticized for mistakes there is little likelihood that he can work as creatively and effectively as he might if he were not apprehensive of criticism.

Admittedly there is disorganization in these cases. But this does not prove that emotions are basically different from physiologically-based motives. When Shackleton's men were so hungry, it was this very physiologically-based motive that made it impossible for them to attend to many of the things around them that otherwise they would have attended to. From a more generalized theoretical standpoint, we can see that any process of an organizing sort, by that very fact, has to be also disorganizing in its effect upon some other processes. When a nation is organized for war, it has to disorganize or interfere with many, many peacetime activities. When a group of people meet as a committee, they may begin by swapping a lot of interesting personal remarks; but when the chairman wants business to start and calls them to order, the organized activity has to interfere with the free talk that would have gone on longer.

Sometimes organized activities are ill-chosen. A gang of criminals does not become socially valuable merely because it is organized. Similarly, when a person becomes so afraid of forgetting in a piano recital that he cannot play well, this fear has unfortunate consequences. It would be better if the person were organized in a different way. But the trouble is merely that the person is organized in ways that he ought not to be; it is not that he is not organized.

All of this needs to be seen from another standpoint, however. The thinking that people have done about emotional processes has hit first on the emotions that are dramatic and easy to see—processes like those of intense fear, or anger, or profound feelings of guilt. But a knowledge of these emotions which could be appreciated easily is not necessarily the most important knowledge.

In other words, the most significant emotional motives are not those that usually make the headlines in newspapers or that furnish the content for sensational movies. Instead, they are the powerful, steady motives that keep a man happily at his work day after day and year after year. They are the motives that make it possible for a woman, year after year, to do the work that is involved in caring for a family and yet experience that work as a privilege rather than as a burden. They are the motives that underlie our friendships, our life as citizens, our enjoyment of the world as a fascinating and wonderful place. And these motives are not primarily the physiologically-based motives; the motives that support the main activities of human life are the less tangible and perceptible from among the emotional motives.

Part II
Methods and Techniques

6

Methods For the Study of Feeling and Emotion

PAUL THOMAS YOUNG

University of Illinois

It is not surprising that there are as many methods for the study of emotion as there are theories. This observation serves to indicate that research findings are limited, and perhaps determined, by the method that is employed. That method and theory are so dependent is the reason that the student of emotion must be concerned with the techniques and methods which are used.

The following selection is the last portion of a chapter by Professor Paul Thomas Young which appeared in T. G. Andrews (Ed.). Methods of Psychology (New York: Wiley, 1948). In the selection Professor Young discusses some of the techniques which have been used in the study of feeling and emotion. The reader will note that Professor Young's research is also discussed in this selection. Some of his other work is included in Section IV.

The selection is reprinted with the permission of the author and publishers. (Copyright 1948 by John Wiley & Sons, Inc.)

Broadly considered, the affective processes include emotions, moods, sentiments, and interests, as well as the simple feelings characterized as pleasant and unpleasant. More narrowly, the affective processes are pleasantness and unpleasantness themselves. The latter are conscious experiences which can be reported and studied from the subjective point of view.

THE INTROSPECTIVE DESCRIPTION
OF FELT EXPERIENCE

Feeling is a conscious experience, and to study it one must employ the introspective method. This method will be illustrated by reference to an investigation by Nafe (1924).

Before the work of Nafe it was commonly assumed that pleasantness and unpleasantness are non-sensory processes. They differ in quality, in intensity, and in temporal course, but they lack attensity (attentive clearness). If one attempts to attend to a feeling of pleasantness or unpleasantness, he finds only sensory processes, especially organic and kinesthetic patterns. These patterns are attentively clear, but they are sensory in nature, not affective.

Nafe argued that earlier experimenters upon affective experience had been too much concerned with arousing feeling. They had made *feelers* of their subjects, rather than *observers of feeling*. To correct this state of affairs, feelings of only moderate intensity were aroused. The subjects were given a variety of stimulus objects in the visual, auditory, olfactory, gustatory, and tactual fields and were trained to observe feeling. Nafe started from the assumption that pleasantness (P) and unpleasantness (U) are *palpable* experiences, i.e., that these experiences in some way or other are observable and reportable.

In an actual experiment Nafe presented a stimulus object intended to arouse a moderately pleasant or a moderately unpleasant sensory experience. He instructed his subjects to attend as exclusively as possible to the affective side of experience and to describe the feeling itself as accurately as possible.

At first the observers had some difficulty in carrying out the instruction, but as the experiment continued they came increasingly to describe P as a bright pressure or pressure-like experience and U as a dull pressure or pressure-like experience. These affective pressures were described as varying in intensity, duration, and voluminousness. They were not precisely localized; usually they were not localized at all. Sometimes they were vaguely localized in some region of the body, and occasionally they were projected out from the body.

In a further experiment upon affective experience, however, Hoisington (1928) reported some observations upon the localization of *P* and *U*. The dull pressures of *U* were localized in the general region of the abdomen, well inside the body. The bright pressures of *P* were localized in the upper part of the body in the region of the shoulders and neck. The pressures of *P* were described as bright, light, expansive feelings in the chest; the pressures of *U* as dull, contracted feelings in the abdomen.

The interpretation of Nafe's result is a different problem. One may ask: Are these bright and dull pressures true sensory processes? If so, what and where are the receptors? Or are the pressure-like experiences merely the sensory concomitants of non-sensory affective processes? Further research will answer these questions.

THE DIRECT REPORT OF AFFECTIVE REACTION

In a good many psychological experiments the subject is instructed to indicate whether he *likes* or *dislikes* some object or activity. There is no attempt at descriptive analysis, as in the foregoing investigation. The verbal report of the subject is commonly supplemented by observations of gross behavior. This method will be illustrated by reference to a study by Richter.

Richter (1942-3) tested over a thousand children, ages five to fourteen, by letting each child taste a small spoonful of unadulterated cod-liver oil and asking him whether he liked or disliked it. The response of each child, verbal and non-verbal, was observed and recorded.

The results were changed into percentages of individuals *liking* cod-liver oil at each age level. These results are summarized graphically in Fig. 1, which shows the results for 328 children tested in one school near the Johns Hopkins Hospital.

In the 5-year group 100 per cent of the girls and 92 per cent of the boys liked the cod-liver oil. Progressively with increasing age, more and more children manifested a dislike for the substance. In the 14-year group only 36 per cent of the girls and 28 per cent of the boys liked it. Incidentally, Richter comments that some children at 14 years had an almost insatiable appetite for cod-liver oil. When allowed to satisfy their craving, they

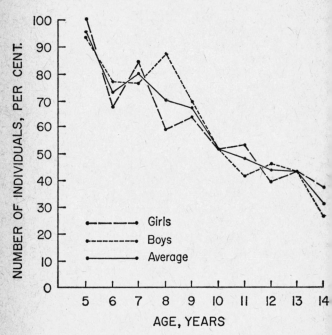

Fig. 1. *Decrease in the palatability of cod-liver oil with increasing age of individual. The curves are based upon a group of 328 Baltimore school children, ages 5 to 14. The percentage of individuals liking the taste of cod-liver oil is shown by the vertical scale. (After Richter, 1942-43.)*

took as much as 16 tablespoonsful in 1 day and continued to take high amounts for 5 to 10 days. After this they took small amounts and finally stated that they no longer liked it.

The psychological procedure in an experiment of this kind is relatively simple. No special training is required of the subject. It is necessary to determine through the words of the subject and by observing his gross behavior whether the affective reaction is one of acceptance or rejection, liking or disliking, yes or no.

OBJECTIVE OBSERVATION IN AFFECTIVE PSYCHOLOGY

When the problems of affective psychology are approached with a strictly objective point of view, they are found to center around the processes of acceptance and rejection and especially around preferential discrimination. The objective approach to affective psychology is illustrated by the studies of Young (1943) upon food preferences of the rat.

On a given trial the animal is offered a choice between two kinds of food presented simultaneously. As soon as he accepts one of the pair, both are removed from his reach. The foods are presented side by side, and their relative positions are interchanged from trial to trial so that, if a rat forms the habit of accepting the food in a given position, this fact can be readily detected. If he develops a preference between the foods, this is clearly apparent in a series of trials.

The foods are placed in glass food tubes, which are shown at F in Fig. 2. At the start of a test the rat is

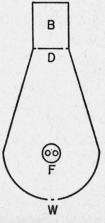

Fig. 2. Ground plan of apparatus for testing food preferences.

locked into a box (B). When a sliding door (D) is raised, the animal is permitted to enter the compartment containing the foods. The unpracticed animal explores the apparatus and discovers the foods in the process. The trained animal runs directly from the box to the foods and takes a bite or sip of one of them. His behavior is observed by the experimenter through a window (W).

After the rat has made a choice or nibbled one of the foods, both are lowered, and the opening in the floor is closed. The experimenter then waits until the rat returns to the box and the sliding door is closed. The time required for a rat to return to the box varies with the amount of training he has had and with the relative palatability of the foods.

The photograph in Fig. 3 gives further details of the technique. The food tubes (F) are held in a turntable (T), which can be rotated 180 degrees, clockwise or counterclockwise, by pulling upon strings (S). The foods can be raised or lowered by an elevator (E), so balanced that it remains indefinitely in the upper or lower position. The door to the box is attached to a lever arm (A), which the experimenter can control by means of a cord (C). Throughout a test a signal lamp (L) flashes once a minute. (In more recent work a buzzer, sounding once a minute, has been substituted for the lamp as a means of time control.) The observation window is seen at W.

A single trial reveals no preference, for behavior may be determined by spatial factors without true preferential discrimination. It requires at least two successive trials, with the relative positions of the foods interchanged, to indicate any preference. A pair of successive runs is thus the true unit of the test. In recent work ten pairs (twenty runs) have been arbitrarily used as a complete test of preference.

Among various results which have been obtained with the method of preference, several are as follows: (1) The foods in a group, when tested in all possible pairs, arrange themselves in a transitive series from high to low palatability. (2) When dietary conditions are held constant, the rats of a group show remarkable uniform-

Fig. 3. *Experimenter's view of the apparatus for testing food preferences.*

ity and stability in the food preferences they reveal. (3) A given food preference can be reversed by permitting a rat to approach satiation upon the preferred food before a test and by then running repeated tests of preference. (4) Food preferences depend upon the diet. By permanently adding an element to the diet, the relative palatability of this dietary component can be permanently lowered. (5) Rats tend to form dietary habits. Not only do they learn to run back and forth on the apparatus to obtain nibbles of food (shuttle habit), but also they sometimes learn to accept the food in a given position (position habit) and sometimes the food of a given quality (food habit). (6) Preferential food habits tend to form in agreement with bodily needs. Once a food habit has been formed, however, it may persist as an independent factor in behavior regardless of whether it meets a bodily need.

A COMMENT UPON THE BASIS OF
AFFECTIVE JUDGMENT

Carr (1925) has proposed a theory that reports of pleasantness and unpleasantness are actually judgments based not upon any unique and characteristic conscious content but rather upon our normal reactions to the stimulating situation. We are so organized, he points out, that we normally react to enhance, maintain, or repeat certain situations and to minimize or avoid others. A situation which normally arouses the positive kind of response is judged to be pleasant, and one which normally arouses the negative response is judged to be unpleasant. Carr adds that motivating factors complicate the problem. For considerations of health we swallow disagreeable medicine, stop smoking, or refrain from foods which we enjoy. Even though we swallow the medicine, we still judge it to be unpleasant because, if freed from considerations of health, we would reject it.

From the point of view of methodology, it is important to indicate that there is a difference between a judgment and the psychological processes upon which that judgment is based. Carr states that affective judgments are based upon the normal reactions of acceptance and rejection. He adds, however, that other factors than the normal reaction may determine the actual acceptance or rejection.

From the subjective point of view the affective judgment "X is pleasant" is not equivalent to the direct psychological report, "Pleasantness was felt." For example, the common statement, "This is a pleasant day" conveys a definite meaning, but it does not necessarily indicate the existence of pleasant feeling at the time the statement was made. As a matter of fact, a person may say, "This is a pleasant day," even though in a grouchy mood of unpleasant depression at the time of the judgment. The present writer has repeatedly found that subjects can describe the quality and intensity of their felt experience. They can trace out its temporal course—the beginning, the waxing and waning, the qualitative shifts, the ending. This is psychological report of existential experience, however, and not affective judgment.

The affective judgment, whether in the form "X is pleasant" or "X is more pleasant than Y," is ambiguous. It tells nothing directly about the affective processes within the subject.

This comment is made to point out that, if an experimenter accepts an affective judgment at face value, he is still ignorant of the psychological basis of that judgment. The experimenter must ask: Upon what is the affective judgment based? He must distinguish between the cognitive process of judging and the affective process of feeling.

METHODS OF IMPRESSION AND EXPRESSION

It has been traditional in affective psychology to classify the available methods as those of *impression* and those of *expression*. This classification implies that the study of consciousness is the central problem of psychology. The methods of impression are concerned with the relation between stimulus object and the conscious feeling it arouses. The methods of expression are concerned with the relation between conscious feeling and its bodily manifestations.

Historically considered, the methods of impression stem from the pioneer work of Fechner upon experimental esthetics. Of the several methods described by Fechner, the one which he designated as the *method of choice* has been developed into several contemporary forms. The forms differ in the number of stimulus objects presented simultaneously for affective judgment.

In the *order-of-merit method* the subject is presented simultaneously with a series of stimulus objects. These may be colored papers, spatial forms, works of art, photographic proofs, or other kinds of material. The subject is instructed to arrange the materials in order from the most to the least agreeable. The statistical analysis of results starts with the obtained orders of merit.

In the *method of paired comparison* the subject is presented with two stimulus objects at a time and is instructed to indicate which he prefers. A series of paired presentations is so planned that in the total series the subject compares each stimulus object with every other one. A record is kept of the choice. From the series of choices it is easy to determine the rank order of the stimulus objects in the group.

The method of paired comparison has also been used with the *successive* presentations of materials such as tones, musical chords, melodies, rhythms. With successive presentations both time orders are used to balance out a possible time error, just as both spatial arrangements are employed with *simultaneous* presentations to balance out possible space errors.

The number of comparisons with a single spatial arrangement or a single time order is equal to $N(N-1)/2$. If N (the number of stimulus objects) is relatively large, the method is not feasible because of the large number of required judgments.

In the *method of single exposure* the subject is presented with only one stimulus object at a time. This stimulus object is then judged or rated by means of a verbal scale of values, a graphic rating scale, or in some other manner. For example, the subject is given two whiffs of a perfume and asked to rate it in terms of the following scale:

$+3$ Very pleasant
$+2$ Moderately pleasant
$+1$ Weakly pleasant
0 Indifferent
-1 Weakly unpleasant
-2 Moderately unpleasant
-3 Very unpleasant

Instead, he may be given a graphic rating scale consisting of a horizontal line of fixed length, marked at one end as *maximally pleasant* and at the other as *maximally unpleasant*. He is instructed to indicate by a mark upon the line his affective rating of the stimulus object.

A technique combining the scale of values and the graphic rating scale has been described by Singer and Young (1941). Another modification, designated as the *percentage-of-pleasantness method*, has been described by Beebe-Center (1932).

In the percentage-of-pleasantness method the subject is instructed to respond in terms of three categories: pleasant (P), indifferent (I), unpleasant (U). Repeated ratings are made of the stimulus objects by the same subject or by a group. On the basis of the ratings a percentage of pleasantness is computed by this formula:

$$\text{Percentage of } P = \frac{P + I/2}{P + I + U} \times 100$$

The formula implies that indifference is statistically equivalent to one-half pleasant and one-half unpleasant. It might be argued that judgments of indifference should be disregarded on the ground that they indicate no affective arousal. We would then be left with the two affective categories: pleasant and unpleasant. These two affective ratings could be handled statistically in a very simple manner, as indicated by the data of Richter upon liking and disliking cod-liver oil.

A discussion of the statistical procedures employed in the analysis of results obtained with the methods of impression is beyond the scope of this chapter. The interested reader is referred to the discussion of psychological scaling methods by Guilford (1936). [A revised edition was issued in 1954.]

Next let us examine the methods of expression. At the turn of the century and in the first decade of the present century a good many experiments were carried out by the methods of expression. The general aim of these experiments was to study the relation between conscious processes, especially feeling and attention, and peripheral bodily changes, such as those in respiration, pulse, blood pressure, and glandular secretion. It was hoped to find some physiological *sine qua non* of pleasantness and unpleasantness, but this hope was not realized. Significant correlations were obtained, but no bodily process was invariably present when the subject reported *pleasant* or when he reported *unpleasant*.

The reasons for this failure are a matter of opinion. Several possible explanations occur to the writer. First, it is likely that the introspections of the subjects were ambiguous. At that time a clear distinction was not drawn between affective judgment (purely cognitive statement of meaning) and true affective report of existential pleasantness and unpleasantness. Second, the experimental techniques were directed exclusively to peripheral changes. In view of the results obtained, it seems likely that the physiological *sine qua non* of felt pleasantness and felt unpleasantness lies hidden within the dynamic interrelationships of central neural processes. Peripheral manifestations do not go to the heart of the problem. Third, it is a historical fact that at about this time American psychologists turned toward objective methods in psychology. Watson's behaviorism relegated the study of consciousness to the ash can. Since the methods of expression imply an interest in conscious feeling, these methods fell into disrepute.

This failure, however, does not imply that the problem is closed. Some day, with sharper definitions of terms and with more adequate physiological techniques, the central physiology of pleasantness and unpleasantness will be discovered.

The instruments employed in the study of bodily changes were for the most part borrowed from physiology. A partial list, with a few modern additions, follows:

PLETHYSMOGRAPH. An instrument for studying changes in the volume of the arm, hand, finger, or other part of the body. Volume changes are due to constriction or dilation of the blood vessels.

SPHYGMOGRAPH. An instrument for recording the pulse, showing changes in the rate, amplitude, or pattern of the beat.

SPHYGMOMANOMETER. An instrument for measuring

blood pressure. Absolute blood pressure can be measured at a given moment. Continuous variations in blood pressure can be measured by setting the instrument at a pressure level between maximal (systolic) and minimal (diastolic) pressure.

PNEUMOGRAPH. An instrument for measuring changes in the rate, depth, and pattern of respiration. (A pneumograph for registering abdominal respiration may be seen in Fig. 4.)

DYNAMOMETER. An instrument for measuring the strength of pull of a group of muscles.

ERGOGRAPH. An apparatus for recording the work done by a group of muscles. An ergograph requires the subject to lift a weight rhythmically by arm or leg muscles.

TREMOGRAPH. An instrument for measuring involuntary muscular tremor in the skeletal muscles. In using the tremograph, the subject is instructed to hold steady his finger or a stylus.

AUTOMATOGRAPH. An apparatus for recording involuntary movement. The subject is required to rest his arm on a suspended board or to place his fingers lightly on a glass plate which rests upon steel balls. Involuntary movements are recorded graphically or photographically.

ATAXIMETER. An instrument for recording body sway.

GALVANOMETER. An instrument used in studies of the skin galvanic reflex for measuring changes in the electrical potential of the body.

VOICE KEYS AND MICROPHONES. Instruments employed for recording vocal reactions.

ELECTROENCEPHALOGRAPH. An instrument for recording changes in electrical brain waves during psychological processes, emotional and non-emotional.

These instruments are commonly employed to investigate bodily changes for their own sake and without reference to conscious experience. Some of the methods used in the objective study of the bodily changes of emotion will be described in the next main section of this chapter. For further discussion of the classical methods of impression and expression see Chapter 2 of Beebe-Center (1932).

PSYCHOLOGICAL TESTS

Two kinds of psychological tests are especially pertinent to the present topic. First, there are tests of attitude, interest, and value. Second, there are tests which reveal emotional and motivational traits of personality.

Tests of attitude, interest, and value reveal some specific readiness of the individual to react positively or negatively. An *attitude* has been defined as a neural or mental readiness to respond toward or against some psychological object. A persistent prejudice against the Japanese or a bias favoring the Catholic Church is an attitude. An *interest* is an activity which one carries on, with enjoyment, for its own sake, such as playing golf or singing. Activities which are unpleasant are called *aversions*. A *value* is that which a person regards as worthwhile.

In testing values, for example, the subject is required to make a discrimination between possible alternatives. Let the reader answer this hypothetical question: Would it be justifiable to remove all the water from Niagara Falls, thus destroying its beauty, to generate electric power? If the answer is yes, economic value is placed ahead of esthetic. If the answer is no, esthetic value is placed first. There is no right or wrong answer. It is a question of what one regards as more worth while.

The Allport-Vernon (1931) test of value requires the subject to make a series of such discriminations. From the scores a profile is constructed to show the relative balance for that individual among six forms of value: theoretical, economic, esthetic, social, political, religious.

The extensive literature upon tests of social attitude has been reviewed by Allport (1935).

After a program of testing and factor analysis, Cattell (1944) described twelve primary factors in personality. Several of these factors are described as emotional or motivational traits. The C factor is described in these terms:

> realistic, facing life vs. demoralized, autistic
> stable, integrated character vs. changeable, characterless, unrealistic
> calm, self-effacing, patient vs. restless, sthenic, hypomanic
> emotionally mature, adjusting vs. infantile, demanding, self-centered

The *E* factor, designated dominance (hypomania) vs. submissiveness, is described in these contrasting terms:

self-assertive vs. self-submissive
willful, egoistic, predatory vs. mild, self-effacing, tolerant
smart, assertive vs. simple-hearted, meek
tough, solid, talkative vs. introspective, sensitive, scared
rigid, tyrannical, vindictive vs. adaptable, friendly
surly, hard vs. good-natured, easy-going

In the *E* factor the emphasis is upon self-assertiveness and submissiveness in social situations. Hence this factor has motivational implications.

METHODS FOR INVESTIGATING BODILY
CHANGES OF EMOTION

An emotion is a natural event. It is something that happens, as does a thunderstorm or a sunrise. It is a complex occurrence, so complex that it must be analyzed piecemeal and from different points of view.

In the older writings of Wundt, James, Titchener, McDougall, and others, an emotion was regarded as a conscious event, and the fundamental problems centered around the relation between the conscious emotion and its bodily expressions. Today psychologists are more interested in the objective aspects of emotion. When viewed objectively, however, the emotion is still exceedingly complex. One must distinguish between the situation which arouses an emotion and the reaction thereto. The emotional reaction itself has both inner and outer aspects. The following example illustrates the different objective aspects.

Cannon [1929] has pointed out that during emotional excitement there is an increase in the number of red blood corpuscles (erythrocytes per cubic millimeter) circulating in the blood stream. This increase can be attributed directly to the action of the spleen. The spleen, a muscular organ, contracts and expands; it is a reservoir for erythrocytes. It renders the organism the service of quickly increasing and later of storing away the red corpuscles in the blood. Contraction of the spleen occurs in carbon monoxide poisoning, in hemorrhage, in the lessening of the oxygen content of the blood, as during asphyxia and muscular exercise, and after injections of adrenalin and pituitrin, as well as during emotional excitement.

Cannon has interpreted this fact. The erythrocytes carry oxygen from lungs to heart, brain, and active muscles. In a biological emergency which might involve a struggle for one's life, this reaction of increase is serviceable in that it facilitates the release of energy within the body. The increase in the number of erythrocytes in the blood is a small part of the pattern of bodily changes aroused by an external situation.

If a dog barks at a cat, the cat's hair bristles, his back arches, he spits and growls, his claws protrude, and there are widespread internal bodily changes, including the increase of erythrocytes in the blood stream. Just what is the emotion?

Some psychologists and physiologists use the term *emotion* to designate certain reflex patterns of response —the rage pattern, crying, laughing, etc.—which are coordinated by neural centers in the region of the hypothalamus and below. Others prefer a broader definition: An emotion is an acute disturbance of the individual, arising from the psychological situation, revealed in conscious experience, in behavior, and through marked changes in the vegetative organs.

The emphasis in this definition upon the psychological situation serves to distinguish emotions from organic appetites, which arise from internal bodily conditions. In the above example the barking of a dog is an environmental event. It arouses internal bodily changes which have environmental significance. The bodily changes of emotion arise from a psychological situation—meeting an enemy or a mate or being socially ostracized.

SIMULTANEOUS RECORDING OF BODILY CHANGES IN EMOTION

For practical purposes it is usually necessary to record only one or two kinds of bodily change in emotion. In lie detecting, for example, a continuous record of respiration or blood pressure or both is sufficient to indicate emotional upset in the prevaricator. Lie detecting, from the point of view of experimental psychology, is really emotion detecting. It rests upon the fact that the involuntary bodily changes of emotion can be observed with the proper apparatus and recorded. Whether the involuntary bodily changes of emotion are due to the telling of a lie cannot be determined from the record, but only from the relation of these bodily changes to the questions asked by the examiner and the total situation. Lie detecting is an art, not an exact science.

In scientific investigations of emotion it is often necessary to record several kinds of bodily change simultaneously in order to see how they are interrelated. To show the simultaneous recording of bodily changes in emotion several illustrations will be given.

Figure 4 shows the subject comfortably seated in an easy chair. A pneumograph attached to the abdomen records the cycle of respiration. The middle finger of both hands is placed in a tremograph to record involuntary muscular changes. A cuff is attached to the left arm

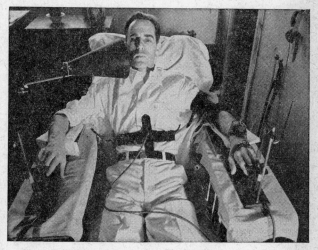

Fig. 4. Subject adjusted to apparatus for recording simultaneous bodily changes in emotion. The subject shown in Fig. 4 is a normal individual employed by the U.S. Public Health Service when the picture was taken. (Photograph, courtesy of Dr. Ralph R. Brown.)

of the subject for obtaining a continuous record of changes in blood pressure. Electrodes in the wrist and palm are for obtaining galvanic skin changes. The head of the subject is near a voice key.

Figure 5 shows the experimenter's apparatus, which is located in an adjoining room. Through a one-way-vision

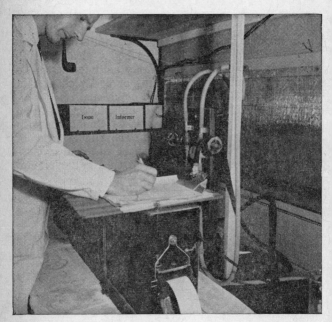

Fig. 5. Darrow's photopolygraph for recording simultaneous bodily changes in emotion. (Photograph, courtesy of Dr. Ralph R. Brown.)

screen the experimenter can observe the subject seated in the easy chair and can, if necessary, communicate with him. Any pertinent observations upon the gross behavior of the subject, as well as a record of the experiment itself, can be written down on the spot. All bodily changes, whether mechanical or electrochemical, are converted into movements, which can be photographically recorded within the instrument shown in this picture.

Figure 6 is a sample strip of photographic record. In the actual trial the word "dopey" was visually exposed, and the subject responded with "junkie." (Dopey is commonly used to mean one who uses narcotic drugs. Junkie means drug addict. Morphine or heroin is frequently called junk in the argot of the addict, and one who uses such drugs may be called a junkie or junker or old dopey.) The break in the voice-response line indicates the moment that the vocal response occurred.

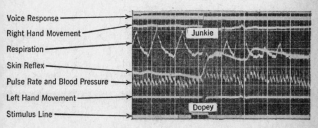

Fig. 6. A sample strip of record obtained from Darrow's photopolygraph. (Photograph, courtesy of Dr. Ralph R. Brown.)

Involuntary hand movements are registered at the top and bottom of the record. The curve of respiration is clearly shown. From the vertical time lines it is possible to determine the fraction of the total respiratory cycle given to inspiration, or the rate of breathing, or to study changes in the pattern or depth of respiration. The curve for the galvanic skin response crosses the respiratory curve, but both can be readily measured and analyzed. Changes in pulse rate and blood pressure are clearly recorded.

At the present time Darrow would probably bring into the picture the more modern electroencephalograph.

ANALYSIS OF PATTERNS OF RESPONSE,
ILLUSTRATED BY THE STARTLE RESPONSE

Everyone has experienced the general muscular contraction which occurs reflexly when there is an unexpected and intense noise, such as the bang of a gun. The startle response is often followed by the emotion of fear, but the reflex itself is typically over before a true emotion can arise.

Landis and Hunt (1939) analyzed the startle pattern in both man and animals. To produce startle, they fired a gun near the subject. Since the gun was of known caliber (0.22 and 0.32 were used), there was at least a rough standardization of the stimulus.

To record the response Landis and Hunt made use of high-speed motion-picture cameras. Startle was photographed with cameras taking 64 exposures per second. In some parts of their work, cameras making as many as 300 to 3000 exposures per second were employed. Later the pictures were projected at the usual rate of 16 per second.

To obtain a photographic record of certain bodily movements, levers were employed. The levers were attached to the back of the trunk and to the knees, so that forward movement of these parts was converted into vertical movement of the levers. Abdominal contraction was recorded by a pneumograph attached to a tambour, which moved a lever in the field of the camera.

From the motion-picture records it was possible to reconstruct the spread of the startle response throughout the body. The startle response usually comes and goes in less than half a second, although the range for the total response varies from 0.3 to 1.5 seconds. Startle begins with closing of the eyelids, both eyes reacting simultaneously. Next there is a widening of the mouth, as though in a grin, but only occasionally does this lead to the baring of the teeth. Then the head and neck are brought forward and down, but the chin is tilted up, so that the features are still directed straight ahead. The muscles of the neck stand out prominently. Then the response sweeps downward. There is raising and drawing forward of the shoulders, abduction and pronation of the upper arms, flexion of the fingers, forward movement of the trunk, contraction of the abdomen, and bending of the knees. A schematic representation of the startle response is shown in Fig. 7.

Observations of startle were made with animals at the Bronx Zoological Park. Although startle was not observed in reptiles and amphibia, the pattern was clearly

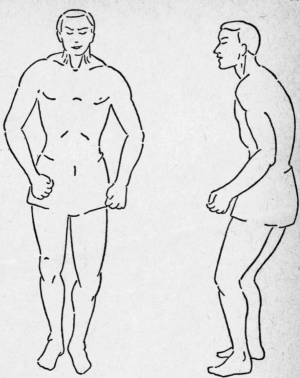

Fig. 7. *Schematic representation of the startle pattern, showing front and lateral aspects of the response to a revolver shot.* (After Landis and Hunt, 1939.)

present in mammals. With animals the most notable addition to the human pattern is the flexion of the ears. Frequently the ears are laid back close to the skull. Sometimes there is a crouching posture with legs braced as if to spring; this suggests biological utility of the response in self-defense. With monkeys and chimpanzees the response is more widespread and complete than with man.

The methodological significance of the work of Landis and Hunt lies in the fact that they have described a technique for the objective investigation of at least one pattern of response. The motion-picture technique can probably be applied to the analysis of other patterns of response which appear as components of emotional behavior, such as the rage pattern, the pattern of disgust, crying, smiling, laughing, and possibly the sexual patterns. Certain physiological psychologists, in fact, have defined an emotion as a *pattern of response*. Although this definition is somewhat narrow, all would agree that the experimental study of patterns of response is a task of major importance.

SURGICAL METHODS IN THE INVESTIGATION OF EMOTIONAL BEHAVIOR

Although the possibilities of applying surgical methods to the investigation of emotion are numerous, only two illustrations are here considered: first, the operation of decortication; second, the technique of implanting electrodes in the hypothalamus for purposes of direct stimulation.

If the cerebral cortex is surgically removed, the preparation can, with care, be kept alive for experimental study and observation. Culler decorticated dogs for experiments upon conditioning, but the animals were also used for observation of emotion. Culler prepared a motion-picture film showing the machine-like behavior of the decorticate dog. In a quiescent environment the dog may walk monotonously around a circular path. If an obstacle is placed in his path, he simply comes to rest. If the skin of such a preparation is rubbed, even lightly, however, there is a display of vicious rage. The pattern of rage includes baring of the teeth, snapping, and biting. There is also snarling or growling, along with diffuse struggling of the entire body. The biting of the animal is localized at the point of stimulation and is so vicious that the experimenter is in real danger when handling the animal. The pattern at the height of its intensity is illustrated in Fig. 8 which is the enlargement of a frame in Culler's film. Incidentally, this pattern of rage is similar to that of a normal dog, as pictured years ago by Darwin.

Other investigators have performed the operation of decortication upon cats. The decorticate cat gives a

Fig. 8. Pattern of rage in a decorticate dog. (Printed by Dr. John T. Cowles from Professor E. A. Culler's film on behavior of the decorticate dog.)

remarkable exhibition of rage, which includes lashing the tail, arching the trunk, protrusion of the claws and clawing movements, snarling or growling, spitting, turning the head from side to side with attempts to bite, rapid panting with the mouth open, movements of the tongue. Along with these bodily changes are others due to excitation of the sympathetic nervous system: erection of the hairs on the tail and back, sweating at the toe pads, dilation of the pupils, increased rate of heart beat, increased arterial pressure, increased blood sugar, abundant secretion of adrenalin.

The pattern of rage in a decorticate or decerebrate animal has been designated *sham-rage* on the assumption that, since the cerebral cortex has been removed, the animal cannot consciously experience an emotion. There is, however, no way of knowing about the possible consciousness of a decorticate cat or dog.

The second illustration of surgical methods in the investigation of emotional behavior is taken from the work of Masserman [1943, 1946] upon the role of the hypothalamus. His method has been to implant electrodes, so that a given center can be stimulated directly by electrical or chemical means. Figure 9 illustrates Masserman's method.

View A shows the frame of the Horsley-Clarke apparatus for orienting and fixing the head of an anesthetized cat. Control bars slide into two curved earplugs (*seen in the foreground*). The upright carrier of the apparatus can be moved to direct electrodes stereotactically into the brain. The electrodes are used to produce electrolytic lesions of nerve tracts and nuclei. Further, one or more needle electrodes (*foreground center*) may be inserted and held *in situ* by means of skull screws (*seen behind the earplugs*). The electrodes make it possible to stimulate a selected neural center with accuracy after the animal has recovered from the operation.

View B is a close-up of the apparatus in use. The head of an anesthetized cat is shown in position. Above is a hypodermic needle for pharmacologic stimulation of the hypothalamus.

View C shows the brain of a cat used in an experiment upon the differential effects of alcohol upon the hypothalamus and the cerebral cortex. The sulci have been outlined on the photograph to show clearly the points of insertion of the separate electrodes.

View D shows a section of the right hemisphere of the brain of a cat. The brain has been marked to show the paths (actually, less than 0.5 millimeter in diameter) of the electrodes through the cortex and into the hypothalamus. The fornix is outlined in dots to aid in orientation. The exact location of the electrodes and lesions was determined for each brain by study of histological sections.

It is not possible to consider in detail the significance of work such as that of Masserman. In general, his research has demonstrated the following: (1) The emotion-like patterns of behavior produced by direct stimulation of the hypothalamus ended abruptly with the cessation of the stimulus. (2) Conditioning did not occur when sensory signals were associated with hypothalamic stimulation as frequently as 480 times. (3) Animals which recovered from the severe metabolic disturbances caused by lesions in the hypothalamus regained their normal emotional reactions.

Fig. 9. Surgical techniques for studying the role of the hypothalamus in emotion. See explanation in text. (After Masserman, 24.)

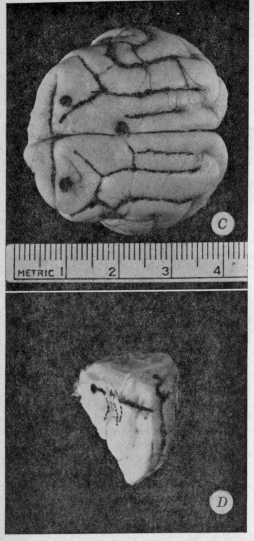

Fig. 9 (cont'd). Surgical techniques for studying the role of the hypothalamus in emotion. (After Masserman.)

These and other findings have led Masserman to infer that, although the hypothalamus is undoubtedly a coordinating center for the sympathetic and motor pathways of emotional *expression*, it is not the source or the seat of affective experience.

EMOTIONAL EXPRESSIONS AND SOCIAL EXPRESSIONS

When Darwin wrote his great book, *The Expression of the Emotions in Man and Animal* [1872], he was concerned in a thoroughly objective manner with the outward manifestations of emotion. He did not consider what it is, whether conscious feeling or neural process or organization of personality, that these outward manifestations express. One result of Darwin's objectivity is that his careful observations are valuable today, even though psychology has made great advancement in the methodology and factual knowledge of emotion.

Today the phrase *emotional expression* is commonly used. It contains, however, a certain ambiguity. The phrase may refer to innate patterns of response, such as crying, smiling, laughing, rage, and disgust, which are common to mankind through the world. The phrase may also refer to individually acquired patterns of response. For example, it is customary in our society to smile in salutation. The smile is learned and enacted as truly as the words that go with it. Superficially, the social expression of smiling may be very similar to the truly reflex pattern. A line of distinction between the innate reflexive pattern and the acquired social expression is not always easy to draw. The distinction was drawn, however, by Landis in interpreting the results of an experiment upon emotion.

Landis (1924) brought real-life situations into the laboratory to arouse genuine emotion. He required his subjects to listen to music, read the Bible, smell ammonia, view pictures of skin diseases, examine pornographic material, read sex case histories, handle live frogs, decapitate a rat, receive electric shocks, etc. The facial responses were photographed. The extent of involvement of the different groups of facial muscles was determined by measuring the distance between dark marks placed on the subject's face before photographing. Measurements of the distances between these marks revealed the groups of muscles involved in a given expression and the extent of the muscular contraction.

For a group of twenty-five subjects Landis failed to discover any fixed pattern of facial expression common to any one of his situations. Each subject tended to use some particular group of facial muscles habitually to the exclusion of others. Landis concluded that emotion, as shown in the face, is commonly not a true pattern of reflex response. He suggested a distinction between innate reflexive patterns and acquired social expressions of emotion.

The same distinction was drawn by the social psychologist Klineberg [1938] on the basis of very different evidence and methodology. Klineberg examined the conventional expressions of emotion in the Chinese novel and upon the Chinese stage.

These conventional expressions differ so widely from those in our own country that some of them would not be understood by a man from our Western civilization. For example, "They stretched out their tongues" is an expression of surprise. "Her eyes grew round and opened wide" usually means anger to the Chinese, and the sentence, "He made his two eyes round and stared at him" can mean only anger. To us this description suggests fear. "He scratched his ears and cheeks" might to us suggest embarrassment, but in the Chinese novel the phrase means happiness. "He clapped his hands" is likely to indicate worry or disappointment.

On the other hand, Klineberg discovered certain expressions in the Chinese novel and on the stage which beyond a question describe the truly reflexive bodily changes of emotion. To illustrate, the emotion of fear is described by the Chinese in such sentences as: "Everyone trembled with a face the color of clay," "Every one of his hairs stood on end, and the pimples came out on the skin all over his body," "A cold sweat broke forth on his whole body, and he trembled without ceasing," "They were so frightened that their waters and wastes burst out of them."

It is obvious, therefore, that a distinction must be

drawn between the innate bodily changes of emotion and the acquired social expressions. In designing any experiments in this field the distinction must be kept in mind. The distinction was not clearly drawn in a group of early experiments upon the expression of "emotion" in the face, in the voice, by gesture and in gross behavior. A good many experiments have been concerned with the agreement among groups of judges in rating photographs. In evaluating these experiments one should ask: To what extent are the bodily changes innate reflexive patterns? To what extent are they acquired conventional expressions? And, in any event, just what is meant by the *expressions* of an emotion?

CONCLUSION

The present chapter is concerned with a representative group of methods used in the experimental study of motivation, feeling, evaluation, and emotion. Although diverse methods are considered, the list is far from complete. On the one hand, a good many other methods are employed in comparative and physiological psychology. These methods are used in the study of animal drives, emotionality and temperament of animals, and conflict and neurosis, and for the analysis of internal bodily processes which release the energy of behavior and regulate its pattern. On the other hand, there are further methods in social psychology, clinical psychology, psychiatry, child development, the psychology of counseling, and other areas of applied psychology. In the applied psychologies at least the following methods are used: the psychoanalytical methods of aided recall, the word-association method, hypnosis, the projective techniques, a variety of tests and psychological measurements not considered in this chapter, the life-history method, and the social case method, as well as the study of individual conflicts, frustrations, and sources of satisfaction. The variety and diversity of methods would be even greater if the scope of the chapter were extended.

In conclusion it is well to ask: Why is there such a diversity of method?

One answer is that the processes under consideration

are exceedingly complex. They are so complex, in fact, that they must be examined piecemeal and from different points of view. There is a diversity of point of view, a diversity of interest, a diversity of aim among investigators, a diversity of problem. And along with these diversities there is, as we might expect, a diversity of experimental method in dealing with such complexity. As stated at the start of this chapter, unity lies not in the methods themselves, for they are many, but in the fact that the methods are all oriented toward the solution of a group of interrelated problems.

The real explanation of the diversity of experimental methods probably lies in the fundamental importance of the processes and problems under consideration. In any theory of personality the dynamics of behavior is a topic of major concern. One cannot understand frustration, conflict, satisfaction, adjustment and non-adjustment, tics, impulsions, traits, habits, and other characteristics of the individual without a sound understanding of motivation, affectivity, and emotion. These processes are basic in importance. And, practically considered, the processes considered in this chapter are of major importance in clinical psychology, psychiatry and psychosomatic medicine, educational psycholoy, the psychology of counseling, the analysis of social problems, and the other fields of applied psychology.

It is because the problems of motivation, affectivity, and emotion are so important and so central, theoretically and practically, that there have been varied attacks upon them. When complex problems of central importance are studied by men with different aims and points of view, it is to be expected that a diversity of method will develop in the attack upon them.

REFERENCES

ALLPORT, G. W. *Attitudes, Handbook of Social Psychology.* C. Murchison (ed.), Worcester, Mass.: Clark University Press, 1935. (Chap. 17.)

BEEBE-CENTER, J. G. *The Psychology of Pleasantness and Unpleasantness.* New York: Van Nostrand, 1932.

CANNON, W. B. *Bodily Changes in Pain, Hunger, Fear and*

Rage; An Account of Recent Researches into the Function of Emotional Excitement. New York: Appleton, 1929.

CARR, H. A. *Psychology, a Study of Mental Activity.* New York: Longmans, 1925. (Chap. 13.)

CATTELL, R. B., Interpretation of the twelve primary personality factors, *Char. Personal.*, 1944, **13**, 55-91.

DARWIN, C. *The Expression of the Emotions in Man and Animal.* London: Murray, 1872.

GUILFORD, J. P. *Psychometric Methods.* New York: McGraw-Hill, 1936. (Part II.)

HOISINGTON, L. B., Pleasantness and unpleasantness as modes of bodily experience. In *Feelings and Emotions, the Wittenberg Symposium.* M. L. Reymert, (ed.). Worcester, Mass.: Clark University Press, 1928. (Chap. 20.)

KLINEBERG, O., Emotional expression in Chinese literature, *J. Abn. Soc. Psychol.*, 1938, **33**, 517-520.

LANDIS, C., Studies of emotional reactions. II. General behavior and facial expression, *J. Comp. Psychol.*, 1924, **4**, 447-501.

LANDIS, C., and HUNT, W. A. *The Startle Pattern.* New York: Farrar and Rinehart, 1939.

MASSERMAN, J. H. *Behavior and Neurosis, an Experimental Psychoanalytical Approach to Psychobiologic Principles.* Chicago: Univ. of Chicago, 1943.

———. *Principles of Dynamic Psychiatry, Including an Integrative Approach to Abnormal and Clinical Psychology.* Philadelphia: Saunders, 1946.

NAFE, J. P., An experimental study of the affective qualities, *Amer. J. Psychol.*, 1924, **35**, 507-544.

RICHTER, C. P., Total self-regulatory functions in animals and human beings, *The Harvey Lectures*, Series 1942-3, **38**, 63-103.

SINGER, W. B., and YOUNG, P. T., Studies in affective reaction. I. A new affective rating scale, *J. Gen. Psychol.*, 1941, **24**, 281-301.

YOUNG, P. T. *Emotion in Man and Animal: Its Nature and Relation to Attitude and Motive.* New York: Wiley, 1943. (Chap. 3 for studies of food preference.)

Part III
Experimental Findings and Observations

7

A Laboratory Study of Fear: The Case of Peter

MARY COVER JONES
University of California, Berkeley

However one may evaluate the assumptions and conclusions of Watson's "behaviorism," it cannot be denied that Watson's ideas stimulated research and furnished psychology with a testable theory of behavior. The following report is concerned with the elimination of fear in a child by the use of conditioning techniques suggested by Watson.

The original article appeared in the Pedagogical Seminary and Journal of Genetic Psychology (*now the* Journal of Genetic Psychology) *1924, 31, 308-315, and is reprinted by permission of the author and the journal.*

As part of a genetic study of emotions,[1] a number of children were observed in order to determine the most effective methods of removing fear responses.

The case of Peter illustrates how a fear may be removed under laboratory conditions. His case was selected from a number of others for the following reasons:

1. Progress in combating the fear reactions was so marked that many of the details of the process could be observed easily.

2. It was possible to continue the study over a period of more than three months.

3. The notes of a running diary show the character-

[1] The research was conducted with the advice of Dr. John B. Watson, by means of a subvention granted by the Laura Spelman Rockefeller Memorial to the Institute of Educational Research of Teachers' College, Columbia University.

istics of a healthy, normal, interesting child, well adjusted, except for his exaggerated fear reactions. A few descriptive notes show something of his personality:

> Remarkably active, easily interested, capable of prolonged endeavor. . . . A favorite with the children as well as with the nurses and matrons . . . Peter has a healthy passion for possessions. Everything that he lays his hands on is his. As this is frequently disputed by some other child, there are occasional violent scenes of protest. These disturbances are not more frequent than might be expected in a three-year-old, in view of the fact that he is continually forced to adjust to a large group of children, nor are they more marked in Peter's case than in others of his age. Peter's I. Q. at the age of 2 years and 10 months was 102 on the Kuhlmann Revision of the Binet. At the same time he passed 5 of the 3 year tests on the Stanford Revision. In initiative and constructive ability, however, he is superior to his companions of the same mental age.

4. This case is a sequel to one recently contributed by Dr. Watson and furnished supplementary material of interest in a genetic study of emotions. Dr. Watson's case illustrated how a fear could be produced experimentally under laboratory conditions.[2] A brief review follows: Albert, eleven months of age, was an infant with a phlegmatic disposition, afraid of nothing "under the sun" except a loud sound made by striking a steel bar. This made him cry. By striking the bar at the same time that Albert touched a white rat, the fear was transferred to the white rat. After seven combined stimulations, rat and sound, Albert not only became greatly disturbed at the sight of a rat, but this fear had spread to include a white rabbit, cotton wool, a fur coat, and the experimenter's hair. It did not transfer to his wooden blocks and other objects very dissimilar to the rat.

In referring to this case, Dr. Watson says, "We have shown experimentally that when you condition a child to show fear of an animal, this fear transfers or spreads in such a way that without separate conditioning he becomes afraid of many animals. If you take any one of these objects producing fear and uncondition, will fear

[2] Watson, J. B., and Watson, R. R., Studies in infant psychology, *Scientific Monthly*, Dec. 1921.

of the other objects in the series disappear at the same
time? That is, will the unconditioning spread without
further training to other stimuli?"

Dr. Watson intended to continue the study of Albert
in an attempt to answer this question, but Albert was
removed from the hospital and the series of observations
was discontinued.

About three years later this case, which seemed almost
to be Albert grown a bit older, was discovered in our
laboratory.

Peter was 2 years and 10 months old when we began
to study him. He was afraid of a white rat, and this fear
extended to a rabbit, a fur coat, a feather, cotton wool,
etc., but not to wooden blocks and similar toys. An
abridgment of the first laboratory notes on Peter reads
as follows:

> Peter was put in a crib in a play room and immediately
> became absorbed in his toys. A white rat was introduced
> into the crib from behind. (The experimenter was behind a
> screen.) At sight of the rat, Peter screamed and fell flat
> on his back in a paroxysm of fear. The stimulus was re-
> moved, and Peter was taken out of the crib and put into
> a chair. Barbara was brought to the crib and the white rat
> introduced as before. She exhibited no fear but picked the
> rat up in her hand. Peter sat quietly watching Barbara and
> the rat. A string of beads belonging to Peter had been left
> in the crib. Whenever the rat touched a part of the string
> he would say "my beads" in a complaining voice, although
> he made no objections when Barbara touched them. In-
> vited to get down from the chair, he shook his head, fear
> not yet subsided. Twenty-five minutes elapsed before he was
> ready to play about freely.

The next day his reactions to the following situations and
objects were noted:

Play room and crib . . . . Selected toys, got into crib
                                        without protest
White ball rolled in . . . . Picked it up and held it
Fur rug hung over crib . . . . Cried until it was removed
Fur coat hung over crib . . . . Cried until it was removed
Cotton . . . . Whimpered, withdrew, cried
Hat with feathers . . . . Cried
Blue woolly sweater . . . . Looked, turned away, no
                                        fear

White toy rabbit of rough cloth . No interest, no fear
Wooden doll . . . . No interest, no fear

This case made it possible for the experiment to continue where Dr. Watson had left off. The first problem was that of "unconditioning" a fear response to an animal, and the second, that of determining whether unconditioning to one stimulus spreads without further training to other stimuli.

From the test situations which were used to reveal fears, it was found that Peter showed even more marked fear responses to the rabbit than to the rat. It was decided to use the rabbit for unconditioning and to proceed as follows: Each day Peter and three other children were brought to the laboratory for a play period. The other children were selected carefully because of their entirely fearless attitude toward the rabbit and because of their satisfactory adjustments in general. The rabbit was always present during a part of the play period. From time to time Peter was brought in alone so that his reactions could be observed and progress noted.

From reading over the notes for each session it was apparent that there had been improvement by more or less regular steps from almost complete terror at sight of the rabbit to a completely positive response with no signs of disturbance. New situations requiring closer contact with the rabbit had been gradually introduced and the degree to which these situations were avoided, tolerated, or welcomed, at each experimental session, gave the measure of improvement. Analysis of the notes on Peter's reactions indicated the following progressive steps in his degrees of toleration:

A. Rabbit anywhere in the room in a cage causes fear reactions.
B. Rabbit 12 feet away in cage tolerated.
C.   "   4   "   "   "   "   "
D.   "   3   "   "   "   "   "
E.   "   close   "   "   "
F.   "   free in room tolerated.
G.   "   touched when experimenter holds it.
H.   "   touched when free in room.
I.   "   defied by spitting at it, throwing things at it, imitating it.

J. Rabbit allowed on tray of high chair.
K. Squats in defenseless position beside rabbit.
L. Helps experimenter to carry rabbit to its cage.
M. Holds rabbit on lap.
N. Stays alone in room with rabbit.
O. Allows rabbit in play pen with him.
P. Fondles rabbit affectionately.
Q. Lets rabbit nibble his fingers.

These "degrees of toleration" merely represented the stages in which improvement occurred. They did not give any indications of the intervals between steps, nor of the plateaus, relapses, and sudden gains which were actually evident. To show these features a curve was drawn by using the seventeen steps given above as the Y axis of a chart and the experimental sessions as the X axis. The units are not equal on either axis, as the "degrees of toleration" have merely been set down as they appeared from consideration of the laboratory notes with no attempt to evaluate the steps. Likewise the experimental sessions were not equidistant in time. Peter was seen twice daily for a period and thence only once a day. At one point illness and quarantine interrupted the experiments for two months. There is no indication of these irregularities on the chart. For example, along the X axis, 1 represents the date December 4th when the observation began. 11 and 12 represent the dates March 10 A.M. and P.M. (From December 17 to March 7, Peter was not available for study.)

The question arose as to whether or not the points on the Y axis which indicated progress to the experimenter represented real advance and not merely idiosyncratic reactions of the subject. The "tolerance series" as indicated by the experimenter was presented in random order to six graduate students and instructors in psychology to be arranged so as to indicate increase in tolerance, in their judgment. An average correlation of .70 with the experimenter's arrangement was found for the six ratings. This indicates that the experimenter was justified from an a priori point of view in designating the steps to be progressive stages.

The first seven periods show how Peter progressed from a great fear of the rabbit to a tranquil indifference

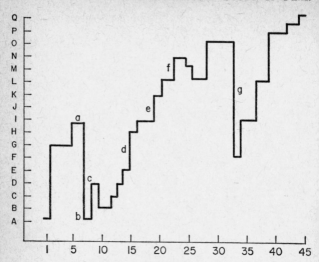

and even a voluntary pat on the rabbit's back when others were setting the example. The notes for the seventh period (see *a* on chart) read:

Laurel, Mary, Arthur, Peter playing together in the laboratory. Experimenter put rabbit down on floor. Arthur said, "Peter doesn't cry when he sees the rabbit come out." Peter, "No." He was a little concerned as to whether or not the rabbit would eat his kiddie car. Laurel and Mary stroked the rabbit and chattered away excitedly. Peter walked over, touched the rabbit on the back, exulting, "I touched him on the end."

At this period Peter was taken to the hospital with scarlet fever. He did not return for two months.

By referring to the chart at (b), it will be noted that the line shows a decided drop to the early level of fear reaction when he returned. This was easily explained by the nurse who brought Peter from the hospital. As they were entering a taxi at the door of the hospital, a large dog, running past, jumped at them. Both Peter and the nurse were very much frightened, Peter so much that he lay back in the taxi pale and quiet, and the nurse debated whether or not to return him to the hospital. This

seemed reason enough for his precipitate descent back
to the original fear level. Being threatened by a large
dog when ill, and in a strange place and being with an
adult who also showed fear, was a terrifying situation
against which our training could not have fortified him.

At this point (b) we began another method of treatment, that of "direct conditioning." Peter was seated in
a high chair and given food which he liked. The experimenter brought the rabbit in a wire cage as close as
she could without arousing a response which would interfere with the eating. Through the presence of the pleasant
stimulus (food) whenever the rabbit was shown, the fear
was eliminated gradually in favor of a positive response.
Occasionally also, other children were brought in to help
with the "unconditioning." These facts are of interest
in following the charted progress. The first decided rise
at (c) was due to the presence of another child who
influenced Peter's reaction. The notes for this day read:

> Lawrence and Peter sitting near together in their high
> chairs eating candy. Rabbit in cage put down 12 feet away.
> Peter began to cry. Lawrence said, "Oh, rabbit." Clambered
> down, ran over and looked in the cage at him. Peter fol-
> lowed close and watched.

The next two decided rises at (d) and (e) occurred on
the day when a student assistant, Dr. S., was present.
Peter was very fond of Dr. S. whom he insisted was his
"papa." Although Dr. S. did not directly influence Peter
by any overt suggestions, it may be that having him there
contributed to Peter's general feeling of well being and
thus indirectly affected his reactions. The fourth rise on
the chart at (f) was, like the first, due to the influence
of another child. Notes for the 21st session read:

> Peter with candy in high chair. Experimenter brought
> rabbit and sat down in front of the tray with it. Peter cried
> out, "I don't want him," and withdrew. Rabbit was given
> to another child sitting near to hold. His holding the rabbit
> served as a powerful suggestion; Peter wanted the rabbit on
> his lap, and held it for an instant.

The decided drop at (g) was caused by a slight scratch
when Peter was helping to carry the rabbit to his cage.

The rapid ascent following shows how quickly he regained lost ground.

In one of our last sessions, Peter showed no fear although another child was present who showed marked disturbance at sight of the rabbit.

An attempt was made from time to time to see what verbal organization accompanied this process of "unconditioning." Upon Peter's return from the hospital, the following conversation took place:

> E.: (experimenter) What do you do upstairs, Peter? (The laboratory was upstairs.)
> P.: I see my brother. Take me up to see my brother.
> E.: What else will you see?
> P.: Blocks.

Peter's reference to blocks indicated a definite memory as he played with blocks only in the laboratory. No further response of any significance could be elicited. In the laboratory two days later (he had seen the rabbit once in the meantime), he said suddenly, "Beads can't bite me, beads can only look at me." Toward the end of the training an occasional "I like the rabbit," was all the language he had to parallel the changed emotional organization.

Early in the experiment an attempt was made to get some measure of the visceral changes accompanying Peter's fear reactions. On one occassion Dr. S. determined Peter's blood pressure outside the laboratory and again later, in the laboratory while he was in a state of much anxiety caused by the rabbit's being held close to him by the experimenter. The diastolic blood pressure changed from 65 to 80 on this occasion. Peter was taken to the infirmary the next day for the routine physical examination and developed there a suspicion of medical instruments which made it inadvisable to proceed with this phase of the work.

Peter has gone home to a difficult environment but the experimenter is still in touch with him. He showed in the last interview, as on the later portions of the chart, a genuine fondness for the rabbit. What has happened to the fear of the other objects? The fear of the cotton, the fur coat, feathers, was entirely absent at our last interview. He looked at them, handled them, and immediately turned to something which interested him more. The reaction to the rats, and the fur rug with the stuffed head was greatly modified and improved. While he did not show the fondness for these that was apparent with the rabbit, he had made a fair adjustment. For example, Peter would pick up the tin box containing frogs or rats and carry it around the room. When requested, he picked up the fur rug and carried it to the experimenter.

What would Peter do if confronted by a strange animal? At the last interview the experimenter presented a mouse and a tangled mass of angleworms. At first sight, Peter showed slight distress reactions and moved away, but before the period was over he was carrying the worms about and watching the mouse with undisturbed interest. By "unconditioning" Peter to the rabbit, he has apparently been helped to overcome many superfluous fears, some completely, some to a less degree. His tolerance of strange animals and unfamiliar situations has apparently increased.

The study is still incomplete. Peter's fear of the animals which were shown him was probably not a directly conditioned fear. It is unlikely that he had ever had any experience with white rats, for example. Where the fear originated and with what stimulus, is not known. Nor is it known what Peter would do if he were again confronted with the original fear situation. All of the fears which were "unconditioned" were transferred fears, and it has not yet been learned whether or not the primary fear can be eliminated by training the transfers.

8

Emotional Development
in Early Infancy

Katharine M. Banham Bridges[1]

As is true of all behavior, emotional behavior is a developmental process which varies as a function of the age and experience of the organism. Both the articles by Professors Watson and Mary Cover Jones were concerned with emotional responses in children and the way in which they were developed and altered. The following article is concerned with observations of the development of emotional behavior in children. This study is one of the earliest and most thorough attempts to evaluate emotion developmentally.

The selection is reprinted from Child Development, *1932, 3, 324-341, with the permission of the author and the publisher. The figure is redrawn.*

The emotional behavior of 62 infants in the Montreal Foundling and Baby Hospital was carefully observed and recorded daily over a period of three or four months. The circumstances attendant upon these reactions were noted, and the whole data was studied from the point of view of development from age to age. A summary of the findings will be presented in the following paragraphs. They will be seen to lend support to the writer's (2) (3) theory of the genesis of the emotions and to add further illuminating detail.

The babies under observation were in separate wards more or less according to age. In different rooms were infants under one month, one to three months, three to six

---

[1] The article was published under this name. Dr. Katharine M. Banham is now at Duke University.

months, six to nine months, nine to twelve months, and twelve to fifteen months. An older group of children between fifteen and twenty-four months of age played together in the nursery.

Table 1 shows the number of children at the different ages whose behavior was observed for this study.

Development in the emotional behavior of the young child comprises 3 main classes of change. From birth onward there is a gradual evolution of the emotions taking place. The earliest emotional reactions are very general and poorly organized responses to one or two general types of situation. As weeks and months go by the responses take on more definite form in relation to more specific situations. It seems to the writer, as already mentioned elsewhere, that in the course of genesis of the emotions there occurs a process of differentiation. Coincident with the partial isolation of certain responses is a combining of the simpler reactions within the unit

TABLE 1

Age in Months	Number of Children
Under 1	3
1- 3	16
3- 6	23
6- 9	18
9-12	11
12-15	20
15-18	8
18-21	5
21-24	6
Over 24	2

responses and the formation of bonds of association between these emotional syndromes and detailed aspects of the provoking situations. In this manner slowly appear the well known emotions of anger, disgust, joy, love, and so forth. They are not present at birth in their mature form.

In addition to the progressive evolution of the emotions, there is, going on at the same time, a gradual change in the mode of response of each specific emotion. Muscles are developing, new skills are being learned. So that the anger, for instance, expressed by the eighteen-month-old differs in detail of form from the anger manifested by the ten-month-old baby. Fresh bonds of association are being made between emotional behavior and the always slightly varying attendant circumstances. Different situations come to have emotional significance for the growing child and subsequently provoke emotional responses. Thus a gradual substitution takes place of the situations which prompt the emotions. In the language of the behaviorists, emotional responses become conditioned to fresh stimuli.

EXCITEMENT, THE ORIGINAL EMOTION

After observing the behavior of babies *under one month* of age, the writer felt more than ever convinced that the infant does not start life with 3 fully matured pattern reactions, such as have been mentioned by behaviorists and named fear, rage and love. Unfortunately the writer was not able to observe the infants within a few hours of birth, but this fact in no way invalidates observations made on children two or three weeks old. Moreover, if the above named emotional responses are really the 3 great primary emotions from which all our adult emotions are derived, surely they may still be observed a month or more after birth. And, even if the process of conditioning begins before or immediately upon birth, one may expect the original emotion-producing stimuli to elicit their natural responses at least for two or three weeks after birth.

It was observed in the hospital that, on presentation of certain strong stimuli the infants became agitated, their arm and hand muscles tensed, their breath quickened, and their legs made jerky kicking movements. Their eyes opened, the upper lid arched, and they gazed into the distance. The stimuli producing such agitation or excitement were: bright sun directly in the infant's eyes, sudden picking up and putting down on the bed, pulling the child's arm through his dress sleeve, holding the arms tight to the sides, rapping the baby's knuckles, pressing the bottle nipple into the child's mouth, and the noisy clatter of a small tin basin thrown on to a metal table whence it fell to the radiator and the floor.

The loud sound startled only four of the one- and two-month-old babies, while six others lay practically undisturbed. None of the infants cried after hearing the noise. The same experiment was tried upon children of successive ages up to fifteen months. Under two or three months the reaction was one of sudden but rather mild general excitement as described above. Children of three or four months and older gave more of a jump and looked definitely in the direction of the sound. Afterwards they remained still with eyes and mouth open, and stared towards the source of the commotion. One baby of eight months stiffened and turned away on the second trial. The corners of his mouth turned down, his eyes moistened and he looked to the adult for sympathy and comfort. Another child of eleven months sat wide-eyed and still, the corners of his mouth drooping as if he were ready to burst into tears. The older childen merely stood, or sat, alert and attentive without further sign of distress.

Lowering the babies suddenly into their cribs, and in some cases lifting them quickly, also startled and excited them. Sometimes they would cry following upon such a surprise. Rocking a quiet child would cause him to open his eyes attentively. But gently rocking a crying infant would often, though not always, cause him to reduce his activity, stop crying, and eventually become tranquil. Gentle handling, slow patting, wrapping in warm blankets, and nursing easily soothed an agitated or crying infant, making him relax and yawn and become sleepy.

Light pinching of the arm left the three- or four-week-old baby unmoved. Deeper pressure caused him to kick slightly, breathe faster and move his arms. A sharp flick on the hand produced similar agitation, but a second rap resulted in a sudden check to breathing followed by a prolonged cry and other signs of distress. The first exciting experience had been found disagreeable and the second rap produced unmistakable distress.

Time after time on waking suddenly from sleep the infants were observed to wave their arms jerkily, kick, open and close their eyes, flush slightly, and breathe quickly and irregularly. Some grunted, some cried spasmodically for a moment or two, while others cried loudly for several minutes. The combined stimulation of light, of sounds, of damp or restricting bed clothes, and the change from sleeping to waking breathing-rate seemed to produce a temporary agitation and often distress. Waking apparently requires emotional adjustment.

The hungry child before feeding would often show restless activity, waving, squirming, mouthing and crying at intervals. The infant who had been lying in one position for a long time and the tired child before falling asleep would also show emotional agitation. Their breath would come jerkily, uttering staccato cries of "cu-cu-cu-ah," and they would thrust out their arms and legs in irregular movements. At the moment the nipple was put into the hungry baby's mouth he again breathed quickly, occasionally cried, waved the free arm, and kicked in excited agitation.

The emotional reactions of the tiny infant are certainly not highly differentiated. The most common response to highly stimulating situations seems to be one of general agitation or excitement. It is a question which word most aptly describes the behavior. The former perhaps conveys more the idea of general disturbance, although the two words are often used synonymously. This vague emotional response to a large variety of circumstances must surely be one of the original emotions, if not the only one.

A kind of general excitement over new and startling or other highly stimulating circumstances may be seen at any age. The behavior manifestations vary from time to time, but the main characteristics of accelerated response, alertness, slight tension or restlessness remain as constant attributes. In the babies, excitement is frequently manifested in kicking movements. The month-old infants kick jerkily with both feet at random. In another month or so, the kicking becomes more regular, the legs being thrust out alternately. By five or six months the babies express their emotions in combined leg thrusts, kicking with one foot, and in swinging the legs from the hips. At fourteen months when the children can stand they will hold onto a support and "mark time" with their feet or stamp. Stamping, jumping and running express excited agitation at a still later age.

Two- and three-month-old babies may be seen to suck their thumbs or fingers rapidly in moments of stress. At seven months and over, children bite, pull and suck their garments as well as their fingers. This behavior seems to produce a gradual subsidence of the emotion. Body-rocking accompanied in many instances by rhythmic vocalizations is another expression of mixed emotion. Hungry, annoyed, excited or restless children will sit and rock for minutes on end. The five-month-old baby lies prone and pushes with his knees, or sways when lying dorsally. Seven-month-old infants support themselves on their arms and rock back and forth murmuring "m̄m̄-ŭm, m̄m̄-ŭm." After nine months they sit up and rock to and fro, or they kneel and bounce up and down holding onto the crib bars. Sometimes they sit and bump their backs against the side of the crib. This kind of behavior was observed in the nursery up to eighteen months of age.

Rhythmical movements were observed not only to be the outcome of emotional excitement or tension, but they were seen to have a soothing and pacifying effect. These must be attempts at adjustment on the part of the organism to reduce tension and restore emotional equilibrium or tranquility. In the light of these observations, it can be easily understood how long walks, games, field sports, singing, dancing, and sea-voyages are found to be so universally health-giving and positively curative for "nervous wrecks."

DISTRESS AND ITS DERIVATIVES

It is a moot question whether "distress" is an original emotion or whether it is a very early differentiated reaction to disagreeably painful and unsatisfying experiences. It may be that it is a part of the general emotional response of excitement which copes more satisfactorily with obnoxious stimuli. Tense muscles resist or remove pressure; activity warms a chilled body and reduces tension; and cries, at first reflex due to the rush of air in and out of the lungs, bring comfort and aid. These responses become differentiated from excitement, associated together and conditioned to the disagreeable stimuli as a result of experience. If such differentiation actually takes place, it must begin immediately after birth. For the two emotions of excitement and distress are already distinguishable in a three-weeks-old infant.

On the other hand, it is possible that there is a native emotional response to pain, particularly muscle pain. The sympathetic branch of the autonomic nervous system is predominantly active and the overt behavior is definitely that of distress. Other stimuli, such as loud sounds and sudden falling merely produce startled excitement. Blanton (1) observed that the infant's cry of colic had a specially shrill character accompanied by rigidity of the abdominal walls. She also noted that infants during the first days of life cried from "(1) hunger; (2) in response to noxious stimuli (including rough handling, circumcision, lancing and care of boils, sores, etc.); and (3) possibly fatigue or lack of exercise." The writer has observed the same phenomena in three-weeks-old babies. But, hunger, rough handling, and fatigue were also noticed on many occasions to produce a restless excitement rather than specific distress.

It is not easy, in the case of the very young infant, to distinguish distress from general agitation. Perhaps the most characteristic marks of the former are greater muscle tension, interference with movement and with breathing, closing of the eyes, and loud rather high-pitched crying. In children of two months and over, the eyes become moist and tears may flow. The crying of the infant *under a month* or even six weeks often seems to be part of the general activity in excitement. Breath comes more or less regularly, the cry emerging on both intake and expiration of air. There are no tears, and the skin does not flush. Movement is free though rather jerky; and the mouth is held open in an elliptic, round, or square shape.

The cry of distress, recognizable in the *month-old* baby, is irregular. There are short intakes of breath and long cries on expiration. The eyes are "screwed up" tight, the face flushed, the fists often clenched, the arms tense, and the legs still or kicking spasmodically. The mouth is open and square in shape or, more usually kidney-shaped with the corners pulled down. The pitch of the cry is high and somewhat discordant, and sounds something like "ah, cu-ah, cu-ah, cu-æh."

Cries of distress were heard from month-old babies in the hospital on the following occasions: on waking suddenly from sleep, struggling to breathe through nostrils blocked with mucous, when the ears were discharging, when lying awake before feeding time, after staying long in the same position, lying on a wet diaper, when the child's buttocks were chafed, and when the fingers were rapped. The three main causes of distress at this age, therefore, seemed to be discomfort, pain, and hunger.

Crying from discomfort and on awakening usually developed slowly, and sounded like "cu-cu-cu-cah-ah—." The cry of pain came suddenly, often after a holding of the breath. The sound was a loud shrill prolonged "ă-ă-ă," and lowered in pitch slightly from the first emission. The cries of hunger were rather like those of discomfort. The former came perhaps more in intermittent waves; the intervening moments being taken up with mouthing or sucking movements. Occasionally the hungry child would utter a sharp loud cry, as if in pain, and then whine or moan for a time.

Two-month-old babies cry less of the total waking time; but slighter, discomforting stimuli seem to cause distress more frequently than in the case of the younger infants. They are more disturbed by a wet diaper, by flatulence, and by tight clothing which restricts movement and makes breathing difficult. Their movements are freer and they tend to move their heads from side to side when they are distressed. While one-month-old babies kick irregularly with jerky movements, the two-month-old kicks his legs alternately and more regularly. He waves his arms up and down when agitated or distressed, as well as in spontaneous play. The sound or sight of an approaching person will not quiet his distress; but being picked up will do so, or being fed if he is hungry.

By *three months* of age a child will cry and show other signs of distress when placed in an unusual position or moved to a strange place; as, for instance, when lain temporarily at the foot of another child's bed. He will wave his arms laterally as well as up and down, and will kick more vigorously. The hospital baby has learned to associate feeding time with the presence of an adult; for, when he is hungry he shows some excitement at the close approach of a person. He stares at the person's face, waves, kicks, breathes faster, and opens his mouth. If no food is forthcoming, he becomes more tense and jerky in his movements and begins to cry. He is distressed at the delay in normal proceedings.

Should the adult remain tantalizingly near for some minutes without either picking up the child or feeding him, his cry increases in intensity, his eyes become moist with tears, he holds his breath longer, and utters prolonged flat "ă-ă-ă" sound reminiscent of an older child's "paddy" or temper cry. The infant's motor responses were all set for being picked up and fed, and then he was thwarted and disappointed. His excitement changed into bitter distress with a semblance of angry vexation.

The slight change in vowel sound of the cry, the long holding of breath combined with more than usually vigorous leg thrusts and arm movements, seemed to suggest that the emotion of anger is beginning to evolve from general distress at about this age. Although for the most part the distress shown at discomfort differs almost imperceptibly from distress in response to disappointment, occasionally the latter includes, to a marked degree, those behavior elements peculiar to the emotion of anger. The situations which evoke these demonstrations of temper in the tiny infant are a stop or check in the progressive satisfaction of a physical need. In the above instance the child's appetite was aroused but not satisfied. Lack of even the first sign of a need being satisfied merely produces vague distress.

A *four-month-old* baby shows distress at the same general sort of situation that troubles the younger child. He is, however, less frequently disturbed by bodily discomfort. He moves about sufficiently to relieve tired muscles and local pressures, and to eliminate gas from his stomach. He cries vigorously at delay in the feeding process and may show decided temper on such occasions. His arms then stiffen and tremble; he screws up his eyes, flushes, holds his breath and utters prolonged and irregular cries on expiration of breath; he kicks violently, pushes with his feet and looks at any adult, presumably to see the effect. He is getting very fond of attention at this age, and will show distress and often anger when a person leaves the room or ceases to pay attention and play with him.

At *five months*, the baby's interest in small objects, such as rattles, stuffed animals and, of course, his milk bottle, causes him to be distressed when these objects are removed. He may express his displeasure as formerly by crying, squirming, waving and kicking, but he may also be heard merely to call out in a protesting tone of voice, "ah aye," without the half-closing of the eyes and the accompanying tensions of crying.

By this age the child may show slight revulsion for certain foods, coughing, spluttering, frowning and crying while he is being fed. Chopped vegetables and soup too thick in consistency were specially disliked by some babies in the hospital. Cereals, milk, and sweetish foods were almost always taken readily. It was noted that babies under three months often refused to drink sterile water. They just let it run out of their mouths without swallowing. There was no emotion involved in this reaction. Similarly, three- and four-month-old babies sometimes rejected their thin vegetable soup, but were not very disturbed about it. A genuine emotional revulsion did not appear till five months or later. Perhaps this is the beginning of the emotion of disgust. Revulsion at nauseating sights and smells, the adult form of disgust, apparently does not develop until two or more years of age.

Several of the babies in the hospital *between six and eighteen months* were observed to splutter and choke, and refuse to swallow spinach more than other vegetables. The mouthfuls that were rejected were usually, though not always, those containing large or stringy pieces of spinach. When the latter was chopped fine it was swallowed a little more easily; but only when it was mixed with other vegetables was it eaten without any protest. There must be factors other than consistency and size of morsel to account for this objection to spinach.

It seemed to the writer that some cans of spinach tasted more bitter than others and were less palatable on that account. In order to find how the children would react to a bitter taste, two teaspoonsful each of unsweetened grape-fruit juice were given to nine children in the nursery. Four of them pursed or curled their lips, 1 turned his head away, and 1 frowned. The others sat still and solemn, and kept tasting their lips attentively for some time. There were certainly individually different reactions to this bitter-sour astringent taste. Several of the children definitely disliked it and none of them seemed to like it. It is possible then that there is a bitter taste to spinach which may in part account for children's aversion to it. Another factor, that of the dark green colour of spinach may influence older children's and adult's feeling reaction towards it. One two-year-old in the hospital on turning away and refusing to eat the vegetable was seen to point to it and say "dirty."

The *six-month-old baby's* attention is usually arrested by the presence of a stranger. His movements are inhibited and he watches the newcomer intently. He is not pleased and one could hardly say he is afraid. But he seems diffident and uncertain what to do, or utterly unable to move for a few moments. At seven months he reacts in the same way to the approach of a stranger, though the general inhibition of movement is greater and lasts longer. After a few moments or several seconds of tension he may begin to cry slowly, or burst suddenly into tears. The whole body is usually rigid and inactive. The eyes, previously wide open, close tight and the head bends. Should the stranger touch the child he will probably turn or draw away. Here is the emotion of fear already differentiated. Frightened distress results when the child through inhibition, ignorance, or inability finds himself unable to respond at all adequately to the situation.

At *seven months* of age an infant calls out protestingly when a familiar person ceases to attend to him, instead of crying distressfully like a four-month-old. He still cries and kicks angrily if some object in which he was deeply engrossed is taken from him. He does so also after being highly excited by a playful adult when the latter goes away or stops playing with him. He now makes prolonged attempts to get at objects out of reach. If he fails to attain his objective he may give up and cry in helpless distress, or he may just grunt in protestation.

A *nine-month-old child* will struggle longer and make more varied attempts to reach the object of his desire. Should he fail to do so after putting forth considerable effort he may become tense and red in the face with anger. He will kick and scream and look for assistance, while tears flow copiously. The cry at this age is becoming exceedingly loud, and tears flow more readily than at the earlier ages. Prolonged crying at four or five months is accompanied by slight lacrimal secretion, but after six months of age tears often flow down the child's cheeks as he cries, especially after an adult's attention has been attracted.

Strangers are still quite terrifying to the nine-month-old baby. His movements are more completely arrested by the unfamiliar presence than those of the six-month-old. He will remain immovable for several minutes unless the newcomer approaches very close to him. In that case he will lie face down or bend his head and probably begin to cry. At ten months of age he may even be so frightened as to flop down suddenly on the bed and scream loudly. Then follows prolonged and tearful crying.

When children of *ten months* and over are hungry, uncomfortable, tired, or fretful and unwell, they will set up a whine or cry as the result of suggestion when another child cries. They do not, however, ordinarily imitate crying when they are occupied and happy. Under these circumstances they may call or babble in a pitch similar to that of the other child's cry. Small objects which can be manipulated interest them so intensely that they can be distracted from a distressing trouble fairly easily at this age. These objects need not necessarily be new so long as they are freshly presented.

Year-old babies often cry suddenly when they feel themselves falling, or when they lose their grip while climbing. If they miss the assistance of a helping hand they will also sit down and cry loudly. Sometimes their emotion is anger at the thwarting or failure of their endeavors. They scream, flush, and tremble in rage. At other times they sit motionless in fright and look for aid or comforting sympathy. When strangers approach the *twelve-* or *thirteen-month-old* baby he may hold his hand behind his ear in a withdrawing motion and stare apprehensively. He may actually hide his eyes behind his hands or look away so as not to see the awe-inspiring or annoying intruder.

At *fourteen months* or thereabouts we may see the real temper tantrum. At least, that is the age when it became noticeable in the hospital. If a child is not given his food or a coveted toy exactly when he wants it he may respond by throwing himself suddenly on the bed or floor. He then screams, holds his breath, trembles, turns red, kicks or thrusts his feet out together. Tears flow and he will wave away anything that is not the desired object. These outbursts may occur frequently for a few weeks, or only spasmodically for another year or eighteen months. The children under observation seemed to have their "off-days" when they were fretful and easily distressed or roused to anger. Such days were usually when they were incubating or recovering from colds, when the hospital routine was disturbed, or after the children had been excited by parents' visits.

Distressful crying becomes less common as the months go by. Extreme hunger and weariness after a long day or great activity may be accompanied by whining and intermittent outbursts of tears. Anger is expressed more in protesting shouts, pushing and kicking, but less in tearful screaming. So long as adults are present, however, the interference and rough handling of another child may bring forth cries and tears. A *fifteen-month-old* may show his annoyance by hitting a child who has taken his toy or who is holding on to the thing he most wants. He may even bite him or pull his hair without a preliminary scream or shout.

The attention of familiar and interested adults is much

sought by children of *fifteen to eighteen months*. If such attention is given to another child there may be signs of deep distress. The neglected one may stiffen, stand motionless, bend his head and burst into tears. Here is perhaps the beginning of jealousy, distress at the loss of, or failure to receive, expected attention and affection. Some children will show aggressive annoyance when another receives the attention they covet. They do this usually by hitting the envied child.

A *twenty-one-month-old* child will show less mistrust of strangers than will a younger infant. He may, however, run away and watch the newcomer for a time at a safe distance. After eighteen months he shows anger at adult interference by obstinate refusal to comply with their requests. He may shake his head and refuse either to be fed or to feed himself. At two he will play with his food, throwing it about instead of eating it, as a spite against some offending or scolding adult. Distress is shown chiefly at pain and acute discomfort, though the child will cry miserably at much less discomfort if a sympathetic adult is close at hand.

The children in the nursery group, *between fifteen and twenty-four months*, were more or less unconcerned when being undressed for the annual physical examination. This part of the procedure was familiar and not unpleasant. Several of the children cried and stiffened somewhat when placed on the table in the examining room. One or two continued to show distress throughout the examination. Others smiled cheerily at the attendant nurse or the doctor, until they felt sudden and unexpected local pressure. All of the children cried at some time during the procedure. The most distressing events were when a flashlight was thrown into the eyes, and when the throat and ears were examined with the aid of the usual tongue-depressor and otoscope. The children had to be held firmly and their movements curbed during these operations.

It was patent to the observer that the children were undergoing rather different emotions according to their fast-developing individual idiosyncrasies. Some were mainly startled and afraid, their movements were paralyzed. Some seemed to be just generally distressed at the unusual proceeding and the discomfort; while others were chiefly annoyed at the interference with their freedom. Several children showed signs of all three emotions. These individual differences probably have their foundation in variants in the physical constitutions of the children, both hereditary and acquired. They are certainly very much determined by the particular experiences the infants have gone through since their birth. A continuous study of behavior week by week reveals the actual differentiation and consolidation of individual traits of temperament.

Two or three of the nursery children over fourteen months developed fears for specific objects or persons. Toy animals that squeaked frightened one or two, causing them to draw away, stare wide-eyed and perhaps cry. This squeak could hardly be called a "loud low sound" such as Watson (4) describes as one of the original fear-producing stimuli. The sound is, however, rather unusual and comes at first as a surprise to the babies. One child was afraid of a particular aggressive little boy. No doubt he had gone up and hit her unexpectedly some time when the nurses were not watching. One youngster showed fear of a dark grey dog with a rough fur, rather different from the soft teddy-bears and other stuffed animals in the nursery.

Parents often remark how their children may suddenly show fear of some surprisingly trivial and inoffensive object. The answer to this may be found in certain partial associations with disturbing events of the past. It may also be found in the particular mental set of the child's mind and body when he came in contact with the object. He may have become suddenly aware of its presence and perceived it as an unwelcome intruder upon an entirely different line of thought or action. Still another phenomenon may account for the peculiar fears and objections of children. Timid behavior may be actually learned and preserved as a social asset, one of the numerous means of drawing attention.

The nursery child who cried and crawled away after touching the rough-haired, stuffed animal was flattered with the attention of all the adults in the room. A nurse brought the dog up to the child, smiling and saying "nice doggie." He looked up at her face, saw her kindly smile, then bent his head and began to whimper again. Another nurse laughed appreciatively as he put his hand to his eye, and tried to coax him with a toy cat. He turned away quickly, cried out again, then looked up to see the effect on the adults. He was having a delightful time out of his apparent fear.

DELIGHT AND ITS DERIVATIVES

Delight is much later in becoming differentiated from general excitement than distress. The baby under a month old is either excited or quiescent. Gentle stroking, swaying and patting soothe him and make him sleepy. When satisfied after a meal he is no longer excited nor even distressed by hunger. And yet he is not positively delighted. He is just unemotionally content, and either tranquil or busy mouthing and staring at distant objects. When he is *over two weeks old* he will sometimes give a faint reflex smile upon light tapping at the corners of his mouth. This is hardly an emotional response.

One- and *two-month-old* babies cry and kick from hunger before they are fed, rather than show delight on presentation of the much desired food. They become calm, however, immediately when given their milk, but not at the mere approach of the adult who brings it. At two months infants will give fleeting smiles upon being nursed, patted, wrapped warmly, spoken to, tickled, or gently rocked. Perhaps this is the beginning of the emotion of delight.

By *three months* of age the emotion of delight is becoming more clearly differentiated from agitated excitement on the one hand and non-emotional quiescence or passivity on the other. The child kicks, opens his mouth, breathes faster, and tries to raise his head upon sight of his bottle. He gives little crooning sounds when being fed, nursed or rocked. He smiles when an adult comes near and talks to him; and he will even stop crying momentarily at the sound of a person's voice. He may also show delight in distant moving objects. One baby in the hospital, for instance, lay and watched the moving leaves of the creeper on the window for a minute or two at a time. Her eyes were wide and her mouth rounded and open. At times she would breathe fast, or inspire deeply, and utter murmurings of "uh-uh-uh." Her arms would wave up and down and her legs kick alternately.

The chief characteristics of delight are: free as against restrained movement; open eyes and expansion of the face in a smile as contrasted with the puckering of the forehead and closing of the eyes in distress; body movements or muscle tension of incipient approach rather than withdrawal; audible inspirations and quickened breathing; soft, lower pitched vocalizations than those of distress or excitement; more or less rhythmic arm and leg movements; prolonged attention to the object of interest; and cessation of crying. Although behavior varies in detail from child to child at successive ages, delight is always recognizable from certain general types of response. Free and rhythmic movements, welcoming and approaching gestures, smiles and vocalizations of middle pitch are most common features.

A *four-month-old* baby laughs aloud when some person smiles and frolics with him. He smiles in response to another's smile and even when anyone approaches his crib, whether they be strangers or not. He spreads out his arms, lifts his chin, and tries to raise his body in approach to the attentive person. He takes active delight in his bath, kicking and splashing the water. Food, though sometimes welcomed eagerly, is often neglected for the more interesting attendant who talks and smiles at him.

At *five months* a child vocalizes his delight in sounds of "uh-uh-ung" in addition to waving, laughing, kicking and wriggling around. He shows special interest in small objects that he can handle and explore. Musical or noisy rattles are popular at this age. When hungry he kicks, breathes fast, and calls out eagerly at the first sign of the person who brings his food. His smiles are more transient, however, and his movements less vigorous on approach of a stranger.

By *six months* of age a child will reach towards a familiar person but will lie still and observe a stranger dubiously. He crows and coos frequently, taking pleasure in his own movements and sounds. In the hospital the babies of this age would watch each other through the bars of their cribs, sometimes laughing and kicking in response to the sight of the other's movements. They would swing their legs rhythmically when lying on their backs, or sway sideways when lying prone.

A *seventh-month-old* baby is becoming increasingly interested in small objects and in the act of reaching and grasping those close at hand. He will even struggle to attain things somewhat out of his reach. When his efforts meet with success he often smiles, takes a deep breath and expresses his satisfaction in a sort of grunt. After a moment or two spent in examination and manipulation of the object, he goes exploring again with fresh vigor. Possibly this is the beginning of the emotion of elation, exhilarating pleasure in personal accomplishments. Resting periods, after the delightful satisfaction of feeding or explorative activity, are often taken up with a rhythmical rocking back and forth, the child supporting himself on his hands and knees.

At *eight months* of age the child seems to take more delight than ever in self-initiated purposeful activity. He babbles and splutters and laughs to himself. Especially does he seem delighted with the noise he makes by banging spoons or other playthings on the table. Throwing things out of his crib is another favorite pastime. He waves, pats, and coos, drawing in long breaths, when familiar adults swing him or talk to him. He will watch the person who nurses him attentively, exploring her, patting gently, and often smiling. Here are perhaps the earliest demonstrations of affection. The child will also pat and smile at his own mirror image. But his behavior is rather more aggressive and inquisitive than really affectionate.

A *nine-month-old* baby is very popular with adults. He laughs frequently, bounces up and down and tries to mimic their playful actions. He pats others babies exploratively but does not show particular affection for them. Strange adults may frighten him at first. But, after studying them for some time in the distance, he will smile responsively and join in play with them. By *ten months* of age the child is taking more interest in other babies. He will mimic their calls and even their laughter. The hospital babies of this age would pat and bang and laugh in imitation of each other.

An *eleven-month-old* baby takes great delight in laughter, not only his own but that of another. He will laugh in order to make another child laugh, then jump and vocalize and laugh again in response. At twelve months of age he will repeat any little action that causes laughter. He is becoming increasingly affectionate. He puts his arms around the familiar adult's neck, and strokes and pats her face. Sometimes he will actually bring his lips close to her face in an incipient kissing movement. He looks eagerly for attention; and may stand holding a support and changing weight from one foot to the other in rhythmic motion, as a solace when neglected.

Between *twelve and fifteen months* a child usually learns to walk with a little help. This performance, though often accompanied by panting and tense effort, causes great delight and even elation when a few steps have been accomplished. The child calls out, smiles and waves ecstatically (i.e. rapidly or jerkily). Without further encouragement from adults, he will then set out again with renewed fervor. When attentive adults are too enthusiastic in their appreciation, the little one may become positively tense with excitement. His efforts may consequently meet with less success, and then he cries in vexatious disappointment.

There is already a noticeable difference between the responsiveness of different *fifteen-month-old* children to demonstrated affection. Some children come readily to be nursed and petted, others require a little coaxing. One or two will kiss back when kissed, while others merely cling closely to the adult caressing them. At this age the children begin to show definite affection for each other. They take hands, sit close to one another, put their arms about one another's neck or shoulders, pat and smile at each other. Eighteen-month-olds will also jabber nonsense amicably together. Again, with regard to playmates as well as adults some children are more affectionate than others.

The variations in affection no doubt have a number

of causal factors. They depend upon the child's physical constitution and his condition of health at the moment. Sick children may be very clinging and affectionate with adults, or, in some instances, refractory and irritable. They may be both by turns. Whether a child is affectionate or not also depends upon the nature of his dominant interest at the moment. Affection for a grown person depends upon the child's attitude towards adults in general; and that again is largely a matter of the amount of fondling or scolding the child has received. Affection for other children is considerably determined by the agreeable or exasperating nature of chance contacts.

Between *fifteen and twenty-one months* the children find increasing enjoyment in walking and running about. They chase each other laughingly and enjoy snatching one another's toys. They come back again and again to adults to be lifted high or swung round. The nursery slide is very popular at this age. One or two of the hospital children pulled away and watched apprehensively in the distance after the first slide. A little encouragement from the nurses and the eager shouts of the other children soon overcame their fear, and they joined the sliding group again.

Gramophone music was listened to intently by almost all the nursery children. Some of them responded by swaying or nodding motions to time. The children at this age were beginning to find individual interests in things and to express their enjoyment each in their own peculiar way. Absorbed preoccupation, tight clasping, biting, and varied manipulations of the attractive object were common expressions of interest. Some children would knock one object against another in play, some would collect things, and others would find pleasure in throwing and scattering toys about. These variations in appreciative interest in things and activities may be the precursors of the more mature emotion of joy.

Most of the eighteen-month-olds in the hospital were anxious to attract attention. They called out or came running to greet an adult. They would smile and hold out their arms to a familiar nurse in expectation of being lifted. A stranger they would watch solemnly for a while. Then they would approach slowly, touch and explore her clothes, or hit and watch for the effect. The children seemed to recognize their nurses at this age, whether the latter appeared in uniform or not. Babies of seven to twelve months, however, would sometimes turn away in fear or hostility when the nurses approached them wearing outdoor clothes.

Slight preferences for certain nurses were noticed as early as six months, but definitely affectionate attachments were observed chiefly between the ages of twelve and twenty-four months. One or two youngsters of eighteen months showed preferences for certain playmates. A twin boy and girl seemed especially fond of each other. The children would be more responsive and playful with those they liked, more delighted at their approach and very anxious to keep them close. Some children were friendly with almost everybody including strange visitors. Others showed more specific and decided likes and dislikes. When a terrifying stranger was present, sometimes a child would show more than usual affection for his familiar nurse, but at other times he would be restrained and aloof from everybody. Similarly when a beloved parent was nursing a child on visiting day he might be hostile to anyone else; but more often he would smile agreeably at everybody including awe-inspiring strangers.

A specific "like" does not necessarily enhance a specific "dislike" by force of contrast, though this does sometimes happen. If the disliked object threatens the satisfaction or enjoyment of the object preferred then the dislike becomes stronger. Similarly a preferred object may be enjoyed with greater intensity in the presence of, or following upon, something disliked. It is a comforting relief from distress. This effect of contrast is perhaps what Freud terms "ambivalence." There are situations, however, where it has no noticeable effect. For instance, as cited above, a child made happy by one person may like everybody for the moment, regardless of previous attitudes towards them. A troubled child may be annoyed with everybody, even his favorite playmates. Strong emotions may thus have a decided "halo" effect.

Although children between *eighteen months and two years* of age tease and hit each other frequently, they show more affection for one another than younger infants. They not only pat and stroke fondly, but they will kiss and hug each other on occasion. The older children in the nursery group were seen to direct the younger ones' activities and point out their errors by gesture and exclamation. There was no evidence, however, of the parental affection and almost self-sacrificing care shown by four-year-olds for their much younger playmates.

Noisy activities delighted the eighteen- to twenty-four-month old youngsters. They took pleasure in tearing and pulling things to pieces and in lifting large but portable objects, such as their own chairs. They jabbered happily to each other at table. One child would repeatedly make strange noises to arouse the attention and laughter of another. With adults they would practice newly learned words and would seek to share their enjoyments. When the children received new toys in the hospital they would cling to them and guard them jealously from the other children. But they would hold them out for the nurses to share in their appreciation. Here is a mark of trusting friendship for their kindly guardians such as the children had not yet developed for one another. They would always rather share the other child's plaything than give up or share their own.

Affection, thus, begins as delight in being fondled and comforted by an elder. It becomes differentiated from general delight and manifested in tender caressing responses at about eight months of age. This earliest affection is essentially reciprocal in nature. Spontaneous affection for adults may be seen, however, by eleven or twelve months of age. Both reciprocal and spontaneous affection for other children make their appearance around fifteen months, but they are not as strong as affection for adults.

Specific affection for the grown-ups who give special attention may be manifested as early as demonstrative affection itself, i.e. eight or nine months. These preferences persist as long as the care and attention continue. Attachments between two children were not observed in the hospital till after fifteen months of age. They were usually very temporary, lasting only a few hours or days. The behavior of a child-friend is so much more erratic and less dependable than that of an adult. Friendships between eighteen- to twenty-four-month-old children would sometimes last, however, for several weeks. There seemed to be no preference in these attachments either for the same or the opposite sex. Little girls would become friends together, or little boys, or a boy and girl would show mutual affection for one another.

SUMMARY AND CONCLUSION

The emotional behavior of young infants as observed in the Montreal Foundling and Baby Hospital seemed to lend support to the writer's theory of the genesis of the emotions. Emotional development was found to take place in three ways. The different emotions gradually evolved from the vague and undifferentiated emotion of excitement. The form of behavior response in each specific emotion changed slowly with developing skills and habits. Different particular situations would arouse emotional response at succeeding age-levels, although these situations would always be of the same general type for the same emotions.

The one-month-old baby showed excitement in accelerated movement and breathing, upon any excessive stimulation. He exhibited distress by crying, reddening of the face and tense jerky movements at painful and other disagreeable stimulations. But he was more or less passive and quiescent when agreeably stimulated.

By three months of age the child was seen to exhibit delight in smiles, deep inspirations and somewhat rhythmic movements when his bodily needs were being satisfied. Between three and four months angry screaming and vigorous leg-thrusts, in response to delay in anticipated feeding, were observed. A few weeks later anger was aroused when an adult's playful attention was withdrawn.

Distress and delight came to be expressed more in specific vocalizations with increasing age. General body movements gave place to precise responses to details of a situation. A four-month-old baby would laugh aloud with delight and cry tearfully when distressed. A child of five months was seen to cough and reject foods of a certain taste and consistency in incipient disgust. He would reach towards objects that caused him delight. By six months of age he showed definite fear when a stranger approached. He remained motionless and rigid, his eyes wide and staring. It is possible that "non-institutional" children might show fear in response to other unusual or unexpected events a little earlier than this. There was little variation in the daily routine of the children under observation, and fear was a rare occurrence.

By seven months of age the child showed positive elation, and renewed his activity as a result of success in his own endeavours. At eight months he began to show reciprocal affection for adults, and by twelve months spontaneous affection. Delight was manifested in much laughter, bouncing up and down, and banging with the hand.

Between nine and twelve months of age the hospital babies would hide their heads, like ostriches, upon the approach of a relatively unfamiliar person. They would scream and become flushed with anger when their efforts or desires were thwarted; and they would cry out in fear and sit motionless after perceiving themselves falling.

It was observed that a child learns to kiss soon after twelve months of age, and by fifteen months he expresses his affection for other children. Anger over disappointment becomes more dramatic in its manifestation. The true temper-tantrum makes its appearance roughly about fourteen months of age. By eighteen months anger at adults is expressed in obstinate behavior; and annoyance at interfering children is manifested in hitting, pulling and squealing.

Eighteen-month-olds would constantly seek the attention of adults, and take great delight in running about and making noises. One or two children of this age showed depressed, and others angry, jealousy when another child received the coveted attention. A few specific fears were noticed; and several children developd particular affectionate attachments.

Thus it seems that in the course of development, emotional behavior becomes more and more specific, both as regards arousing stimuli and form of response. Distress, though more readily aroused, comes to find adequate expression in a variety of actions, and delight becomes sensitive appreciation and joy in numerous pursuits. The emotions, evolve slowly, and the exact age of differentiation is difficult to determine.

A diagram showing the approximate ages of the appearance of the different emotions, as observed in the Montreal Foundling Hospital, is given in Figure 1. Study

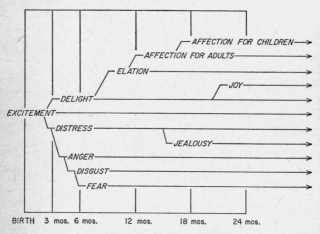

Fig. 1. Showing the approximate age of differentiation of the various emotions during the first two years of life.

of a number of children in private homes might suggest a somewhat different age arrangement. Readers of the Journal of Genetic Psychology will note that a greater number of different emotions are attributed to the two year level than were suggested in a previously published diagram, (3) based on a study of nursery school children.

Emotional behavior and development are very much determined by particular events and experiences and the routine of living. It is, therefore, to be expected that "institution babies" will show some deviations in their reactions from those of children at home. The former will probably exhibit fear of a larger number of things than other children, due to their very limited experience.

On the other hand, they may show greater tolerance of interference, as a result of much practice in self-control in the nursery. They may also be more affectionate with other children, in consequence of the many happy play-hours spent together.

The daily round of feeding, washing, dressing and sleeping, however, has so many factors in common for all babies, that the observations made on the emotional development of a few hospital children, and the suggested inferences presented above, may have at least some general significance for infants brought up under other circumstances.

REFERENCES

1. BLANTON, MARGARET GRAY, The behavior of the human infant during the first thirty days of life, *Psychol. Rev.*, 1917, **24**, 456-483.
2. BRIDGES, K. M. B. *The Social and Emotional Development of the Pre-School Child*, London: Kegan Paul, 1931, p. 277.
3. ————, A genetic theory of the emotions, *Journal of Genetic Psychol.*, 1930, **37**, 514-527.
4. WATSON, J. B., Experimental studies on the growth of the emotions, *Ped. Sem.*, 1925, **32**, 2, 328-348.

9

Emotional Behavior of the Rat

NORMAN L. MUNN

Bowdoin College

The study of emotional behavior has not been restricted to human behavior. Lower animals have several advantages for experimentation and experimenters have found that animals as different as the rat and the chimpanzee can provide useful information on emotional behavior.

The following selection, by Professor Norman L. Munn, reviews findings and techniques of research on emotional behavior in the commonly used rat. The selection is taken from the Handbook of Psychological Research on the Rat *(Boston: Houghton, 1950), and is reprinted with the permission of the author and publisher.*

Emotional behavior, or what has more generally been referred to as "temperament," is clearly evident in rats. Calvin Hall (1941) defines temperament "approximately" as "consisting of the emotional nature, the basic-needs structure, and the activity level of an organism" (p. 909). The items covered in Hall's survey of research on temperament in animals are timidity (under which he lists his own studies of emotionality or "fearfulness"), aggressiveness, wildness and savageness, activity, persistence, and speed of reaction. In this section we consider research on timidity, savageness, wildness, and general emotionality, with special reference to the inheritance of such traits. Since a large amount of research has concentrated specifically on fear in rats, this topic is given separate consideration.

Using a five-point scale, R. M. Yerkes (1913) rated aspects of temperament in wild gray rats and in tame laboratory rats. Savageness, according to Yerkes, is expressed by such responses as exposing and gnashing the teeth, biting, and squeaking; wildness by hiding, random and excited behavior, urination and defecation; and timidity by chattering or gnashing of teeth, cowering, apparent trembling, urination and defecation. Yerkes reports that when he crossed wild with timid rats, the progeny had an intermediate temperament. Ada Yerkes (1916) carried the research further and found that differences in temperament between the stock rats and exceptionally timid rats are greater than differences in learning ability. Utsurikawa (1917) and Sadovnikova-Koltzova (1925) also reported results suggesting genetically determined differences in temperament among rats. Rasmussen (1939) suggests that wildness depends to some extent on whether or not the offspring are reared by a wild mother and whether or not they are reared with other wild rats. The most comprehensive researches on the problem begin with Stone's study of wildness and savageness.

Stone (1942) rated different strains of rats for wildness and savageness under standard conditions of obsevation. Observation was carried on over a period of ten consecutive days. Eleven behavior items were involved in the ratings, six of them suggesting wildness and five savageness. Six types of animals were involved: (1) wild animals trapped in a basement, (2) wild descendants of these trapped animals, (3) first generation crosses between the trapped animals and tame albinos, (4) crosses between the half-breeds and albino rats, (5) yellow hooded rats, and (6) pure albinos of Wistar stock. The ratings differed for these six strains, the differences in some instances being small and in others large. Stone says that "Differences in the trait of wildness and savageness were clearly displayed by our half-breeds and full-wilds as compared with the albinos, quarter breeds, and yellow hoods prior to the age of 20 days. This fact, together with that of the persistent difference shown in later life, strongly suggests that the differences arise from hereditary rather than environmental factors" (p. 35).

Both Yerkes and Stone, in their researches on savageness, wildness, and timidity assumed that defecation and urination under emotion-provoking circumstances are indicative of wildness. Calvin Hall (1943b) examined the possibility that quantitative aspects of defecation and urination could be used as measures of emotionality. Rats were observed in a standardized field situation, the strangeness of which was assumed to be an emotion-provoking situation. Defecation and urination were regarded as emotional if they ceased after repeated experience with the situation. Much of the research arising out of this investigation deals with validation of the emotionality test itself. When Hall correlated the number of trials in which the animals failed to eat (generally regarded as a sign of emotionality) with the number of trials during which they defecated, he found the coefficient of correlation to be .82 with a probable error of .04. Urination yielded a corresponding correlation of .70 ± .06. These correlations suggest that the test is actually measuring what it purports to measure, namely, individual differences in emotionality. Most of the validation data appear to support Hall's contention that urination and defecation in the rat provide valid information on differences in emotionality. (See, especially Hall, 1934a; and Tryon, Tryon, and Kuznets, 1941a.) O'Kelley (1940) has alone questioned the validity of Hall's test.

There is evidence that differences in emotionality are inherited. Calvin Hall (1941) has presented data (Table 1) for eight filial generations of selectively bred "emotional" and "non-emotional" rats. The table represents cross-matings of rats exhibiting no excretion in the standard test and cross-mating of rats exhibiting excretion for a number of trials. One will observe that the results of crossing are different for the emotional and non-emotional strains. In the former the mean number of days during which emotional excretion occurred increases with further crossings. In the latter there is no consistent change. The magnitude of the difference between the two groups increases with continued inbreeding and the magnitude of the critical ratio also increases. It is evident that these differences are due primarily to an increase of emotionality in the emotional strain. Hall said that no hybridizing experiments had at that time been carried out and that the genetic basis of emotionality was

TABLE 1

A statistical summary of seven generations of two rat strains selectively bred for emotional (E) and unemotional (NE) behavior[a]

Generation	Means		Sigmas		Critical Ratios
	E	NE	E	NE	
P	3.86		3.54		
F_1	3.07	.46	3.36	.77	4.74
F_2	4.72	1.94	4.12	2.28	2.50
F_3	3.92	1.02	3.64	1.30	6.00
F_4	4.69	1.40	3.89	1.43	7.00
F_5	4.96	.41	3.85	1.18	8.44
F_6	6.87	.51	3.28	1.13	12.72
F_7	7.82	.17	3.18	.47	20.40
F_8	8.37	1.07	2.94	2.46	14.29

Means represent average number of days during which emotional defecation and urination occurred out of a total of 12 trials in the field.

[a] From Hall (1941), p. 921.

thus unknown. He concluded, "It is evident, however, that differences in fearfulness rest in part on a genetic basis" (p. 921).

Tryon, Tryon, and Kuznets (1941a) found that they could rate, with a reliability approximating .80, the emotional behavior of rats as evidenced in hiding, avoidance, and vocalization. Their ratings showed some relation to defecation scores, especially in females, where the correlation was .83. In males the correlation was .34. In a later study, focused on emotional responses in novel maze situations, Tryon, Tryon, and Kuznets (1941a) found almost perfect agreement in their ratings of emotionality in a given situation. Responses in a given situation were highly related, but those in different situations were relatively independent.

Billingslea (1940, 1941, 1942) has made an extensive investigation of the intercorrelations between indices of emotion and various other responses in rats, responses like fighting, timidity in the home cage, delay in starting in a runway, and running in an activity wheel. His factor analysis (1942) leads him to posit three simple factors: emotionality, freezing, and timidity.

Applying Hall's test of emotionality to 73 gray Norway rats and 73 Wistar albino rats, Farris and Yeakel (1945) aimed to discover whether the relatively wild gray rats would prove more emotional than the albinos. Averages for number of days either urinating or defecating in the field were 6.8 ± .467 for grays and 5.3 ± .527 for albinos. The difference of 1.5 was, however, not statistically reliable. Slightly over one half of the gray rats achieved high scores (8 to 12) and almost one half of the albinos fell in the range of low scores (0 to 3). This difference was statistically significant, the Chi square test indicating that it would occur by chance only once in 100 times. The number of fecal boluses excreted during the tests did not differentiate the two groups. There was a statistically significant relation between wildness and the number of tests in which excretion occurred. The differences in emotional behavior observed in this research are assumed to arise from differences in the genetic constitution of the gray and albino rats.

Rather consistent differences in temperament go with differences in coat color. This has been demonstrated by Keeler and King (1942).

An opportunity to study the relation between temperament and coat color came after an epidemic of mutations in a strain of gray Norway rats, produced substrains of piebald, ruby-eyed dilute, black, curly, albino, albino waltzer, cinnamon, and stub. Character sketches of these strains were derived from independent descriptions given by five people who had worked with them over a long period. In addition, the voice of each substrain was recorded with an oscillograph. Sample character sketches are as follows:

> *Mutant albino:* Cringe when approached after being completely tamed. When tamed, about as apt as the tamed grays to bite or fight back when picked up. When not tamed, as wild and vicious as the grays. When dropped on the floor they attack the caretakers as grays may do. Voice may be high, sustained whistle with fundamental tone at a frequency of 2800 cycles per second and having no over-

tones, whereas the rough, loud gray Norway voice may have a fundamental at 400 with overtones at 2200 and 4400.

Black: Sluggish. Already tame by nature. If very excited they may click their teeth, but are not apt to bite. Many only whine softly when picked up with tongs. Voice may be high, sustained tone with fundamental at 1100 to 2600.

Stub: Dwarfed, frequently tailless. Always fighting each other. Go out of their way to pick trouble. Do not mind their own business as do gray rats, but throw their bodies against the cage wire when anyone approaches. Voice is a high squeak with great amplitude at high frequencies. The fundamental is at 1100. Both 2200 and 4400 predominate with the peak at 6600.

Keeler and King conclude that the basis of temperament and behavior is inherited in gene-controlled patterns, the effects of a single gene being distributed irregularly throughout the whole field of response, like dabs of a particular color in a polychrome print. The complete basic-response picture is the sum-total of the effects of genes and their interactions in all parts of the field of response (p. 246). The non-agouti gene is thought to be the principal factor in producing tame albino rats, not domestication, as some have thought. A detailed analysis is given of the contributions of three genes (albino, black, and piebald) to alleged domesticative modifications in a strain of tame albino rats studied by Donaldson (1924). The results of this analysis lead the investigators to conclude: "It seems probable that the tame albino rat, at least the strain studied, was not domesticated by painstaking selection over long periods of time, but was modified in morphology principally by the introduction of three coat color genes, and in behavior particularly by the (non-agouti) black gene" (p. 249). The final conclusion is that "temperament and behavior are inherited in gene-controlled parcels and that personality may be synthesized by combining various behavior-modifying genes" (p. 249).

Gray Norway rats, as well as black rats derived from crossing gray and albino rats, were subjected by Keeler (1942) to several tests involving "annoying" and other emotion-provoking situations. On the basis of these tests it was concluded that there is a much larger incidence of wildness in the gray Norway than in the black rats. Keeler attributes this to presence in the black animals of the non-agouti gene.

The findings discussed in this section give ample evidence of emotional response in rats and also agree in suggesting the strong influence of heredity on determination of individual differences in emotionality.

FEAR OF CATS AND SNAKES

Do rats have an innate fear of cats? Several investigators have argued that they do, and researches have centered around the question of which sense is primarily involved, vision, olfaction, or hearing.

The fact that some rats display unusual behavior in the presence of cats is well established (Small, 1899; Kunkel, 1919; Griffith, 1919, 1920; McDougall and McDougall, 1927; Curti, 1935, 1942; and Vojtonis, 1936). Griffith and Curti agree that a large proportion of their rats exhibited what Curti calls "freezing" in the presence of cats; holding a fixed pose for as long as thirty minutes.[1] Griffith (1920) describes the response as follows:

> The exploratory movements were totally inhibited. The otherwise tense position of the rats was varied by a slight trembling and a sort of spasmodic contraction in the region of the viscera. At the end of five minutes, the cat was removed. During this time the rats had not changed their tense position, the head being held up and out, the feet planted squarely on the floor, the body slightly crouching, the respiration accelerated for a few moments and then momentarily retarded (p. 21).

Since "freezing" appears in rats never before confronted by a cat, it seems that the response is unlearned.

An intensive study of fear in rats was carried out by

[1] This is different from the so-called "freezing" behavior of rats placed in a strange situation, as in a maze. See Riess (1945, 1946) and Nissen (1946). Vojtonis (1936) observed that some rats display "quietude" and others a "death-feint" when confronted by a cat. These responses are perhaps equivalent with the "freezing" mentioned by American investigators.

Griffith (1920). His experiments involved substitution of a dog, a cat in a sealed glass jar, and a cloth cat for a cat whose odor might be sensed by the rat. Under these conditions, no fear response was elicited. Nor did anosmic rats show any fear reaction in the presence of cats. Griffith thus concluded that fear of cats by the white rat is a fear of the odor of cats.

The hypothesis that odor provides the stimulation for "freezing" and related responses in the presence of cats was tested by Curti (1935). The most relevant of her experiments is one in which the rat was in a supposedly airtight glass cage from which it could be stimulated visually by the cat, but not smell it. Great care was taken to have the rats and cats handled by different persons so that odors would not be transmitted in this way. But the description of the box leaves some doubt as to its insulation from outside odors. The investigator reports that "every possible crack was stuffed with cotton, and since the whole apparatus was very carefully constructed to be airtight, no odor from the cat could possibly reach the rat." Of 16 rats tested singly, none "froze" in response to the cat. Three rats in a group of three all "froze" when the cat was presented. The fact that these three rats "froze" in the "absence of odor" is regarded as evidence against Griffith's view that odor is a necessary stimulus for this response. Other experiments by Curti led her to suggest that visual perception of the cat's movements underlies "freezing."

In a later investigation (1942), Curti found that blind rats also display the "freezing" response. All of 9 blind rats "froze" in the presence of cats. The same objective situation had elicited "freezing" from only 3 out of 11 seeing rats. In addition to suggesting that blinding increased the "timidity" of rats, Curti came to the conclusion that "visual stimulation is by no means necessary to the arousal of such fear behavior." It is suggested that a specific adequate stimulus for the behavior may not exist. One may take this to mean that, where odor is present (as in the experiment with blind rats), odor may elicit the behavior and that, where visual stimulation is present, as in the case of rats presumably removed from stimulation by the odor of cats, visual stimulation is adequate. Auditory stimulation has not been excluded. If blind and anosmic rats should show "freezing" in response to cats, one would guess that auditory stimuli, suggested by Curti as possibly important, are also adequate. Perhaps any two of these stimuli (odor and sound, vision and odor, or vision and sound) are required. More research must be done if these questions are to be settled.

The whole question of the rat's instinctive fear of cats is equivocal. If the behavior is instinctive (that is, unlearned and phylogenetic) it should appear in all normal rats which have had no previous contact with cats. It is clearly not universal even in white rats. Nevertheless, in those rats which do display "freezing," it is apparently unlearned.

Kellogg (1931) found no evidence indicating that albino rats are afraid of snakes, although several other animals displayed responses when confronted with a snake. Richardson (1942), on the other hand, reports an innate fear of snakes in the wood rat. The behavior includes "thumping of the hind feet . . . a specialized reaction of the adult wood rat" and hasty random movements suggesting panic. No "freezing" such as that found in white rats in the presence of a cat is reported.

FEAR AS A DRIVE

We shall see in later discussions that rats escaping from water or from an electric shock tend to learn more quickly than under less exciting conditions. Mowrer and Lamoreaux (1946) assume that the fear aroused in such situations is learned but that it plays an important role in further learning. Rather generally, however, the motivation in such situations is assumed to spring from an innate fear of water and electric shock. Mowrer has also used the term *anxiety* in this connection.

Behavior aroused by a fear or anxiety-producing situation often persists after the original stimulus (e.g., shock) has ceased. Such persistence is very nicely demonstrated in Miller and Hart's film "Motivation and

Reward in Learning." [1] Here a rat, after finding that it can terminate shock in the floor by turning a small wheel, vigorously continues to turn the wheel even though shock has been terminated. According to Miller (1948), such behavior is motivated by a continuing fear or anxiety. He calls this an acquired drive to distinguish it from the primary (innate) fear of the shock itself. Miller has shown, moreover, that one may utilize such a continuing response (or the fear that underlies it) as motivation for further learning. Rats first learned to escape shock by running from a white compartment into a black one. They continued to run into the white compartment when shock was no longer given. Then a small wheel was introduced and the entrance to the black compartment was closed. By rotating the wheel a rat could open the door and escape. Without any further shock, the animals learned to escape from the white compartment by turning the wheel. When the wheel was made inadequate and a bar was introduced, they learned to operate the bar, again without shock. In a somewhat comparable experiment, May (1948) increased the motivating value of a buzzer by pairing it with electric shock. One possible interpretation would be that fear of the shock was transferred to the buzzer, which then became a stronger motivating stimulus than before.

In situations like the above, what is the explanation? Is learning based upon persistence (perseveration) of the fear or is it based upon the continued fear-arousing potency of the white compartment? One gathers that the latter interpretation is favored by Miller. If this is the correct interpretation, then the phenomenon under discussion is another example of what Anderson (1941) has called "externalization of drive." The only difference is that Anderson's studies deal with hunger motivation instead of fear. One might say that in these studies a food box without food aroused appetite as, in Miller's experiment, a white compartment without shock aroused fear.

It is of course also conceivable that merely a running response was retained. In other words, that the white

[1] PCR 2013 (1948), State College, Pennsylvania.

compartment continued to elicit running without any concomitant fear or anxiety. In this case one would have an example of what Woodworth called a "mechanism becoming a drive" and what Allport refers to as "functional autonomy."

REFERENCES

ANDERSON, E. E. 1941. The externalization of drive. I. Theoretical considerations, *Psychol. Rev.*, **48**, 204-224.

BILLINGSLEA, F. Y., 1940. Analysis of intercorrelations between emotionality and other behavior salients in the rat, *Psychol. Bull.*, **37**, 430-431.

————. 1941. The relationship between emotionality and various other forms of behavior in the rat, *Psychol. Bull.*, **37**, 582.

————. 1942. Intercorrelational analysis of certain behavior salients in the rat, *J. comp. Psychol.*, 3., 203-211.

CURTI, M. W. 1935. Native fear responses of white rats in the presence of cats, *Psychol. Monog.*, **46**, No. 210, 78-98.

————. 1942. A further report on fear responses of white rats in the presence of cats, *J. comp. Psychol.*, **34**, 51-53.

DONALDSON, H. H. 1924. The Rat: data and reference tables (2nd ed.). Philadelphia: Wistar Institute of Anatomy.

FARRIS, E. J. and YEAKEL, E. H. 1945. Emotional behavior of Gray Norway and Wistar Albino rats, *J. comp. Psychol.*, **38**, 109-118.

GRIFFITH, C. R. 1919. A possible case of instinctive behavior in the white rat, *Science*, **50**, 166-167.

————. 1920. The behavior of white rats in the presence of cats, *Psychobiol.*, **2**, 19-28.

HALL, C. S. 1934a. Drive and emotionality: factors associated with adjustment in the rat, *J. comp. Psychol.*, **17**, 89-108.

————. 1934b. Emotional behavior in the rat: I. Defecation and urination as measures of individual differences in emotionality, *J. comp. Psychol.*, **18**, 385-403.

————. 1941. Temperament: a survey of animal studies, *Psychol. Bull.*, **38**, 909-943.

KEELER, C. E. 1942. The association of the black (non-Agouti) gene with behavior in the Norway rat, *J. Hered.*, **33**, 371-384.

KEELER, C. E. and KING, H. D. 1942. Multiple effects of coat color genes in the Norway rat, with special reference to temperament and domestication, *J. comp. Psychol.*, **34**, 241-250.

KELLOG, W. N. 1931. A note on fear behavior in young rats, mice and birds. *J. comp. Psychol.*, **12**, 117-121.

KUNKEL, B. W. 1919. Instinctive behavior in the white rat, *Science*, **50**, 305-306.

McDOUGALL, K. D. and McDOUGALL, W. 1931. Insight and foresight in various animals—monkey, raccoon, rat and wasp, *J. comp. Psychol.*, **11**, 237-273.

MAY, M. A. 1948. Experimentally acquired drives, *J. exp. Psychol.*, **38**, 66-77.

MILLER, N. E. 1948. Studies of fear as an acquirable drive: I. Fear as motivation and fear-reduction as reinforcement in the learning of new responses, *J. exp. Psychol.*, **38**, 89-101.

MOWRER, O. H. and LAMOREAUX, R. R. 1946. Fear as an intervening variable in avoidance conditioning, *J. comp. Psychol.*, **39**, 29-49.

NISSEN, H. W. 1946. "Freezing" behavior in rats. *Science*, **103**, 27.

O'KELLY, L. I. 1940. An experimental study of regression. I. Behavioral characteristics of the regressive response, *J. comp. Psychol.*, **30**, 55-95.

RASMUSSEN, E. W., 1939. Social facilitation in albino rats, *Acta. Psychol.* (Hague), **4**, 275-294.

RICHARDSON, W. B. 1942. Reaction toward snakes as shown by the wood rat. Neotonia abigula, *J. comp. Psychol.*, **34**, 1-10.

RIESS, B. F. 1945. A possible explanation of "freezing" behavior in rats, *Science*, **102**, 570.

———. 1946. "Freezing" behavior in rats and its social causation. *J. soc. Psychol.*, **24**, 249-251.

SADOVNIKOVA-KOLTZOVA, M. P. 1925. Genetic analysis of temperament in rats, *J. exp. Zool.*, **45**, 301-318.

SMALL, W. S. 1899. Notes on the psychic development of the young white rat, *Amer. J. Psychol.*, **11**, 80-100.

STONE, C. P. 1942. "Maturation and instinctive functions" and "Motivation" in Moss, F. A. (ed.). *Comparative Psychology*, rev. ed. New York: Prentice-Hall, 32-97.

TRYON, R. C., TRYON, C. M. and KUZNETS, G. 1941a. Studies in individual differences in maze ability. IX. Ratings of hiding, avoidance, escape and vocalization responses, *J. comp. Psychol.*, **32**, 407-435.

———. 1941b. Studies in individual differences in maze ability. X. Ratings and other measures of initial emotional responses of rats to novel inanimate objects, *J. comp. Psychol*; **32**, 447-473.

UTSURIKAWA, N. 1917. Temperamental differences between

outbred and inbred strains of the albino rat, *J. anim. Behav.*, **7**, 111-129.

Vojtonis, N. 1936. (An experimental study of genetic primary forms of behavior motivation.) *Refleksi Instincti, Naviki*, **1**, 77-99. *Psychol. Abs.*, 1936, 2988.

Yerkes, R. M. 1913. The heredity of savageness and wildness in rats. *J. anim. behav.*, **3**, 286-296.

Yerkes, Ada W. 1916. Comparison of stock and inbred albino rats. *J. anim. behav.*, **6**, 267-296.

10

On the Nature of Fear

D. O. HEBB

McGill University[1]

*The following selection could have appeared under
"Problems and Theory," since Professor Hebb draws
upon his research and observation of chimpanzees to
complement his theory of neuropsychological action.
The purpose of the research reported in this paper was
to discover how fear develops in primates in an attempt
to understand the development of similar emotional
behavior in humans.*

*The reader who finds Professor Hebb's approach re-
warding will find a more thorough discussion of his
theory in a more recent work,* The Organization of
Behavior: a neuropsychological theory (*New York:
Wiley, 1949*).

The selection is reprinted from the Psychological
Review, *1946,* **53,** *259-276, with the permission of the
author and the American Psychological Association.*

In the course of an experiment dealing with individual differences of behavior among chimpanzees, observations of fear were made which held an immediate
interest. Besides extending the information concerning
the causes of anthropoid fear which is provided by the
work of Köhler (23), Jacobsen, Jacobsen and Yoshioka
(17), Yerkes and Yerkes (42), Haslerud (10), Mc-
Culloch and Haslerud (31), and Hebb and Riesen
(14), the new data brought up again the question of
mechanism. Analysis of the behavior leads, in the present discussion, to a review of the whole problem and

[1] The author wrote this while at the Yerkes Laboratories of
Primate Biology.

an attempt to formulate a hypothesis of the causes and nature of fear.

NATURE OF THE DATA

Validity and reliability. The validity of naming fear in chimpanzees, or recognizing something in animals which can be identified with fear in man and the reliability of naming have been discussed elsewhere (13). There it was shown that the recognition of emotion in an animal is possible in the same way as in another human being. Fear named in an animal means either that there was actual avoidance of some object or place, or that the observer inferred from incidental behavior ('associated signs') that avoidance was imminent and likely to appear with further stimulation. When such inferences are made with confidence by experienced observers, it appears that they are valid and reliable, the criterion being the animal's subsequent behavior.

Definition of fear behavior. The symbol 'W,' for withdrawal, was recorded when the animal actually moved away from a test object in such a way as to show that he did not move by coincidence, but was responding to the test situation. The evidence was of several kinds: (1) when change of position of the test object produced a corresponding movement of the animal, maintaining his distance from it; (2) when the original movement was abrupt and coincided exactly with the appearance of the test object; (3) when there was coincident evidence of unusual excitation, such as erection of hair, screaming, threatening gestures directed at the test object, or continued orientation of gaze at the object while moving directly away from it. On occasions one of these three forms of evidence alone, if exceptionally clear, might provide the basis for an entry of 'W' in the record; usually, at least two were present before the entry was made. In many instances the experimenter was certain that an animal would be afraid to approach the test object, but did not record his opinion since the formal behavioral criteria were not met.

EXPERIMENTAL METHOD

The experimental procedures were part of a study of individual differences of emotionality and temperament, and not planned to meet the problem of defining the adequate stimulus to fear. Thus the range of test objects was limited, and the order in which they were presented does not permit an exact comparison of the excitatory value of each.

Test objects. The test objects were representations of animals, from reptile to man, varying considerably in completeness and verisimilitude. They fall in three classes: primate objects, pictures of primates, and non-primate objects. It was not expected that the pictures would induce fear—they were used for another purpose —but they were presented in the same way as the other objects and consequently are useful as control material.

Primate objects. There were 9 objects 'representing' primates. The responses to these are the main interest of the study.

(1) An adult chimpanzee head, three-fifths life size, made of papier-maché and painted to appear reasonably lifelike.

(2) An unclothed doll representing a human infant, one-half life size.

(3) An infant chimpanzee's head and shoulders, nearly life size, modelled in wax and painted—about as lifelike as the adult chimpanzee head.

(4) The cadaver of a chimpanzee infant, newborn, fixed in formalin.

(5) A lifelike, full-sized human head from a window-display dummy.

(6) The skull of a 5-year-old chimpanzee, with movable jaw controlled by a string.

(7) The roughly mounted skin of a spider monkey, with head and shoulders movable by means of string.

(8) An unpainted plaster of Paris cast of the visage of an adult chimpanzee without the ears or the rest of the head, made from a death mask.

(9) The cured and flexible hide of a 5-year-old chim-

panzee, somewhat denuded of hair; the proportions of
the skin about the head and face were distorted out of
recognition, but the hands and feet were recognizable.

The pictures are not described in detail, since they
are important here only as 14 emotionally unexciting
objects, presented in the same way as the others.

Nonprimate objects varied greatly in verisimilitude,
from a careful replica of a snake to a 'bug' which was a
rectangular block of wood on coiled-spring legs.

(1) A dog's head and forequarters, of cloth, slipped
over the hand and manipulated from inside with the
fingers; this common toy is surprisingly lifelike in its
movements.

(2) A model of an imaginary white 'grub,' 4 inches
long, with long white legs.

(3) A grub identical in proportions and color, one-
third as large.

(4) A rubber tube, ½ inch diameter, 24 inches
long, with a roughly carved wooden snake's head at
one end; so mounted, with string inside the tube, that
it could be given a snakelike movement without apparent external agency.

(5) A rectangular wooden 'bug,' 6 inches long. It
was capable of an oscillating movement, since it was
mounted on six coiled-wire legs, and had oscillating
'antennae.'

(6) A 'grasshopper,' a mechanical toy with moving
legs.

(7) A similar 'turtle.'

(8) A rubber dog, 3½ inches high.

(9) A brightly colored cloth dog, 7 inches high.

(10) A painted wax replica of a coiled 24-inch-
snake.

Procedure. Test objects were presented to the animals while they were in their own living cages. The
animal or pair of animals was first brought to the front
of the cage by an offer of a small amount of food. The
hinged top and front of the presentation box (which
was wheeled from cage to cage) was then lifted, exposing one test object to the chimpanzee. At the end
of 15 seconds the test object was set in motion, if it
had movable parts; if not, it was moved forward about

6 inches nearer the animal. The presentation box was closed at the end of another 15 seconds; total exposure was thus 30 seconds. The box had three compartments, and three objects were shown in succession on each experimental period, once or twice a week. The objects were shown to all animals in the same order with the same time intervals.

EXPERIMENTAL RESULTS

With a fixed order of presentation to all subjects, there is a probability that the serial position of a test object will affect the degree of response to it, either by negative adaptation or cumulative effect. There were marked indications that such effects occurred. Some animals apparently learned that the test objects, at first terrifying, would not move out of the presentation box; others began to show fear in the later trials before the box was opened at all.

The total number of animals making fear responses to any object, therefore, is not a wholly satisfactory index of its relative effectiveness in provoking fear. However, there is evidence that the amount of such error is limited. In each group of three objects one or more pictures were included. The number of avoidance responses was consistently low for these pictures, while remaining high for objects such as dog or snake, known from the work of others (Yerkes, Haslerud) to be fear provoking. This means that transfer or generalization effects were limited. Also there was no sign of a steady increase or decrease of fear responses as the experiment progressed. The animals' responses were highly selective. Preliminary observations, and tests made after the completion of the experiment, also make it clear that such objects as a head without the body attached are in themselves capable of eliciting panic, and that the number of fear responses to human or chimpanzee head, recorded experimentally, is not due to an association of these test objects with the others.

The table presents the number of fear responses to each test object, separating primate, pictorial and non-primate objects. The table gives the order of presenta-

Number of animals (from a total of 30) making fear responses to 'primate' test objects, 'pictures,' and 'nonprimate' objects (M) indicates that the object was put in motion during the presentation

		Primate	Picture		Nonprimate	
Test	I	Adult ape head: 7	Picture: 0	Dog head (M):	10
	II	Doll: 4	Picture: 1	Large grub:	3
	III	Infant ape head: 3	Picture: 2	Rubber tube (M):	3
	IV	Infant: 1	Picture: 1	Wood-wire bug (M):	3
	V		Picture: 0	Mechanical	
			Picture: 1	grasshopper (M):	4
	VI	Human head: 12	Picture: 0	Rubber dog:	5
	VII	Skull (M): 24	Picture: 4		
	VIII	Monkey (M): 16	Picture: 4	Small grub:	2
				Mechanical	
				turtle (M):	8
	IX	Cast of ape visage 14	Picture: 0	Cloth dog:	8
	X	Ape hide: 5	Picture: 0		
	XI		Picture: 0	Cast of snake:	21
			Picture: 0		
			Picture: 0		
		Total = 86	Total = 13	Total =	67
		Mean = 9.6	Mean = 0.9	Mean =	6.7

tion and also shows which three objects were grouped together for each test period. It is assumed, partly on the basis of evidence not presented here, that what particular pictures were used is irrelevant and that the number of animals avoiding the pictures is an index of the 'spread' of fear from exciting to neutral objects. From a total of 30 animals the mean number making fear responses to each primate test object was 9.6; to pictures, 0.9; to nonprimate objects, 6.7. These scores, it must be remembered, are the number of actual overt withdrawals which met the criteria set up in advance for a definable fear response. They take no account of signs of fear which were peculiar to an individual animal. Also, they are the number of such responses made while animal and test object were separated by a stout wire mesh. Tests in other circumstances show a higher percentage of avoidance, and show also that the relative effectiveness of two objects as causes of fear may vary somewhat according to the mode of presentation. In the conditions of the experiment, the following are the most effective stimuli, in descending order: *skull* (with moving jaw); painted wax *snake*; *monkey* (with moving head); plaster cast of *chimpanzee visage*; and *human head*. Least exciting are, in ascending order, chimpanzee infant; small wax grub; infant chimpanzee head; large wax grub; moving rubber tube ("snake"); and moving wood-and-wire 'bug.'

SUPPLEMENTARY OBSERVATIONS

The chimpanzee's fear of toy animals and snakes is of course well known (23, 42). The data which are new and which were the occasion of this report are those showing that the chimpanzee is excited by, and avoids, parts of chimpanzee or human bodies. It was evident that such a conclusion had important implications, and that further observations would be desirable as a control of the data. Control observations, accordingly, were made after the formal experiment was completed. Their purpose was to discover whether some peculiarity of the actual experimental objects, or some detail of procedure, might have been the true cause of fear; or whether the behavior falls into a more general class related to the common human avoidance of a mutilated face and of dead bodies.

Preliminary experiments had already shown that all the adult chimpanzees were excited at the first sight of a chimpanzee head modelled in clay and carried in the hand from cage to cage. A majority showed avoidance, which was outright panic in five or six of the thirty subjects. In the supplementary observations an unpainted plaster cast of the clay model, and also an actual head from a dead chimpanzee, produced definite avoidance.

With different presentations the results were essentially the same, although intensity of response varied, in part with adaptation to sight of so many similar objects. Avoidance was observed when a head was carried by hand; when it was exposed by removing a cloth or opening a box; and when the head was first put in the chimpanzee's cage and the animal admitted afterward. In another observation the head was placed behind a small ledge, so that the actual termination of the neck was not visible (although the chimpanzee 'knew' from familiarity with the cage in which the test was made that there was no space large enough for a body beneath the head). The chimpanzee was then admitted from a detaining inner room from which none of the preparations could be seen. A marked fear response occurred immediately, before the lapse of enough time to make the unresponsiveness of the head abnormal. Thus lack of movement in the test object did not determine the fear, nor yet an actual perception of the termination of the neck.

A painted human eye and eyebrow (sawn from a plaster manikin's head) produced marked avoidance.

Finally, observations were made with anesthetized chimpanzees as stimulus objects. Four adults were shown an anesthetized infant, two years old, carried by two members of the staff. The infant was recovering from nembutal, and made some spontaneous movements of an arm and hand. Three of the four adults were very excited and one at least afraid, in spite of the fact that they had often seen young chimpanzees being carried by the staff. A more deeply anesthetized adult was taken on a low, flat, two-wheeled barrow up to the cages of nine of the adults. Definite fear was shown by six, aggression (possibly related to fear) by two others, and the remaining animal was almost certainly afraid but remained at a distance without showing definable avoidance.

The fear evoked by a detached face or head in the formal experiment, therefore, was not a product of some uncontrolled detail of procedure or of the construction of the test objects. Any of a number of related stimuli have the same effect, in a number of situations.

From the data it appears that *either* lack of responsiveness in a whole animal, *or* an evident lack of a body when the head or part of the head is seen, can determine the fear. The first conclusion depends on the observations with anesthetized animals as stimuli. The second follows from the fact that avoidance of an isolated head was immediate and certainly was not delayed long enough for an unusual unresponsiveness, as such, to have become apparent before fear occurred.

SPONTANEITY OF THE FEAR

The fears observed must also have been spontaneous,[2] and not conditioned by some association of the test objects with a more primitive source of fear such as pain. This is shown by the following considerations.

There are two ways in which fear of a detached head or an anesthetized animal could be due to learning. Fear might occur (1) because the subjects recognized part of a whole which they had learned to fear in the past, or (2) because of an earlier association of a class of objects (detached heads, abnormally unresponsive chimpanzees) with a more primitive cause of fear.

(1) The first explanation can be ruled out. The dummy human head represented an ordinary young

[2] The term 'spontaneous' is used here to mean that the fear is not built up by association, as a learned response. The term is not synonymous with 'innate' since there are definite factors of past experience involved, as will appear in the later discussion.

man whom the adults of the colony might have teased or injured, as they often tend to do with strangers whose general appearance is similar to that of members of the laboratory staff, but whom they would not have feared. The cast of a face was a faithful replica of the chimpanzee Lita's, made from a death mask. She had died not long before the experiment began, and certainly would not have been a source of fear to any of the other chimpanzees with cage wire intervening, as in the conditions of the experiment. The anesthetized infant in his normal state would not have been feared by an adult; and the anesthetized adult who was used as a stimulus object was Don, who is dominated by almost all of the other adults of the colony. The test object which aroused fear therefore did not do so because it was recognized as part of a whole which in its normal completeness would have caused the response.

(2) The second possibility to be examined is that an association had been formed earlier between the class of stimulus objects and some event such as pain, loud noise, or a fall. For animals born in the bush and captured when their mothers were killed this is a real possibility. But nine of the adolescent and adult subjects of the experiment were born and reared in captivity and definitely had no opportunity to make such associations. None of these had seen a detached human or chimpanzee head; a few of them had seen a dead chimpanzee, but no more primitive cause of fear would be associated with the sight. The nine animals who are known not to have such associations showed on the average rather more frequent and stronger avoidance than the remaining twenty-one animals.

These facts require the conclusion that the fears discussed are spontaneous. Further support for the conclusion is found in the behavior of human beings.

HUMAN AVOIDANCE OF MUTILATED
AND DEAD BODIES

Human emotional responses to the dead and to such things as the sight of a major operation or of a badly mutilated face cannot reasonably be attributed to conditioning. The responses tend to be strongest on the first experience, which eliminates direct conditioning as an explanation and requires the supporting assumption of a preliminary verbal conditioning which forms the whole basis of the response. But if avoidance were so readily established, with no innate tendency toward fear of the conditioned stimulus itself, one could easily keep children from playing in dangerous places or train adults to drive automobiles carefully—by verbal instruction alone. This is the essence of Valentine's (39) brilliant criticism of Watsonian theory and my rejection of the explanation by conditioning rests upon his argument. What he did was to show how easy it is to condition fear of some things, how hard with others, and thus demonstrated the existence of emotional susceptibilities which are the basis of spontaneous and almost spontaneous fears.

Watson's (40) theory of fear has rightly had a profound effect upon psychological thought, and a radical departure from his ideas is not easily accepted. Yet the present situation is that the theory has been demolished, with no good substitute in sight. Jones and Jones' (22) experiment on the human fear of snakes constituted a strong and radical attack on Watson's theory. The evidence adduced by Valentine (39) reinforced the attack with evidence from a variety of fears. He has shown that there is a wide range of situations, not easily defined or classified, which have some tendency to evoke human fear. Finally, Hebb and Riesen (14) have shown the existence of a spontaneous fear of strangers in infant chimpanzees, where the customary appeal to the subject's unknown past experience is impossible and the explanation by conditioning ruled out.

Watson's work, consequently, provides no more than a starting point in determining the causes of fear and gives no reason to reject the conclusion that human fear of dead or mutilated bodies is spontaneous. The conclusion is also not affected by the fact that an almost complete adaptation to such stimuli is possible, nor by the fact that some persons may not have an emotional disturbance at their first sight of an opera-

tion, autopsy or dissection. It has sometimes been
assumed that if a fear is not general it must have been
learned by those who do have it: that an innate fear
should be found in all persons. This argument of course
is quite invalid, in view of the existence of individual
genetic differences, and it has been seen that some of
the chimpanzee fears discussed in this paper are not
found in all animals and yet cannot be ascribed to
learning.

The evidence therefore is that both in man and in
chimpanzee there occur spontaneous fears of mutilated
and unresponsive bodies. The chimpanzee knows
nothing of anesthesia, has no abstract conception of
death, and presumably may confuse a model of a head
and the real thing. Considering the intellectual differences between the species and the extent to which
man's behavior is influenced by speech, one must say
that human and chimpanzee fear susceptibilities, with
dismembered or inert bodies as stimulus objects, are remarkably similar. In this fact there is further support for
the idea that such fears are spontaneous and not asso-
tiative or conditioned.

So that this conclusion will be seen in the proper
perspective, the reader is reminded that the importance
of learning is not minimized. There are essential factors
of past experience in the fears which have been discussed; and the hypothesis which is to be presented lays
a good deal of emphasis on learning as an element in
the development of any fear.

CENTRAL VERSUS SENSORY FACTORS

DETERMINING FEAR

The first step in an analysis of fear is a better definition of the problem and of its relation to other psychological investigations.

It should be specified that the problem is not simply
that of the subcortical motor integration of fear behavior. The earlier studies of Bard (2) had the effect
of concentrating attention on the hypothalamus, but it
is now evident that more must be taken into account.
The analysis by Lashley (24) and Masserman (32)

has limited the emotional functions of the diencephalon to a motor integration. More recently, Bard (3) has described rage in a cat lacking *only* the hypothalamic region which he formerly considered to be essential to emotional activity. In view also of the marked differences of the stimuli which are effective in each case, and the absence of 'after-discharge' in the decorticate preparation, it is evident that the processes of normal and decorticate emotions cannot be equated. Fear behavior has been demonstrated by Bard in the decorticate cat, but only with auditory stimuli. An essential problem remains in understanding cortico-subcortical interaction and the important role of perception in the fear responses of the normal animal.

The evidence presented has shown that the chimpanzee's fear of a detached head is in some way related to the physical lack of an attached body or of movement, or both. But our real interest is not in the physical properties of the stimulus object but in the way they act on the organism. The first question to be asked concerns the existence of a sensory control of the response: can one find any property of the sensory excitation which in itself determines the occurrence and form of the response?

The answer seems to be no. In the first place, the physical lack in the stimulus object cannot be equated with a sensory lack by saying that the sight of a head without the normally associated sight of a body causes fear, for the statement would not be true. When a chimpanzee sees a man's head only, without movement and with the rest of the man's body out of sight behind a door, he is not afraid. There are certainly sensory cues which distinguish the two situations (*i.e.*, detached head, *vs.* attached head with body hidden) but I have not been able to find any generalization that distinguishes the purely sensory[3] event which causes fear from the one which does not. In the second place,

---

[3] 'Sensory' in the present discussion is defined as referring to activity, in afferent structures, which is directly determined by environmental events; roughly, activity in the receptor organ and afferent tracts, up to and including the corresponding sensory projection area.

it has been shown that the fears are spontaneous. If they were also sensorily determined, it would follow that there are innate connections from the sensory cells excited in seeing any chimpanzee or human head to the motor centers determining avoidance; or in a more *Gestalt* formulation, that the dynamic properties of every such sensory excitation have an innately selective action on those particular motor centers. It would follow further that this sensori-motor relationship is consistently inhibited and nonfunctional throughout the animal's lifetime, no matter how many times he sees a human or chimpanzee head, unless by chance the head has been cut off from its owner. The improbability of such ideas is evident. They seem to be a product of the assumption (quite reasonable in itself) that the form of a response is fully determined by the sensory event that precipitates it: since a physical lack in the stimulus object cannot excite receptor cells, the assumption means that the part of the stimulus object which is present is an adequate excitant of fear, and, since the whole object does not cause fear, that the part which is missing is normally an inhibiter or in some way prevents an innately determined response to the other part. Such reasoning will be found to lead rapidly to absurdities. Doubt is then cast on the original assumption, and the alternative conclusion is indicated that the determinant of certain strongly marked anthropoid fears is not any property of the sensory excitation alone but may have to be sought in some interaction of sensory events with other cerebral processes.

This argument depends on the accuracy of the analysis which has been made of the stimulating conditions in which fear of dismembered or inert bodies is observed. Other interpretations are possible, but seem either to beg the question or to amount to the same thing. (One might say, for example, that it is strangeness or mysteriousness that produces fear of a decapitated head and of an inert chimpanzee being carried by human beings. Actually, reference to strangeness only strengthens the preceding argument, as we shall see in a moment.) Nevertheless, it would be unwise to depend too strongly on the evidence of behavior into which so many complicating factors of experience may enter. Let us turn to fear of strangers (14) and of sudden noise (8). The theoretical interpretation suggested by fear of a dismembered body gains decisive support from these other observations and in turn makes their theoretical significance clearer.

The growing chimpanzee is persistently afraid of strange persons, objects and places, although the response is not always predictable in the individual case. Hebb and Riesen (14) have shown that the fear of strangers by chimpanzee infants is spontaneous and cannot be accounted for as a conditioned response. Also, a slight change of clothing may produce fear of a familiar attendant who was not feared before. To assume that the form of the response on seeing something strange is controlled alone by some property of the sensory event is to assume that *any* visual excitation is primarily a cause of fear and that other responses are substituted merely by repetition of the stimulation. Fear of strangers would mean that the visual excitation from any human or chimpanzee face (strange chimpanzees are feared as much as strange men) or any pattern of clothing is an innately adequate excitant of fear; for any pattern whatever may be strange, depending on accidents of experience. The idea seems absurd in itself, and is definitely contradicted by observations of the behavior of an infant chimpanzee blindfolded from birth to the age of four months, when the avoidance of strangers by normal animals is beginning (Nissen[4]). In Senden's (35) comprehensive review of the literature on persons born blind and given their sight after infancy, there is no mention of fear aroused by the first visual form-perception; and Dennis (7) explicitly denies that fear occurs in these persons. Fear of a strange person is therefore not determined by a particular property of the sensory excitation, but by some discrepancy of the pattern from those which have been frequently experienced by the subject—by a complex

[4] Personal communication from Dr. H. W. Nissen. The experiment was not an investigation of emotional behavior, and detailed records on this point were not kept. But it is known with certainty that there was no avoidance evoked by the chimpanzee's first visual perception of human beings.

relationship, that is, of the sensory event to pre-existent cerebral processes.

A similar meaning lies in the fact noted by English (8) that a noise must be sudden to cause fear. When auditory intensity is built up gradually, the response is hard to elicit. The same is true of loss of support. An unexpected drop is the one that causes fear, not one for which preparation has been made verbally or by playful swinging of infant subjects. Jones (21) has shown that unexpectedness is an essential feature of a number of fear-provoking situations. In all such fears the major determinant cannot be the afferent excitation alone but involves a relationship of that excitation to concurrent cerebral activity.

These facts actually raise no new theoretical issue. Their effect is to sharpen the definition of a problem which has been formulated in various ways by other writers. That both sensory and central processes are involved in the control of behavior and must be distinguished for theoretical purposes is implied by the concept of 'operants' (Skinner, 37) and of 'stimulus trace' (Hull, 16) no less than by the 'expectancy' of Cowles and Nissen (6), Mowrer (34) and Hilgard and Marquis (15). It is the real problem of attention and of the selectivity of response to the several properties of a sensory event (Leeper, 27; Lashley, 26). The problem is made explicit by Hilgard and Marquis's "central process which seems relatively independent of afferent stimuli" (p. 275), Beach's (4) 'central excitatory mechanism,' and Morgan's (33) 'central motive state.' Every serious attempt in recent years to analyze the neural mechanisms of the more complex forms of behavior has found the need of distinguishing, as more or less independent factors, sensory and central states or processes; in other words, of denying that the direction of transmission of a sensory excitation is determined by the properties of that excitation alone, even when the stable changes of learning have been taken into account. This is thoroughly consistent also with modern electro-physiology. All parts of the brain are continuously active and there are reasons for believing that the activity may be self-maintaining, and even self-initiating (1,

18, 29, 30, 41). An afferent excitation does *not* arouse inactive tissue, but modifies an activity already in existence. The conclusion, therefore, that there are non-sensory factors in the determination of certain fears agrees with existing theory.

It must be added that the conclusion is not necessarily trivial. Current opinion recognizes the necessity of postulating central determinants of behavior but it has done so reluctantly, always with reference to a single, rather narrow aspect of behavioral theory, and apparently without recognizing how generally the necessity has actually cropped up in psychological analysis. The preceding discussion may do no more than suggest a change of emphasis, but the change is one which, as I shall try to show, has a considerable effect on theory. Besides drawing attention to facts of behavior which are usually forgotten, it reveals some order in the facts and makes possible a coherent hypothesis of the nature of fear.

DEVELOPMENT OF AN HYPOTHESIS

Avoidance of strangers provides a possible starting point for a theory of the nature of fear. An essential feature of the stimulating conditions is the divergence of the object avoided from a familiar group of objects, while still having enough of their properties to fall within the same class. It is a most important fact that the fear or shyness does not develop at first vision, as the already cited data of Nissen, Senden (35) and Dennis (7) show. Common experience indicates also that the fear is minimized or absent if the growing infant has always been exposed to sight of a large number of persons. It is therefore dependent on the fact that certain perceptions have become habitual, a limited number of central neural reactions to the sight of human beings having been established with great specificity by repeated experience. The idea that there are such habits of perception was developed by Gibson (9) and further supported by later studies of the effect of set upon perception (5, 27, 43). A number of facts relating to the development of intelligence, and its changes with advancing age, have the same import (11, pp. 286, 289). From this point of view, it might be proposed that fear occurs when an object is seen which is like familiar objects in enough respects to arouse habitual processes of perception, but in other respects arouses incompatible processes.

Such a treatment of the fear of strangers would amount to an interference, incongruity or conflict theory. It might subsume fear of mutilated bodies as well, by classifying them as strange objects, and could be extended to cover fears due to pain and sudden loud noise, which obviously tend to disrupt concurrent psychological processes. But farther than this such a conflict theory will not go. There might be some difficulty in applying it even to the fear of strange objects, when the strangeness is apparently due to incompleteness in a familiar object (as with the chimpanzee's fear of a detached head); and conflict cannot account for causes of fear such as darkness (39) in which a sensory deficit is the effective condition, or nutritional disturbance (38).

Moreover, a fundamental question would remain as to the meaning of 'conflict,' and why an incompatibility between two perceptions should produce the incoördinations of emotional behavior. This is the crucial question, and in trying to answer it I believe we can find the possibility of a more comprehensive hypothesis, according to which conflict is only one of several ways in which a true source of fear occurs. If two perceptual processes, which cannot coexist, cannot even alternate without producing gross disturbances of behavior (which is what the conflict notion implies), ordinary unemotional behavior must depend on an essential temporal integration in cerebral processes, and fear may be a direct result of their disorganization. Let us ask what such ideas would involve.

It has already been seen that sensory and central processes contribute separately to the control of behavior. For convenience, let us designate the specific pattern of cellular activity throughout the thalamo-cortical system, at any one moment, as a 'phase.' Behavior is directly correlated with a phase sequence which is temporally organized (4), in part by the inherent properties

of the system (the constitutional factor) and in part
by the time relations of various afferent excitations in
the past (the factor of experience). The spatial organization of each phase, the actual anatomical pattern of
cells which are active at any moment, would be affected
by the present afferent excitation also. Subjectively, the
phase sequence would be identified with the train of
thought and perception. Now each phase is determined
by a neural interaction, between the preceding phase
and the concurrent afferent excitations. Lorente de Nó's
(29) discussion of the dynamics of neural action shows
that two or more simultaneous neural events might rein-
force each other's effects and contribute to a single, de-
terminate pattern of subsequent cerebral activity; or on
the contrary might be indeterminate, in the sense that
slight changes of timing and intensity could lead to
marked and sudden fluctuations of pattern. A phase sequence, that is, could be stable or unstable, and one can
assume that vacillating, unpredictable and incoördinated
behavior is the expression of unstable cerebral activity.
Also, the effect of learning in general is to increase the
predictability and coördination of behavior. The element
of learning in emotional behavior will be discussed more
specifically, but in the meantime we may speak of the
cerebral processes controlling predictable, coördinated
behavior as 'organized,' and recognize the tendency of
learning to establish and maintain cerebral organization.

Disorganization could occur in several ways, some of
which may be called conflict. (1) A sensory event might
disrupt the concurrent phase sequence. The event might
be one whose facilitation has been integrated into other
phase sequences, and the disruptive only because it is
'unexpected.' If so the disruption would be brief, another
well-organized phase sequence would be promptly established, and one would speak of the subject as having
only been 'startled.' The disruption would be brief but
it would occur; a well-organized phase could not be set
up instantaneously, independent of facilitation from the
preceding phase. On the other hand, the sensory event
might fail to set up another organized sequence, and so
initiate a prolonged disturbance; or might like loud
noise, and especially pain, tend persistently to break

down cerebral organization. (2) Simultaneous sensory events might have facilitations which are enough unlike to make the following phase sequence unstable, even though each event separately might be capable of integration with the concurrent phase. Evidently (1) and (2) would be modes of conflict, one sensory-central, the other sensory-sensory.[5] But disorganization might also result (3) from the absence of a usually present sensory process. Cerebral organization involves learning. If a sensory activity A has always been present during adaptation to a sensory event B, facilitation from A would necessarily affect the final pattern of cellular activities which constitutes the adaptation to B, and might be essential to it. If so, B in the absence of A could again produce behavioral disturbance (if B without A occurs often enough, however, another adaptation would be established). Finally, (4) metabolic and structural changes in the central nervous system could obviously be a source of disorganization, by changing the time relations between the activities of individual cells, apart from any unusual conflict or sensory deficiency.

Attention must now be turned to the way in which cerebral processes tend to maintain their organization, in order to round out the picture of fear behavior. Whatever else may be true of it, avoidance certainly averts or minimizes disruptive stimulation. When we distinguish between the disruption and the processes tending to avert it, and assume that the degree of disruption may vary, we obtain the valuable result of seeing how a single mechanism of fear could on different occasions produce perfectly coördinated flight, a less coördinated avoidance accompanied by trembling and so on, startle, or the paralysis of terror: when cerebral disruption is extreme, it might presumably prevent any coördinated action, even flight.

It seems evident that the so-to-speak homeostatic

[5] Logically, another category of 'central-central' conflict would be possible, which might have some meaning with regard to emotional disturbances and anxiety arising from a conflict of ideas or beliefs. Such a concept might be applied to fear of socialism or of catholics and emotional disturbances due to such purely intellectual ideas as those of Galileo or Darwin.

processes which maintain the dynamic equilibrium of unemotional behavior are to a great extent processes of learning, operating in either of two ways. On the one hand there is negative adaptation to strange objects, which implies that a sensory-central conflict may be banished by an effect of learning on the central organization alone. The sensory event remains the same, yet disturbance disappears. With still further exposure, the formerly strange object may become not merely tolerated but 'liked' and 'pleasant,' which is to say that the originally disturbing sensory event now actively supports cerebral integration.

On the other hand, learning may contribute to this integration indirectly, by reinforcing a mode of behavior (avoidance) which minimizes or removes the disturbing sensation. The incoördinations of emotional behavior, its most characteristic feature, are unlearned; they are apt to be most marked on the first occasion on which they are aroused by any particular stimulus. But the coördinated element of the behavior tends to become more prominent on repetition of the stimulus and to increase, while the unlearned incoördination is decreasing. It thus appears that the coördinated avoidance which occurs in fear behavior of normal animals is mainly learned.

There is indeed a primitive innate avoidance (manifested e.g. in the flexion reflex of Sherrington's (36) spinal animals, and the cowering of Bard's (3) decerebrate cats), but the avoidance which operates most efficiently to maintain coördinated effector activity is acquired. In the normal mammal at least, simple avoidance appears as a conditioned response to cues which in the past have preceded a disruptive stimulation. When a disruptive event is sudden and without warning the response is never an uncomplicated avoidance, a smooth and economical coöperation of effector organs, but involves startle, trembling, sweating, vocalization and so on. The optimum toward which behavior tends, with repetition of such disturbances, is a response (to premonitory cues) which completely averts the disturbing sensory event. At this final stage of learning, avoidance is fully effective in maintaining integrated cerebral action, and no emotional component is left in the behavior. Thus avoidance without wear occurs. In the avoidance that does involve fear the learning process is not complete or premonitory cues have not been available, and the belated avoidance appears side by side with the excess of effector activity that justifies the inference of cerebral disorganization.

The reciprocal relationship of learning to the disruption of integrated behavior is most simply illustrated by an adult's unemotional avoidance of a hot stove which as an infant he may once have feared. Another illustration is provided by observation of adult chimpanzees where the course of learning in a very unusual social situation could be followed from its beginning. The experimenter, disguised with a grotesque false face and a change of clothing, approached each animal's cage wearing heavy gloves and acted the part of a very aggressive individual, instead of the cautious role one ordinarily takes with the chimpanzee. The results suggested an interpretation similar to that of Bridges* who concluded that an infant's fear develops out of primitive undifferentiated excitement. The first response by a number of animals was a generalized excitement and marked autonomic activity. An animal might be 'friendly' and viciously aggressive, almost in the same breath, or show erection of hair and scream and yet solicit petting. Attack, flight, and the friendly pattern alternated unpredictably. As the stimulus was repeated over a 5-weeks' period, the autonomic activity decreased and one or other of the various patterns dominated. Eventually each animal's behavior became predictable, but it appeared often to be a matter of chance whether the original disturbance would develop into fear, aggression or (less often) friendliness. When avoidance became dominant, the animal would move back out of reach while the experimenter was still distant, with a marked decrease of the excessive effector activity. Learning was clearly involved. We shall also see that the possibility, suggested by this example, that the learning may take more than one form, has a bearing on the theoretical relation of fear to other emotional patterns.

The hypothesis implicitly developed in this discussion

[* See the article by Bridges included in this volume.]

can now be made explicit. The immediate source of fear is a disruption of a coördination, principally acquired, in the timing of cellular activities in the cerebrum. The disruption may be due to conflict, sensory deficit or constitutional change. With disruption there at once occur processes tending to restore the integration of cerebral activities; in fear these include either liminal or subliminal (13) activation of processes determining avoidance. Optimally, avoidance tends toward completely averting the cerebral disruption, and at this stage avoidance without fear would be said to occur.

CLASSIFICATION OF SPECIFIC FEARS

The value and limitations of the hypothesis will be clearer if we next see how it would be related to specific causes of fear.

(1) *Fears due to 'conflict.'* Here may be included fears induced by pain, loud noise, dead or mutilated bodies, and strange persons and animals. Pain and loud noise appear to have a primitive disrupting action, not psychologically analyzable nor dependent on any previous experience. To this extent fear of such things is in a special class. It is also noteworthy that there is little adaptation to the repetition of pain and sudden intense noise except in very special conditions (28).

Fear of the strange and of dead and mutilated bodies is included under the heading of conflict on the assumption that strange objects arouse incompatible perceptual and intellectual processes. If it should be concluded however that the effective condition is a perceptual deficit, fear of the strange should be included in the following category (2). Finally, fear of snakes and certain small mammals may belong either in this or the following category. Although some basis for including them in the present category might be proposed it would be much too speculative, and it is best to let such fears stand for the present as not fully accounted for.

(2) *Fears due to sensory deficit.* Loss of support, darkness and solitude, as causes of fear, have in common an absence of customary stimulation.

Proprioceptive and pressure stimulation due to maintained position in space is practically always present, and it is plausible to suppose that the afferent excitation from these sources would have an essential part in maintaining experientially organized, or habitual, modes of cerebral action. With loss of support, however, the proprioception accompanying maintenance of posture against gravity, and exteroception from the surfaces on which the body's weight rests, are decreased or abolished. Redistribution of blood pressure and changes of position of the viscera would no doubt also lead to positive stimulation, but it seems unlikely that this is an effective cause of fear, in the infant. In the adult of course such stimulation would have become conditioned by experience. (If it should be true that positive visceral stimulation is the main cause of fear in an infant dropped for the first time, the fear should be classed in the preceding category (1), as one of those aroused by an unaccustomed stimulation.)

Fears induced by darkness and solitude (39) do not occur with time relations such that the emotional excitation can be attributed to the positive visual activity of the 'off-effect.' The response appears to be a genuine reaction to deficit (25), intelligible only on the assumption of the present discussion that a 'response' need have no direct *sensory* excitant. The violent attempts of the growing chimpanzee to avoid isolation, even in full daylight, seem to require a quite similar interpretation. Köhler (23) has shown that the effective condition here is the social deprivation, as such. Just as a few patterns of postural stimulation are a practically constant feature of the afferent influx to the brain, and visual stimulation during waking hours, so social perceptions are frequent (though intermittent) and might be expected to become an integral element in the organization of cerebral action patterns. It is important to note that this would be a function of experience, and that no fear of darkness or of being alone should be expected in the subject who has only infrequently experienced anything else. Such a subject would develop a different cerebral organization, in which the perceptions referred to would play no essential part. It is also implied that in early infancy neither darkness nor isolation would have any emotional effect; and that as psychological development continues the patterns of cerebral action might toward maturity become so stable as to be relatively independent of any particular set of perceptions. Some adults, or most adults in a particular culture, might have no fear of darkness and isolation.

(3) *Constitutional disturbances and maturation.* Spies et al. (38) have provided exceptionally clear evidence that the psychotic fears so frequently found in pellagra are, in some instances at least, directly due to nutritional disturbance (see also Jolliffe, 20). When the psychosis is acute (before irreversible neural damage has been done), fear of friends and relatives and of hallucinatory creatures may clear up dramatically upon administration of nicotinic acid. The patient regains insight rapidly, can recall his fears clearly, but also is puzzled at the lack of any incident that might have caused them. Controls made to exactly define the action of nicotinic acid rule out psychological influence as essential either to the mental illness or its cure. Such fears must be regarded as originating in a disturbance of the metabolism of the individual cell, changing (for example) the timing of its detonation cycle and thus its relationship to the activity of other cells. In other words, metabolic changes would have disrupted the orderly sequence of cerebral events which is postulated here as the basis of normal unemotional behavior.

It is also evident that endocrine factors might at times produce a similar effect, partly accounting for the increased shyness and emotional instability of adolescence. The gonadal hormones must be supposed to have a selective action on certain central neural cells (4, 25) changing their properties of excitability and thus disrupting to a greater or less degree the neural organizations into which those cells have entered. With the passage of time reorganization would occur and shyness would decrease.

I do not of course suggest that constitutional changes are the only cause of shyness, or even the main cause. In its most pronounced form it must be thought of simply as an avoidance of strangers; and the next most important factor, after the sight of a strange person, may well be the fact that as the child matures others begin to behave toward him in a different way, according to his age. The child is confronted by 'strange' behavior, and situations which are strange to him. Thus shyness can be treated mainly as avoidance of the strange. It is not impossible however that structural and endocrine changes may also play a part in the emotional instabilities of youth. One thinks of maturation as slow and gradual; but there is actually little evidence on this point, and spurts of growth might well make a significant modification of cerebral organizations established by earlier experience. In general terms, such an approach makes intelligible the sporadic appearance of the 'imaginative, subjective or anticipatory fears' classified as such by Jersild and Holmes (19). The fears referred to by Jersild and Holmes are markedly subject to maturation during a period of rapid and irregular growth, and when one observes them in the growing child it is characteristically hard to discover any sufficient cause in experience.

THE RELATIONSHIP OF FEAR TO RAGE
AND OTHER STATES

Fear and rage are notoriously related, and it is impossible to frame any statement of the causes of rage (12) which would not on some points comprise causes of fear as well. The question, whether there is in fact any definite distinction, has been raised elsewhere (13). The hypothesis developed here suggests a kinship between the two emotions which may be put as follows:

The fundamental source of either emotion is of the same kind, a disruption of coördinated cerebral activity. Flight and aggression are two different modes of reaction tending to restore the dynamic equilibrium, or stability, of cerebral processes. The question may be left open at present whether there are different kinds of disturbance, one kind leading to rage, the other to fear. It seems almost certain that such a difference exists between extremes, but with no clear dichotomy; for in some situations, as I have suggested above, it appears to be a matter of chance whether aggression or flight will dominate behavior. Each of these modes of response tends to restore integrated cerebral action, one by modifying the disturbing source of stimulation, the other by removing the animal from it.

Fawning would be another mode of reaction which would tend to modify disruptive stimulation (by placating the source). It is evident also that the hypothesis of this paper opens a wide field of speculation concerning a number of socially and clinically familiar conditions, such as shame, grief, chronic depression and so on. To deal with these varied emotional disturbances, the first step would be to classify the source of disturbance as modifiable by the subject's responses, or unmodifiable; and to further classify the modifiable according to the mode of overt reaction which would be effective. Thus shame or grief would arise from unmodifiable conditions; fear primarily from situations which are (or appear to the subject to be) modifiable by retreat; and so on. Finally, neurosis and some forms of psychosis would be regarded as a chronic condition of cerebral disorganization which according to the hypothesis might be initiated either by severe and prolonged conflict, or by a metabolic disturbance.

It would be idle at present to carry speculation farther, but it has been worthwhile observing that a theoretical relationship of fear to other emotional patterns is provided. If the proposed hypothesis is on the right track, the details of the relationship will become evident when more is known of the physiology of the cerebrum.

CONCLUSIONS

The conclusions of this paper may be put as follows:

(1) Anthropoid fears of inert, mutilated or dismembered bodies are spontaneous: that is to say, although experience of a certain kind is a prerequisite and learning is definitely involved, the avoidance of such objects is not built up by association with a more primitive cause of fear.

(2) These and a number of other fears are evidently

not determined by a sensory event alone, and the behavior is not intelligible except on the assumption that its control is a joint product of sensory and 'autonomous' central processes. Consequently no amount of analysis of the stimulating conditions alone can be expected to elucidate the nature of fear, or to lead to any useful generalization concerning its causes.

(3) An adequate hypothesis of the nature of fear cannot be framed in psychological terms alone, but must utilize physiological concepts of cerebral action. No common psychological ground can be discovered for all the various causes of fear. What is there in common, for example, between the characteristically high level of the auditory and low level of visual stimulation which induces fear in children? or between fear of strangers, which decreases, and fear induced by pain, which tends to increase, with repetition?

The hypothesis developed here has made a considerable synthesis of formerly unrelated facts, although it remains vague on some crucial points. It proposes in brief that fear originates in the disruption of temporally and spatially organized cerebral activities; that fear is distinct from other emotions by the nature of the processes tending to restore cerebral equilibrium (that is, *via* flight); and classifies the sources of fear as involving (1) conflict, (2) sensory deficit or (3) constitutional change. By distinguishing between processes which break down and those which restore physiological organization in the cerebrum, the variability of fear behavior is accounted for.

The conceptions of neurophysiological action on which this is based were developed originally as an approach to other problems, and will be presented in detail elsewhere.* When this is done, and the neurophysiological implications are made explicit, it may appear that a basis has been laid at last for an adequate theory of emotion and motivation—something which is lacking in psychology at present.

[* A more detailed statement of Professor Hebb's viewpoint may be found in Hebb, D. O. *The Organization of Behavior: A Neuropsychological Theory.* New York: Wiley, 1949.]

REFERENCES

1. Adrian, E. D., Electrical activity of the nervous system, *Arch. Neurol. Psychiatr.*, 1934, 32, 1125-1136.

2. Bard, P., On emotional expression after decortication with some remarks on certain theoretical views, *Psychol. Rev.*, 1934, 41, 309-329.

3. ———. Neural mechanisms in emotional and sexual behavior, *Psychosom. Med.*, 1942, 4, 171-172.

4. Beach, F. A., Analysis of factors involved in the arousal, maintenance and manifestation of sexual excitement in male animals, *Psychosom. Med.*, 1942, 4, 173-198.

5. Carmichael, L., Hogan, H. P., and Walter, A. A., An experimental study of the effect of language on the reproduction of visually perceived form, *J. exp. Psychol.*, 1932, 15, 73-86.

6. Cowles, J. T., and Nissen, H. W., Reward-expectancy in delayed responses of chimpanzees, *J. comp. Psychol.*, 1937, 24, 345-358.

7. Dennis, W., Congenital cataract and unlearned behavior, *J. genet. Psychol.*, 1934, 44, 340-350.

8. English, H. B., Three cases of the "conditioned fear response," *J. abnorm. soc. Psychol.*, 1929, 24, 221-225.

9. Gibson, J. J., The reproduction of visually perceived forms, *J. exp. Psychol.*, 1929, 12, 1-39.

10. Haslerud, G. M., The effect of movement of stimulus objects upon avoidance reactions in chimpanzees, *J. comp. Psychol.*, 1938, 25, 507-528.

11. Hebb, D. O., The effect of early and late brain injury on test scores, and the nature of normal adult intelligence, *Proc. Amer. phil. Soc.*, 1942, 85, 275-292.

12. ———. The forms and conditions of chimpanzee anger, *Bull. Canad. Psychol. Assoc.*, 1945, 5, 32-35.

13. ———. Emotion in man and animal: An analysis of the intuitive processes of recognition, *Psychol. Rev.*, 1946, 53, 88-106.

14. ———, and Riesen, A. H. The genesis of irrational fears, *Bull. Canad. Psychol. Assoc.*, 1943, 3, 49-50.

15. Hilgard, E. R., and Marquis, D. G. *Conditioning and Learning*. New York: Appleton, 1940.

16. Hull, C. L. *Principles of Behavior: An introduction to Behavior Theory*. New York: Appleton, 1943.

17. Jacobsen, C. F., Jacobsen, M. M., and Yoshioka, J. G. Development of an infant chimpanzee during her first year, *Comp. Psychol.*, Monog., 1932, 9, 1-94.

18. JASPER, H. H., Electrical signs of cortical activity, *Psychol. Bull.*, 1937, **34**, 411-481.

19. JERSILD, A. T., and HOLMES, F. B. *Children's fears.* New York: Teachers College Bureau of Publications, 1935.

20. JOLLIFFE, N., The neuropsychiatric manifestations of vitamin deficiencies, *J. Mt. Sinai Hosp.*, 1942, **8**, 658-667.

21. JONES, M. C., Emotional development. In A *Handbook of Child Psychology*, 2nd ed. (C. Murchison, ed.). Worcester, Mass.: Clark Univ. Press, 1933, 271-302.

22. JONES, H. E., and JONES, M. C., A study of fear, *Childhood Educ.*, 1928, **5**, 136-143.

23. KÖHLER, W. *The Mentality of Apes.* New York: Harcourt, 1925.

24. LASHLEY, K. S., The thalamus and emotion, *Psychol. Rev.*, 1938, **45**, 42-61.

25. ———, Experimental analysis of instinctive behavior, *Psychol. Rev.*, 1938, **45**, 445-471.

26. ———, An examination of the "continuity theory" as applied to discrimination learning, *J. gen. Psychol.*, 1942, **26**, 241-265.

27. LEEPER, R., A study of a neglected portion of the field of learning. The development of sensory organization, *J. genet. Psychol.*, 1935, **46**, 41-75.

28. LIDDELL, H. S., Animal behavior studies bearing on the problem of pain, *Psychosom. Med.*, 1944, **6**, 261-263.

29. LORENTE DE NÓ, R., Transmission of impulses through cranial motor nuclei, *J. Neurophysiol.*, 1939, **2**, 402-464.

30. ———, Cerebral cortex: architecture. In *Physiology of the Nervous System*, 2nd ed. (J. F. Fulton, Ed.). New York: Oxford Univ. Press, 1943, 274-301.

31. McCULLOCH, T. L., and HASLERUD, G. M., Affective responses of an infant chimpanzee reared in isolation from its kind, *J. comp. Psychol.*, 1939, **28**, 437-445.

32. MASSERMAN, J. H., The hypothalamus in psychiatry, *Amer. J. Psychiatr.*, 1942, **98**, 633-637.

33. MORGAN, C. T. *Physiological psychology.* New York: McGraw-Hill, 1943.

34. MOWRER, O. H., Preparatory set (expectancy)—a determinant in motivation and learning, *Psychol. Rev.*, 1938, **45**, 62-91.

35. SENDEN, M. v. *Raum- und Gestaltauffassung bei operierten Blindgeborenen vor und nach der Operation.* Leipzig: Barth, 1932.

36. SHERRINGTON, C. S. *Integrative Action of the Nervous System.* New York: Scribner, 1906.

37. SKINNER, B. F. *The Behavior of Organisms: An Experimental Analysis.* New York: Appleton, 1938.

38. SPIES, T. D., ARING, C. D., GELPERIN, J., and BEAN, W. B., The mental symptoms of pellagra. Their relief with nicotinic acid, *Amer. J. med. Sci.*, 1938, **196**, 461-475.

39. VALENTINE, C. W., The innate bases of fear, *J. genet. Psychol.*, 1930, **37**, 394-419.

40. WATSON, J. B. *Behaviorism.* New York: Norton, 1924.

41. WEISS, P., Autonomous versus reflexogenous activity of the central nervous system, *Proc. Amer. phil. Soc.*, 1941, **84**, 53-64.

42. YERKES, R. M., and YERKES, A. W., Nature and conditions of avoidance (fear) response in chimpanzee, *J. comp. Psychol.*, 1936, **21**, 53-66.

43. ZANGWILL, O. L., A study of the significance of attitude in recognition, *Brit. J. Psychol.*, 1937, **28**, 12-17.

11

Use of Conditioned Autonomic Responses in the Study of Anxiety

John I. Lacey, Robert L. Smith, and Arnold Green

Fels Institute for the Study of Human Development, Yellow Springs, Ohio

The evidence furnished by Watson and other investigators that emotional behavior could be understood by the established laws and principles of conditioning opened several new approaches to the study of emotion. The following selection indicates one method for conditioning emotional behavior by a technique in which the subject is unaware that conditioning is occurring.

The selection is reprinted from Psychosomatic Medicine; May-June, 1955, with the permission of the authors and publisher.

Experimental studies of "complex guiding processes . . . formed, retained, and used without the person's being aware of the process at any step," to quote Leeper, are relatively few, and are limited mainly to studies of hypnosis or of concept formation. Simple Pavlovian conditioning, however, with its impressive accumulation of quantitative findings and principles upon which special investigations may be based, may prove to be a more rigorous and efficient tool for the experimental demonstration and study of such unconscious processes. It has been known for many years that the conditioning process in human subjects is responsive to the subjects' cognitions of and attitudes towards the experimental situation. (7) Rather than viewing these facts as obstacles to the study of "pure" laws of conditioning, we are exploring the utility of the conditioning experiment as a tool for (*a*) objectively demonstrating unconscious emotional processes; (*b*) studying the difference it makes whether a cognitive and emotional process is conscious or not; and (*c*) developing experimentally derived principles and generalizations about unconscious affect.

We have undertaken the study of unconscious anxiety using a conditioning procedure which is an adaptation of a method first described by Diven (4). Our procedure is described in full in an earlier report. (9)

PROCEDURE

To the subject, who is a male freshman at Antioch College, it appears that he is participating in a study of the physiological cost of mental-motor coordination. He is seated comfortably in an armchair with his eyes closed. Over a loudspeaker he hears a word, perhaps the word "copper." This is the signal to him to begin a combined mental-motor performance: he must produce aloud as many single-word associations to the word "copper" as he can and at the same time he must tap a telegraph key at as even a rate as possible. He continues this combined performance until he hears the word "stop" over the loudspeaker. He then "relaxes" and waits for the next word, again with eyes closed.

From time to time he receives an electric shock on his left upper arm, which produces a violent muscular spasm. The shock burns and stabs, but he is more disturbed by the muscular cramp and by his lack of control of an important part of his body. He has accepted the experimenter's explanation that the purpose of the shock is to stimulate the muscles he uses in tapping. He wonders how many shocks he is going to get, and he is aware that he is rather tense and anxious about them. He tries to ignore this concern, the better to get on with the difficult job of producing an even tapping performance and a long list of associations.

He soon becomes aware that shock is never administered until he hears the word "stop," but that shock does does not conclude each association-tapping episode.

He wonders if he gets shocked when his tapping performance has been erratic, or when he produces too few associations. But the pressure of events is too much for him and he has no time to think clearly about these and other possibilities; he must tap and associate, associate and tap.

He can discover no rationale to the shocks. He is aware that "there are an awful lot of farm words," and that "some words are repeated a lot." Why, oh why, did he let himself in for this? It is on the whole a rather unpleasant experience.

The experimenter, of course, perceives the situation differently. The subject is chain-associating for 15 seconds each to a phonographically recorded list of 40 stimulus words, at intervals of 45 seconds. Four words are repeated six times each. Two of the words, "cow" and "paper," are critical words. The members of one group of subjects—the cow-shock subjects—will be shocked each of the six times they complete chain-associating to the word "cow"; the members of a second group of subjects—the paper-shock subjects—will be shocked each of six times they complete chain-associating to the word "paper."

The shock is of constant current (13 ma.) and constant wave shape and frequency, and is delivered to a motor point of the upper arm, in the region of the musculospiral nerve, so as to produce violent flexion at wrist and elbow, with rigid extension and adduction of the fingers. For the entire hour of the experiment, three physiologic variables are being simultaneously and continually recorded. These variables are plantar skin resistance, digital blood flow, and heart rate.

In the word list there are also 8 words with obvious rural meaning (plow, corn, chicken, haystack, grain, sheep, tractor, and farmer), and 8 words with no specifically rural connotations (clock, book, soft, gray, copper, blue, smooth, and yellow). These rural and non-rural words, and the words "cow" and "paper" appear in temporally counter-balanced positions throughout the word list.

After the conditioning session, the subject will be carefully interviewed. An extinction session will follow immediately, in which, unknown to the subject in advance, no shocks will be administered as the subject responds to the same list of 40 words.

RESULTS

1. Unconscious Conditioning and Generalization

As conditioned word and shock were repeatedly paired, evidence appeared of discrimination between the words "cow" and "paper." Cow-shock subjects came to exhibit greater autonomic changes upon hearing and responding to the word "cow" than they did to the word "paper." Paper-shock subjects did the reverse. The degree of autonomic discrimination increased with increased numbers of reinforcements (the electric shock following association to "cow" or "paper").

This differential reaction appeared *in anticipation* of the disturbing shock, i.e. in the 15-second interval between the presentation of the word and the shock. These physiologic changes that follow a signal of future painful stimulation constitute an operational description of an elementary state of anxiety. This anxiety is unconscious in the sense that the subject never "knew" when the shock was coming. Despite intensive questioning and prodding in the interview following the conditioning session, they could not verbalize the association between word-signal and shock. This unawareness was found in 22 of 31 subjects.

This unconscious anxiety was not limited to the conditioned words themselves. It spread to other symbols. Both cow-shock and paper-shock subjects developed autonomic discrimination between rural and nonrural words. Cow-shock subjects came to react more to rural words than to nonrural words, whereas paper-shock subjects developed the reverse reaction. This generalized response was also a function of the number of reinforcements and, indeed, was stronger and more reliable than the primary anxiety response.

These phenomena were represented and analyzed in detail in our first report. (9) Let us turn now to the results of further analyses.

2. Conscious and Unconscious Conditioning Compared

First, what are the differences between conscious and unconscious anxiety? To answer this question, we compare the responses of our unaware group with those secured from a group of 20 "informed aware" subjects.

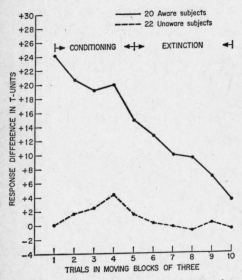

Fig. 1. *Comparison of the acquisition and loss of conscious and unconscious anxiety, in moving blocks of three trials; i.e., the first block of trials includes the first, second, and third trials; the second block includes the second, third, and fourth trials, and so on. A positive response difference indicates greater heart rate reaction to the conditioned word than to the control word (see text).*

These latter subjects were treated exactly as the unaware subjects, with the single exception that at the beginning of the experiment they were specifically told after which word they were to be shocked. Ten members of this group were shocked after associating to the word "cow," ten after the word "paper." Figure 1 shows the results for heart rate response, which is the only physiologic variable we have exhaustively analyzed to date.

On the X-axis are plotted trials in moving blocks of three. This technique was adopted to smooth out temporal irregularities. The first block of trials compares the average of the first three reactions to the word "cow" with the average of the first three reactions to the word "paper"; the second block compares the second, third, and fourth set of responses; the third block compares the third, fourth, and fifth reaction; and so on.

On the Y-axis are plotted the *response-differences, i.e.,* the average response to "cow" minus the average response to "paper" for cow-shock subjects, and the reverse for paper-shock subjects. A positive response-difference, then, signifies greater response to the conditioned word-stimulus than to the control word-stimulus.

These response-differences are expressed in an abstract system of measurement rather than in beats per minute. The abstract unit of measurement, the intrasubject autonomic lability score, simultaneously compensates for individual differences in over-all cardiac reactivity, and for varying "resting" levels of heart rate, and is fully described in our earlier report.

The solid line shows the results for the 20 aware subjects; the broken line for 22 unaware subjects. Of the latter, 10 are cow-shock subjects and 12 are paper-shock subjects.

A dramatic quantitative and qualitative difference is seen in this figure. Informed aware subjects instantly show a tremendous overreaction to the conditioned word-stimulus. For the first block of three trials, their average reaction to the critical word is 24 T-units (2.4 standard deviations) greater than to the control word-stimulus. This overreaction slowly but consistently exhibits adaptation, but persists throughout the period of observation. Having verbally forewarned the subject that one word was a signal of a forthcoming painful and unpleasant experience, a strong emergency response was immediately induced, which did not grow as a function of repeated reinforcements, but instead showed steady and gradual adaptation.[1]

---

[1] Cook and Harris have reported similar results for aware conditioning of the galvanic skin response to a light stimulus. The significance of these findings, and the obstacle they present

This conscious anxiety response was not eliminated easily; even repeated omission of the reinforcing shock did not destroy the subject's apprehension and anxiety. The curve exhibits no sharp break during the extinction session. The apparent linearity of the curve makes it difficult to say whether the extinction procedure itself was effective, or whether the continued decline is to be attributed only to a continued process of adaptation.

The results for the unconsciously formed anxiety responses are radically different. Note, in the first place, that the autonomic discrimination is considerably less. The data of Table 1, which summarizes the performance, block by block, of the aware and unaware subjects, show that this quantitative difference is statistically significant throughout the experimental session until the final block of extinction trials. In the second place, a typical conditioning curve is found. The unconscious anxiety response, unlike the conscious one, grew as a function of repeated nonreinforced trials.[2]

3. Conscious and Unconscious Generalization Compared

We turn now to a consideration of the effect of awareness-unawareness upon semantic generalization as indicated by heart-rate responses. By the term "semantic generalization" we refer to the phenomenon that the primary conditioned response is not limited to the conditioned word-stimulus itself, but spreads to other word-symbols meaningfully related to the conditioned word. (12, 13)

In Figs. 2A and 2B, the results for 10 informed aware cow-shock subjects are shown by the solid line, and those for 10 unaware cow-shock subjects by the broken line. Results are not presented for paper-shock subjects because no conclusive evidence was secured in our first analyses (9) that they exhibited generalization, although

---

to easy application of modern behavior theory have been ignored. Response strength grows as a function of repeated reinforcements only under certain conditions not yet completely specified. The cognitive variable is obviously an important one.

[2] The drop in the curve, before any extinction trial, from Block 4 to Block 5, between which a rest period and the interview occurred, is analyzed in our first report of these experiments. (9)

TABLE 1

Comparison of the formation and extinction of conditioned heart-rate discrimination between a critical and noncritical word for 22 unaware subjects and 20 aware subjects

Trials	Means		Medians		Ranges		p^a
	Aware subjects	Unaware subjects	Aware subjects	Unaware subjects	Aware subjects	Unaware subjects	
1, 2, 3	24.1	0.0	23.0	-0.5	+4.3 to +50.0	-15.3 to +16.3	< .01
2, 3, 4	20.7	1.7	20.0	0.0	0.0 to +41.3	-18.7 to +20.7	< .01
3, 4, 5	19.2	2.5	17.6	2.2	-1.0 to +44.0	-8.3 to +23.0	< .01
4, 5, 6	19.9	4.4	20.5	3.6	+2.0 to +38.7	-4.7 to +25.0	< .01
5, 6, 7	14.9	1.5	17.3	0.8	-11.3 to +41.0	-10.0 to +13.3	< .01
6, 7, 8	12.7	0.2	14.2	0.2	-6.3 to +36.0	-13.0 to +15.7	< .01
7, 8, 9	10.0	-0.2	11.0	1.2	-6.3 to +31.3	-12.0 to +10.3	< .01
8, 9, 10	9.5	-0.9	10.7	-0.6	-4.0 to +22.0	-17.7 to +15.0	< .01
9, 10, 11	6.8	0.3	6.2	-0.8	-6.7 to +23.3	-10.0 to +26.0	.01 < p < .05
10, 11, 12	3.4	-0.6	2.8	-0.2	-15.0 to +22.3	-10.6 to +15.0	.05 < p < .10

Entries are response-differences: heart-rate response in T-score form to the conditioned word minus response to the control word. Conditioning is reflected in Trials 1 through 7, extinction in Trials 8 through 12. Between Trials 6 and 7, the session was interrupted for an interview, which produced a decrement in the conditioned response.

^{a} Confidence levels computed by a nonparametric test, the Wilcoxon-White unpaired replicates test (18) which, for the N's involved, does not give accurate estimates of the .001 level. The first eight p's are considerably below the .01 level.

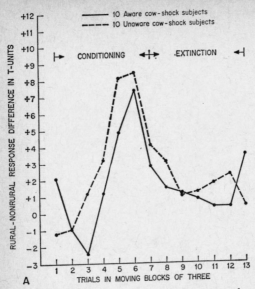

Fig. 2A. *Comparison of the acquisition and loss of generalized anxiety in aware and unaware subjects. A positive response-difference means greater heart rate response to rural words, excluding the conditioned word "cow," than to nonrural words. The first block of trials compares reactions to the first rural and nonrural words; the second block compares reactions to the second, third, and fourth rural words with reactions to the second, third, and fourth nonrural words, and so on.*

it was conclusively shown that their results differed significantly from those for cow-shock subjects.

Figure 2A shows the obtained results in their original form. To make the differences between the two groups more explicit, Figure 2B shows the results when the initial response-differences shown by the two groups in the first block of trials (response to first three rural words minus response to first three nonrural words) are equated and set equal to zero. Unaware subjects, it can be seen, developed progressively greater response to rural words than to nonrural words. The extent of the autonomic discrimination between the two classes of words grew as a function of repeated reinforcements of the word "cow," and then declined under the influence of

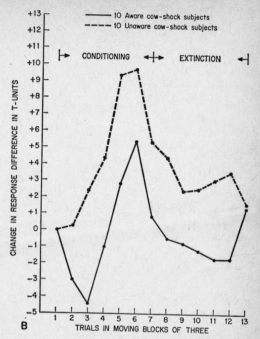

Fig. 2B. *Data of Fig. 2A when the initial response-differences of the two groups are equated and set equal to zero.*

an extinction procedure. Aware subjects, despite the greater precision of their conscious understanding, nevertheless also show generalization. Their discrimination between which symbols are "dangerous" and which are not, however, is somewhat better than that of the unaware subjects. This is seen in the less regular development of a generalized response exhibited by the aware subjects, and in the fact that quantitatively they show less generalization than the unaware subjects.

Statistical analyses of these differences were performed using the data of Table 2, where we compare (*a*) the rural-nonrural response-difference to the words "book" and "corn," before the first reinforcement of "cow" occurred; (*b*) the rural-nonrural response-difference to the words "smooth" and "tractor," after the subject has been

TABLE 2

Response-differences in T-units between heart-rate reactions to rural and nonrural words for 10 aware cow-shock subjects and 10 unaware cow-shock subjects

Subject	Aware Subjects			Unaware Subjects		
	Zero preceding reinforcements	Five preceding reinforcements	Five preceding extinctions	Zero preceding reinforcements	Five preceding reinforcements	Five preceding extinctions
A	+1	+2	−15	+6	+11	+12
B	+2	+23	−13	−16	+8	+29
C	−1	+11	0	0	+15	+13
D	+13	+20	−19	−18	+12	−10
E	−2	+18	−13	−8	+8	−13
F	−6	−6	+17	0	+17	−3
G	−8	+32	+28	−5	+9	−8
H	+11	+14	+15	−6	+16	−8
I	+25	+13	+7	−6	+14	−6
J	+8	+14	+2	−40	+8	+12
Average	+4.3	+14.1	+0.9	−8.7	+11.8	+1.8
Median	+1.5	+14.0	+1.0	−5.5	+11.5	−4.5
Range	−8 to +25	−6 to +32	−19 to +28	−40 to +6	+8 to +17	−10 to +29

Reaction to a nonrural word is subtracted from reaction to a rural word. The words compared are as follows: no preceding reinforcements, book and corn; five preceding reinforced or non-reinforced trials, smooth and tractor.

given five shocks following "cow"; and (c) the response-difference to the words "smooth" and "tractor" in the second session, after the subject has had five non-reinforced trials on the word "cow." These words are selected for the sake of uniformity with the mode of analysis used in our first report (9) and because in that report we show that the change in autonomic discrimination for these words is indeed a function of the experimental procedure, and not of the words themselves.

It can be seen by comparing the second and third columns in Table 2 that 8 of the 10 aware subjects showed larger response-differences in favor of rural words after five preceding reinforcements than they did before "cow" and shock were paired. Ten out of 10 unaware subjects developed this generalized response. By a nonparametric test, the Wilcoxon paired replicates test, (19) the trend is significant at better than the 5 per cent level of confidence for aware subjects, and at better than the 1 per cent level for unaware subjects. The increase is, on the average, larger for the unaware subjects. This difference between aware and unaware subjects is significant at the 5 per cent level, by Wilcoxon's unpaired replicates test. (19)

It might appear from Table 2 that, although unaware subjects show greater *change* in the rural-nonrural response-difference from zero to five preceding reinforcements, they show less actual discrimination between rural and nonrural words. For zero preceding reinforcements, the average response-difference is +4.3 for aware subjects and −8.7 for unaware subjects. This difference is significant at between the 5 per cent and 2 per cent levels of confidence, by the Wilcoxon test. After five preceding reinforcements, the aware subjects are still showing a greater average response-difference than the unaware subjects, the figures being +14.1 and +11.8 respectively. This small difference, however, is not statistically significant. As Figure 2A shows, moreover, when we use the more reliable procedure of comparing responses to three rural words with responses to three nonrural words, the amount of generalization becomes and remains quantitatively greater for unaware subjects after the second block of trials. Unfortunately, these differences, too, are not statistically significant, and this particular quantitative issue is left for future experimentation to answer. The data taken as a whole suggest that the verbal forewarning given the aware subjects induced some semantic generalization prior to reinforcement. Repeated reinforcements, however, did not cause the generalized response to increase as regularly and dramatically as it did in unaware subjects, and unaware subjects soon came to show greater generalization than aware subjects.

In extinction, too, the aware and unaware groups differ. After five preceding extinction trials, eight out of ten aware subjects show either a loss of relative overreaction to a rural word or develop overreaction to a nonrural word, as compared with the results after five preceding reinforcements. The trend is significant at the 5 per cent level of confidence. Of the unaware subjects, seven show a loss of the generalized response, but the extinction trend is not significant.

4. Effect of Chronic Anxiety Level

Our freshmen subjects had been administered[3] a battery of psychological tests upon entrance to Antioch. The Taylor Manifest Anxiety Scale (17) which several experiments have shown to be related to ease of conditioning and extinction (1, 6, 14-16) was a part of this battery. We scored only 35 "nonsomatic" items, omitting those items of this questionnaire inventory that deal with somatic complaints of headache, gastrointestinal upsets, ease of blushing, and the like. Those scoring in the upper and lower thirds of the entering freshman class in the frequency of complaints such as sleep disturbance, frightening dreams, feelings of worry, tension, unhappiness, restlessness, irrational fears, and inability to concentrate were classified as high anxiety and low anxiety respectively. The range of scores for the high anxiety group was from 13 to 29; for the low anxiety group from 0 to 7. Half of each of the experimental groups were high anxiety, and half low anxiety.

[3] We are indebted to Mrs. Ruth Churchill, Antioch College Examiner, for the administration and scoring of these tests.

We wanted to determine the effect of such psychometrically identified anxiety levels upon the acquisition and spread of new anxiety responses, and to determine whether the relationship held for both consciously and unconsciously conditioned anxiety.

The results are shown in Fig. 3. While none of the differences obtained meets the criteria of statistical significance, they are worth presenting because the results show a consistent pattern, and have biological and psychological importance. We are, moreover, continuing the investigation of the problem in a new series of experiments.

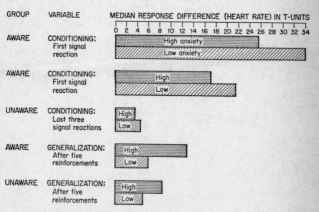

Fig. 3. *Relationship of chronic anxiety level to the acquisition and spread of new anxiety responses. High and low anxiety subjects were identified by the Taylor Manifest Anxiety Scale (see text).*

The first two sets of the bar graphs in the figure show that for both the first and last presentations of the critical word-signals, the low anxiety aware subjects exhibit a larger response-difference than the high anxiety aware subjects. As can be seen in the third set of bar graphs the unaware subjects show the same effect, at the characteristically diminished level of autonomic discrimination and activity. For these unaware subjects, too, the effect is made clear only by averaging the last three conditioning trials, because of the previously mentioned temporal irregularities in conditioning.

The final two sets of bar graphs show an apparent reversal. Both for aware and unaware subjects, the low anxiety subjects show less generalization.

Low anxiety subjects, then, seem to condition better but generalize less.

The two sets of findings point to a common interpretation: low anxiety subjects make more accurate discriminations than high anxiety subjects. In the first place, low anxiety subjects, during conditioning, respond accurately; the dangerous signal (the conditioned word-stimulus) brings forth an appropriately larger emergency response than the nondangerous signal (the control word). In the second place, the low anxiety subjects limit their emergency responses to the appropriate stimulus more than high anxiety subjects, and therefore do not show as much generalization. These differences in accuracy and precision, in appropriateness of response, hold for both conscious and unconscious conditioned anticipation of shock.

CONCLUSIONS AND DISCUSSION

First of all, it is clear that situational anxiety can be easily induced by the conditioning process at an unconscious level. We have been impressed with the rapidity with which such anxiety responses are formed. Two or three reinforcements suffice to produce observable changes. Anxiety responses in rats, as others have noted (2, 5, 8, 11), require many fewer pairings of conditioned and unconditioned stimuli than other responses. The human organism, too, seems extremely sensitive to danger even in the slight degree employed in our experiments. We are anxiety-prone.

Secondly, this situational anxiety is not limited to the truly dangerous symbol. It spreads to meaningfully related symbols at both the conscious and unconscious levels. Unlike other studies of generalization, we find that the generalized response was of greater magnitude than the primary response.

Third, the role of conscious understanding in enabling more accurate, appropriate, and reality-bound responses is given quantitative expression in both conditioning and generalization curves.

Fourth, it appears that the chronic anxiety level of the individual may be a factor in the ease with which he acquires and generalizes new anxiety responses.

These results, and the current developments of the basic technique in our laboratory, lead us to the belief that the conditioning procedure, with its simplicity, objectivity, and possibility for experimental manipulation and quantification, is a valuable experimental tool for the analysis of elementary forms of unconscious and conscious anxiety. When used with due regard for the realities of the enormously more complex and more subtle anxiety processes with which we deal clinically, it may provide greatly increased precision of our clinical tools and concepts.

REFERENCES

1. Bitterman, M. E., and Holtzman, W. H., Conditioning and extinction of the galvanic skin response as a function of anxiety, *J. Abnorm. & Social Psychol.*, 1952, **47**, 615.

2. Brown, J. S., Kalish, H. I., and Farber, I. E., Conditioned fear as revealed by magnitude of startle response to an auditory stimulus, *J. Exper. Psychol.*, 1951, **41**, 317.

3. Cook, S. W., and Harris, R. E., The verbal conditioning of the galvanic skin reflex. *J. Exper. Psychol.*, 1937, **21**, 202.

4. Diven, K., Certain determinants in the conditioning of anxiety reactions, *J. Psychol.*, 1937. **3**, 291.

5. Gwinn, G. T., Resistance to extinction of learned fear-drives, *J. Exper. Psychol.*, 1951, **42**, 6.

6. Hilgard, E. R., Jones, L. V., and Kaplan, S. J., Conditioned discrimination as related to anxiety, *J. Exper. Psychol.*, 1951, **42**, 94.

7. Hilgard, E. R., and Marquis, D. G., *Conditioning and Learning.* New York: Appleton, 1940.

8. Kalish, H. I., Strength of fear as a function of the number of acquisition and extinction trials, *J. Exper. Psychol.*, 1954, **47**, 1.

9. Lacey, J. I., and Smith, R. L., Conditioning and generalization of unconscious anxiety, *Science*, 1954, **120**, 1045.

10. Leeper, R., Cognitive processes. In Stevens, S. S. (ed.) *Handbook of Experimental Psychology.* New York: Wiley, 1951.

11. MILLER, N. E., Learnable drives and rewards. In Stevens, S. S. (ed.) *Handbook of Experimental Psychology*. New York: Wiley, 1951.
12. OSGOOD, C. E. *Method and Theory in Experimental Psychology*. New York: Oxford, 1953.
13. RAZRAN, G. Stimulus generalization of conditioned responses, *Psychol. Bull.*, 1949, **46**, 337.
14. SPENCE, K. W., and FARBER, I. E., Conditioning and extinction as a function of anxiety, *J. Exper. Psychol.*, 1953, **45**, 116.
15. SPENCE, K. W., and TAYLOR, JANET A., Anxiety and strength of the UCS as determiners of the amount of eyelid conditioning, *J. Exper. Psychol.*, 1951, **42**, 183.
16. TAYLOR, JANET A., The relationship of anxiety to the conditioned eyelid response, *J. Exper. Psychol.*, 1951, **41**, 81.
17. ———, A personality scale of manifest anxiety, *J. Abnorm. & Social Psychol.*, 1953, **48**, 285.
18. WHITE, C., The use of ranks in a test of significance for comparing two treatments, *Biometrics*, 1952, 8, 33.
19. WILCOXON, F. *Some Rapid Approximate Statistical Procedures*. Stamford, Conn.: American Cyanamid Co., 1949.

12

The Alarm Reaction

P. C. CONSTANTINIDES AND NIALL CAREY
University of British Columbia

The work of Hans Selye and his collaborators on the effects of stressful experiences has interested students of emotion in that this type of work indicates relations between bodily change and emotional behavior.

The following paper indicates the type of research which is being conducted on stress and adaptation and is reprinted from Scientific American, 1949, *180*, 20-23, *with the permission of the author and publisher.*

In biology and medicine it is becoming increasingly difficult to see the forest for the trees. The specialization of modern research leads into ever-narrowing paths. One man spends an entire lifetime studying a single hormone, another an enzyme, another the circulation of the kidneys. Year by year the data pile up; yet in some respects this vast accumulation of facts is leading us no nearer to an understanding of the living organism as a whole. Biologists have pushed so far into their individual tunnels of exploration, and there are so many tunnels, that the relation of one finding to another may elude discovery for years. Obviously we have reached a point where it is highly desirable to widen the view, to conduct researches in breadth as well as in depth.

At the Institute of Experimental Medicine and Surgery, the University of Montreal, Dr. Hans Selye and his team of biologists have been pursuing such an investigation for more than a decade, with stimulating results. They have been studying the generalized reactions of a whole animal to the stresses produced by its environment. A living organism consist of salts, enzymes, hormones, energy and a host of other elements, each of which may react in a specific way to some assault from outside; but the response of the organism as a whole is more than the sum of all these reactions. Life, and even death, is a chain reaction, and it is this linked process that Selye's group has been examining.

The particular focus of the investigation is the adaptation of animals to various types of severe or prolonged injury that affect large sections of the body. From this work has come the discovery that the animal organism possesses a general defense mechanism which it automatically mobilizes against any damage, whatever the cause. The principal agent of the mechanism is the endocrine system. As the officers of the defense, the hormones call upon various organs of the body for extraordinary efforts. If the stress becomes too great, the animal is destroyed by its own defenses, for ultimately the strain is conveyed to the heart and the circulatory system. Thus the research leads directly to a study of high blood pressure, hardening of the arteries and heart failure—the principal causes of death among human beings today.

Selye started this work some 12 years ago as the result of certain unexpected findings during some experiments on rats. He was investigating their specific responses to various drugs, poisons and gland extracts. He injected heavy doses, sufficient to kill the rats in a day or two, and made a careful autopsy of every animal. He was surprised to find that every substance he injected produced exactly the same result in three of the animals' organs: (1) the adrenal glands swelled to twice their usual size and changed in color from yellow to brown; (2) the thymus withered away; and (3) the stomach lining was spotted with bleeding ulcers. The puzzling fact was that these reactions were caused by such widely diverse substances as atropine, strychnine, formalin, crude pituitary extracts—all entirely different in chemical structure and mechanisms of action. The only factor that the many agents had in common was that all were injected in quantities dangerous to life. Selye reasoned that the responses he observed must represent a nonspecific reaction to general damage as such, regardless of the specific agent that caused the damage.

If this were true, other types of acute stress ought to provoke the same response. Selye tested this assumption by subjecting animals for some hours to cold, to excessive muscular exercise, to fasting, to emotional excitement and to numerous other kinds of injuries. Sure enough, all these nonchemical types of stress elicited in the animals the same unmistakable "alarm reaction" (AR), as he called it.

It was soon discovered that certain characteristic chemical changes in the tissues and body fluids always accompanied the AR. Among the first to be studied were the sugar and the chloride ions of the blood. During the first few hours of exposure to stress, it developed, both of these fall to subnormal concentrations. After a few more hours, they rise above normal values. The two periods are known respectively as the "shock phase" and the "counter-shock phase" of the AR.

As a result of a great amount of work, done mostly in Canada and the U. S., we know considerably more about the AR today. Its anatomical and biochemical aspects have been studied in many other species besides the rat. There is no doubt that it represents a general defense reaction against sudden stress in many higher vertebrates, including man.

The most dramatic changes during the AR occur in the adrenal glands. The two adrenals of an average human adult weigh together not more than 10 grams—about one 7,000th of the total body weight. But they are extremely important organs; if they are destroyed, as in Addison's disease, death is inevitable. With the exception of the brain centers for breathing and vascular tonus, there is no other equally small part of the body whose destruction or removal results in so quick a death. You can remove both legs, two thirds of the liver or a whole kidney and life will not be endangered; but if you remove an animal's adrenals, it loses its resistance to the slightest damage and dies within a few days. Obviously, then, the adrenals hold a key position as regulators of vital functions.

The gland has a capsule, or cortex, enclosing a marrow, or medulla. It has been known since the beginning of the century that the medulla produces adrenalin, a hormone that constricts blood vessels, raises the blood pressure, and mobilizes sugar from the liver in emergency situations. The function of the cortex—the only portion that enlarges in the alarm reaction—is a more recent discovery. It is now known that the cortex produces hormones indispensable to life, storing them in fat droplets, or lipids, which give the cortex its yellow color. All of these hormones are steroids, that is, fat-soluble compounds with the same basic chemical structure as the sex hormones, the cancer-producing hydrocarbons, the active ingredient of digitalis and certain other substances. At least 20 adrenal cortex hormones are known.

These are the messengers that marshall the alarm reaction. During the first hours of the AR, the hormones in their lipid vehicles are rapidly discharged from the adrenal cortex into the bloodstream and race to the tissues of the body. There they perform their various functions, of which two are definitely known: (1) They keep the composition of the fluid cell environment constant, mainly by retaining salts, particularly sodium, in the solution between the cells. The most important salt-retaining hormone is desoxycorticosterone, more commonly known as DCA. (2) They promptly build up sugar, a ready energy donor, from other materials, particularly proteins.

How important these two functions are can easily be judged from the fact that animals whose adrenals are removed die with their blood almost drained of salt and sugar. On the other hand, the injection of salt-retaining and sugar-forming adrenal hormones can prolong the life of such animals considerably; it also raises their resistance to otherwise fatal stress.

Yet the adrenal itself does not act independently. It is merely an executive of higher coordinating centers, from which it receives orders as to when to act, how much to act and what hormones to discharge. The adrenal cortex, like almost all other endocrine glands, is under the direct command of the anterior part of the pituitary gland —the "leader of the endocrine orchestra." If the pituitary is removed, the adrenal cortex shrinks and becomes inactive. It can regain its normal size and function only if a new pituitary gland is transplanted into the animal or if pituitary extracts (i.e., hormones) are injected.

Fundamentally, then, the AR is controlled by the pituitary. Remove this gland, and no AR can occur; when the animal is placed under stress there is no activation of the adrenals, no thymus destruction, none of the other typical AR changes. Yet the pituitary cannot act alone: an animal whose pituitary is left intact but whose adrenals are removed shows no AR in response to stress.

Thus a long series of experiments clearly outlined the AR mechanism. Acute stress acts on the anterior pituitary through some unknown pathway; the pituitary replies by mobilizing the adrenals, which discharge their hormones, which in turn destroy the thymus and effect most of the other changes. This process has been found to be set in train by hundreds of damaging agents. There are, however, a few interesting exceptions. Certain stress agents can destroy the thymus directly in animals whose adrenals have been removed. A significant fact is that all these "unusual" agents have something to do with cancer.

After the alarm reaction was established, the next major step in the experiments was an investigation of animals' long-range responses to stress. What would happen if the organism were exposed to continuous, prolonged stress of an intensity below the lethal level, a stress strong enough to strain the defenses almost to the limit, yet not sufficiently overwhelming to silence all defense at once?

Animals were subjected to sublethal daily stress with the same agents for several weeks instead of a few days. During the first few days, the organism responded with the usual AR. It showed the typical organic and chemical changes; growth and sex functions ceased, and all the signs of an intense tissue breakdown were present.

As the stress continued unabated, the animals that survived the AR began to recover. The adrenals started to refill their empty stores with lipids and reverted to normal size; the thymus began to regain its mass, and such substances as sugar and chlorides in the blood rose to normal or even higher levels. At the height of that state the organism had in some way accomplished an adaptation to the continuing stress. Its organs and their functions were apparently returning to normal. In some instances it was difficult to distinguish such animals from control animals not under stress. This stage, lasting from a few weeks to a month or more, was called the "stage of resistance."

It should be noted, however, that resistance increased only against the one type of stress employed from the beginning. If, in the middle of this recovery period, the stress against which adaptation developed was replaced by a different one, the animals succumbed immediately. Quantitative experiments with graded amounts of stress showed that while the animal's specific resistance to the initial agent increased, its resistance to any other stress decreased.

The adaptation to the original stress was not permanent. As the strain continued after the recovery period, the animals became progressively weaker; the adrenals enlarged again and discharged their lipids; the thymus lost the mass it had recovered; sugar and chlorides fell to dangerous levels; after a few weeks all defenses collapsed and life ceased. This last "stage of exhaustion" was similar to the initial alarm reaction. The end was like the beginning.

Thus the struggle of life against stress was found to consist in three successive acts, all aiming at a balance which was not quite attained during the AR, was achieved during the stage of resistance but was lost again during the stage of exhaustion. Evidently the war of the organism against damage was waged at the expense of a finite capital of "adaptation energy." The whole battle was named the "general adaptation syndrome" (GAS).

The establishment of the GAS opened a number of fascinating fundamental problems. Life as a whole could be regarded as a GAS that ends when adaptation energy runs out. More immediately, the phenomenon suggested some studies of great medical interest.

Some types of stress are so severe that an animal can

develop resistance for only a very short period; others permit a prolonged adaptation before the animal becomes exhausted. Animals can adapt themselves to cold, for example, for periods as long as two or three months. And such animals presented quite unexpected changes. The arteries were enormously thickened and their bore was narrowed almost to obliteration in numerous districts of the body; the heart was abnormally large and filled with nodules very like those appearing in human rheumatic disease; the kidneys were largely destroyed through hardening and closing of their vessels—as in human nephrosclerosis—and the blood pressure rose more than 50 per cent. In other words, long-lasting stress had produced in these animals hypertension and cardiovascular disease.

This was a finding of the highest importance in experimental medicine. It suggested that these diseases might be caused by the pituitary-adrenal mechanism, perhaps by the excessive production of their hormones. If one could produce the changes found in these animals by loading the organism with large quantities of pituitary and adrenal hormones, then at least some forms of degenerative diseases would appear to be the consequences of "over-adaptation," i.e., the defense mechanism that an animal develops during the stage of prolonged resistance to stress.

The experiment was made. A number of animals were dosed with large amounts of these hormones. Extracts would not do for this purpose, for one can never be sure how much hormone they contain or that they include everything produced by the gland in the natural state. Fortunately the previously mentioned adrenal hormone desoxycorticosterone, or DCA, was available in pure, crystalline form. Because chemists have not succeeded in synthesizing any pituitary hormones, it was decided to use the whole anterior lobe of this gland, powdered and suspended in water. In laboratory terms the product, "lyophilized anterior pituitary," is referred to as LAP. Continuous injections of large amounts of DCA or LAP are equivalent to the prolonged and excessive secretion of hormones by the adrenal or the pituitary, respectively.

The results were remarkable. In three weeks the animals

that were injected with DCA developed severe hypertension and hardening of the kidneys. Those treated with LAP showed a strikingly similar picture, though after a somewhat longer interval.

In medical research one can never lose sight of the ultimate objective, namely, the cure of patients. The investigator first devotes every effort to reproducing a disease in animals, and when he has succeeded he turns to the endeavor to destroy that disease. In searching for ways to combat the diseases produced by too much hormone production, one of the most obvious targets would be to try to neutralize the hormonal excess, in other words, to find a chemical antidote. Logical as it seems at first sight, this is too complicated a task at present. In the first place, we do not yet know the chemical mechanism of the hormones' action. Secondly, we must not forget that the organism needs those hormones, even if by overproducing them it poisons itself with its own defense substances.

A more practicable approach was suggested by experience in the treatment of other endocrine diseases. Some of these diseases can be alleviated by control of the diet. A case in point is diabetes, in which the basic trouble is a hormone deficiency. In moderate cases diabetes can be completely controlled by a diet low in sugar.

It was conceivable that the experimental hypertension produced in animals by overdoses of hormones or by stress might flourish on some diets and be suppressed by others. The animals were therefore subjected to a great variety of diets, a process which had to be pursued by trial and error because there was little indication as to what diets might be helpful.

From the many tests, two facts emerged clearly. One was that experimental hypertension produced by DCA was markedly affected by salt in the diet. A high salt intake increased both the frequency and the intensity of the pathological changes caused by that hormone. Contrariwise, when the animal was fed a salf-free diet, it was immune to hypertension, even when considerable amounts of DCA were injected. The second finding was that hypertension caused by stress or LAP was not affected by salt at all but was influenced by protein in the diet. A low-protein diet afforded considerable protection to the animals, while a high protein intake aggravated the damage.

Thus sodium favored the adrenal hormones, and proteins favored stress or the pituitary hormones in their injurious effect on blood vessels and blood pressure. The why and wherefore of these results is still unknown. It may be that DCA cannot act without the simultaneous presence of sodium. Perhaps the pituitary manufactures adrenal-stimulating hormones from food proteins. Research on these questions is now going on. One of the present objectives is to find out whether it is the total quantity of proteins that counts or a protein constituent, i.e., an amino acid.

In any event, these experiments tend to strengthen the case for the widely held belief that some forms of human cardiovascular disease are due to hormonal derangements. Medical experience has taught doctors that patients with high blood pressure fare best on a low-sodium, low-protein diet. This is exactly what the animals needed to withstand the destruction of their blood vessels by prolonged stress or by hormones.

The research of Selye's group yielded another key fact, namely, that in this whole general process the kidneys are somehow deeply involved. They are early victims of damage in the resistance phase of the GAS or during the inundation of the body with pituitary and adrenal hormones. But they also seem to be something more than passive targets. A great deal of work since the turn of the century has shown that the kidney itself can become the active cause of the most malignant hypertension. There is considerable evidence now that under certain abnormal conditions parts of the kidney tissue may stop their normal function, which consists in filtering the blood and producing urine, and start producing hormones that raise blood pressure. In the rat, this was beautifully demonstrated by what is now known as the "endocrine kidney" of Selye. By a surgical operation that interferes with the blood supply of one kidney, the whole organ is transformed into an endocrine gland, and in a few days the blood pressure rises to fatal levels. It is a particular feature of the endocrine kidney technique that only one kidney is transformed into a gland while the other gets all the damage.

Correlation of the evidence derived from all the numerous experiments on the GAS has led Dr. Selye to formulate the following current hypothesis: Long-lasting stress provokes an excessive production of adrenal- stimulating hormone in the anterior pituitary; this forces the adrenal cortex to an intensive discharge of DCA-like hormones which, among other things, affect the kidney in such a way as to release hypertensive substances.

In a sense the research is only beginning. Its implications are tremendous. In the GAS we seem to see the merest outlines of a great biological chain reaction which can be set off by almost any stress and which may frequently lead to the suicide of the organism. Some of the links in this chain are still missing, but its essential structure has been amply confirmed. As a result, large-scale research in this field is now starting in many laboratories.

Should further research prove that chronic stress can produce the same disorders in man as in animals, it would appear that the most frequent and fatal diseases of today are due to the "wear and tear" of modern life. One might question whether stress is peculiarly characteristic of our sheltered civilization, with all its comforts and amenities. Yet these very protections—modern labor-saving devices, clothing, heating—have rendered us all the more vulnerable and sensitive to the slightest stress. What was a mild stress to our forebears now frequently represents a minor crisis. Moreover, the frustrations and repressions arising from emotional conflicts in the modern world, economic and political insecurity, the drudgery associated with many modern occupations—all these represent stresses as formidable as the most severe physical injury. We live under a constant strain; we are losing our ability to relax; we seek fresh forms of physical or mental stimulation.

Thus it would not be surprising to find that much of our organic disease derives from psychological trauma, with the general adaptation syndrome as the bridge that links one to the other. If this be true, medicine may eventually find a cure for the consequences of stress; but prevention of the basic causes will remain a task that lies beyond its reach.

13

Ulcers in "Executive" Monkeys

JOSEPH V. BRADY

Walter Reed Army Institute of Research

The common "ulcer" has maintained its share of interest from psychologists since it has long been suspected that gastrointestinal lesions, as well as other diseases, are related to emotional behavior and personality. Many studies have indicated a causal relationship between the "ulcer" and emotion.

The following selection indicates a technique by which "ulcers" were produced in a monkey as a result of the "emotional" schedule forced upon the subject.

The report is reprinted from Scientific American, *1958,* **199**, *95-100, with the permission of the author and publisher.*

Physicians and laymen alike have long recognized that emotional stress can produce bodily disease. Psychic disturbances can induce certain skin and respiratory disorders, can set off attacks of allergic asthma and may even play a part in some forms of heart disease. Of all the body's systems, however, the gastrointestinal tract is perhaps the most vulnerable to emotional stress. The worries, fears, conflicts and anxieties of daily life can produce gastrointestinal disorders ranging from the "nervous stomach," which most of us know at first hand, to the painful and often disabling ulcers which are the traditional occupational disease of business executives.

Emotional stress appears to produce ulcers by increasing the flow of the stomach's acid juices. The connection between emotional disturbance, stomach secretion and ulcers is well documented. A recent study of 2,000

Army draftees, for example, found that those who showed emotional disturbance and excessive gastric secretion during their initial physical examination developed ulcers later on under the strains of military life.

But not every kind of emotional stress produces ulcers, and the same kind of stress will do so in one person and not in another. Experimental investigation of the problem is difficult. Animals obviously cannot provide wholly satisfactory experimental models of human mind-body interactions. They can, however, be studied under controlled conditions, and it is through animal experiments that we are finding leads to the cause of ulcers as well as to the effect of emotional stress on the organism in general.

Various investigators have succeeded in inducing ulcers in experimental animals by subjecting them to physical stress. But the role of the emotional processes in such experiments has been uncertain. Experiments on dogs by George F. Mahl of Yale University Medical School indicate that a "fear producing" situation lasting many hours increases the animals' gastric secretions, but these animals do not develop ulcers. William L. Sawrey and John D. Weisz of the University of Colorado produced ulcers in rats by subjecting them to a conflict situation: keeping them in a box where they could obtain food and water only by standing on a grid which gave them a mild electric shock. But this experiment, as Sawrey and Weisz themselves pointed out, did not prove conclusively that emotional stress was the crucial factor in producing the ulcers.

Our studies of ulcers in monkeys at the Walter Reed Army Institute of Research developed somewhat fortuitously. For several years we had been investigating the emotional behavior of these animals. In some of our experiments we had been keeping monkeys in "restraining chairs" (in which they could move their heads and limbs but not their bodies) while we conditioned them in various ways. Since these procedures seemed to impose considerable emotional stress on the animals, we decided that we ought to know something about their physiological reactions. Preliminary investigation showed that stress brought about dramatic alterations in the hor-

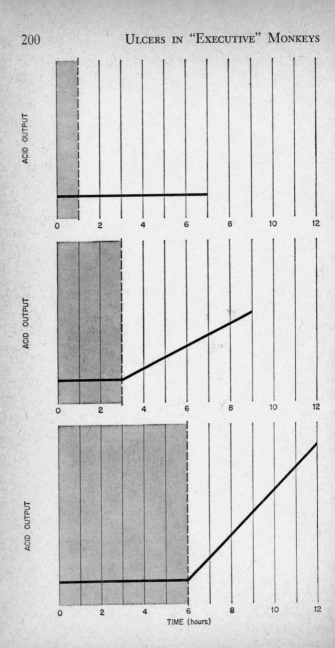

mone content of the animals' blood, but a more extensive study of 19 monkeys was brought to a halt when many of them died.

At first we considered this merely a stroke of bad luck, but the post-mortem findings showed that more than bad luck was involved. Many of the dead monkeys had developed ulcers as well as other extensive gastrointestinal damage. Such pathological conditions are normally rare in laboratory animals, and previous experiments with monkeys kept in restraining chairs up to six months convinced us that restraint alone did not produce the ulcers. Evidently the conditioning procedures were to blame.

One of the procedures which showed a high correlation with ulcers involved training the monkey to avoid an electric shock by pressing a lever. The animal received a brief shock on the feet at regular intervals, say, every 20 seconds. It could avoid the shock if it learned to press the lever at least once in every 20-second interval. It does not take a monkey very long to master this problem; within a short time it is pressing the lever far oftener than once in 20 seconds. Only occasionally does it slow down enough to receive a shock as a reminder.

One possibility, of course, was that the monkeys which had developed ulcers under this procedure had done so not because of the psychological stress involved but rather as a cumulative result of the shocks. To test this possibility we set up a controlled experiment, using two monkeys in "yoked chairs" in which both monkeys received shocks but only one monkey could prevent them. The experimental or "executive" monkey could prevent shocks to himself and his partner by pressing the lever; the control monkey's lever was a dummy. Thus both animals were subjected to the same physical stress (i.e., both received the same number of shocks at the same time), but only the "executive" monkey was under the psychological stress of having to press the lever.

We placed the monkeys on a continuous schedule of

Stomach acidity of executive monkeys, as shown in these highly simplified charts, did not increase during avoidance sessions (shaded) but rather during the subsequent rest periods. The greater increase followed a six-hour session; no rise followed a one-hour session.

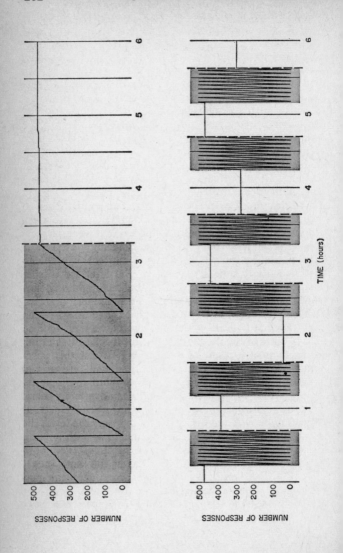

alternate periods of shock-avoidance and rest, arbitrarily choosing an interval of six hours for each period. As a cue for the executive monkey we provided a red light which was turned on during the avoidance periods and turned off during the "off" hours. The animal soon learned to press its lever at a rate averaging between 15 and 20 times a minute during the avoidance periods, and to stop pressing the lever when the red light was turned off. These responses showed no change throughout the experiment. The control monkey at first pressed the lever sporadically during both the avoidance and rest sessions, but lost interest in the lever within a few days.

After 23 days of a continuous six-hour-on, six-hours-off schedule the executive monkey died during one of the avoidance sessions. Our only advance warning had been the animal's failure to eat on the preceding day. It had lost no weight during the experiment, and it pressed the lever at an unflaging rate through the first two hours of its last avoidance session. Then it suddenly collapsed and had to be sacrificed. An autopsy revealed a large perforation in the wall of the duodenum—the upper part of the small intestine near its junction with the stomach, and a common site of ulcers in man. Microscopic analysis revealed both acute and chronic inflammation around this lesion. The control monkey, sacrificed in good health a few hours later, showed no gastrointestinal abnormalities. A second experiment using precisely the same procedure produced much the same results. This time the executive monkey developed ulcers in both the stomach and the duodenum; the control animal was again unaffected.

In a series of follow-up experiments which is still in

Responses of monkeys were recorded automatically. Slope of the lines shows the rate of lever-pressing (vertical lines indicate resetting of stylus). Upper chart shows responses of an executive monkey during the last half of a six-hour avoidance session (shaded area) and the first half of a six-hour rest period; shocks were programmed every 20 seconds. Monkeys kept on this schedule developed ulcers. Lower chart shows responses during a 30-minutes-on, 30-minutes-off schedule with shocks programmed every two seconds. Monkeys on this schedule failed to develop ulcers, despite more intense activity and presumably greater psychic stress.

progress we have tried to isolate the physiological and psychological factors which produce the "laboratory ulcers." For example, one of our groups suggested that the "social" interaction between the two monkeys might be important. Certainly the most casual observation showed that considerable "communication" was going on between the two animals, who were seated within easy chattering distance of each other. We therefore studied several pairs of animals isolated from each other in soundproof "telephone booths." Unfortunately isolation failed to protect the executive monkeys, for they continued to develop ulcers.

More recently, however, we have found a factor or group of factors which does seem to be critical in producing ulcers. What we have learned seems to pivot on our chance selection of six hours as the interval for shock-avoidance and for rest in the conditioning procedure. We made this discovery when we sought to improve on the results of our experiments. Though laboratory animals can rarely be made to develop ulcers, we had come upon a procedure that seemed to produce ulcers "to order." The only uncertainty was the length of exposure required. This varied greatly among individual monkeys; some came down with ulcers in 18 days, others took as long as six weeks. If we could develop a technique guaranteed to produce ulcers in, say, 10 days, we could stop the shock-avoidance sessions on the eighth or ninth day, apply various therapeutic measures and study the monkey's response to them.

It seemed reasonable to assume that we might induce ulcers more rapidly and dependably by simply increasing the stress on the animals. We therefore put several monkeys on an 18-hours-on, six-hours-off schedule. After a few weeks one of the animals died, but of tuberculosis, not ulcers. The rest continued to press their levers week after week with no apparent ill effects. Finally, when it began to seem as if we might have to wait for the animals to die of old age, we sacrificed them—and found no gastrointestinal abnormalities whatever!

We put another group on an even more strenuous schedule: 30 minutes on and 30 minutes off, with the shocks programmed for every two seconds rather than every 20. Again one of the animals died, this time of a generalized virus infection unrelated to ulcers. The others, after weeks of frantic lever pressing, showed no gastrointestinal changes.

We had to conclude that the crucial factor was not the degree or even the frequency of stress but was to be sought in the relationship between the length of the stress period and that of the rest period. The six-hours-on, six-hours-off schedule had produced ulcers (and occasionally other somatic disorders) despite individual differences in monkeys, variations in diet and maintenance routines and gross alterations in preliminary physiological tests. No other schedule we had tried produced ulcers at all.

This unexpected finding suggested that we should investigate what was going on in the monkeys' stomachs during the conditioning procedure. A standard technique for investigating gastric processes in experimental animals makes use of an artificial opening, or fistula, in the animal's abdominal and stomach walls through which the contents of its stomach can be sampled. Such fistulas have played an important role in expanding our knowledge of the gastro-intestinal system. In the early 19th century the famous U. S. Army surgeon William Beaumont made the first systematic study of the digestive process with the cooperation of a young Canadian who had a fistula due to an imperfectly healed gunshot wound. More than a century later Steward G. Wolf, Jr., and Harold G. Wolff at the Cornell University Medical College, with the help of a man who had a similar injury, conducted a pioneer investigation of the relationship between emotional stress and ulcers. They found that situations which produced feelings of anxiety or aggression in their subject stepped up his gastric secretions and engorged his stomach wall with blood. Physiological changes of this sort, they believed, are the precursors of ulcers.

Edwin Polish of our department of neuroendocrinology has been studying the stomach acidity of some of our executive monkeys by means of artificial fistulas. His measurements, though far from complete, seem to provide one possible explanation of the results of our experiments.

The stomach secretions of the executive monkeys do indeed become considerably more acid, but not (as one might expect) during the avoidance periods. When the animals are actually pressing the levers the acidity of their stomachs rises little. The significant increase in acidity begins at the end of the avoidance session and reaches a peak several hours later, while the animal is presumably resting. This finding suggests a close relationship between the formation of ulcers and the cyclic character of the six-hours-on, six-hours-off procedure. Emotional stress, it appears, must be intermittent—turning the animal's system on and off, so to speak—if it is to cause ulcers. Continuous emotional stress seems to permit a stable adjustment (at least for a while) under which ulcers do not develop. It is tempting to consider the analogy of the vacuum tube or light bulb which seems to last much longer under conditions of continuous current than when it is subjected to frequent heating and cooling.

Like most analogies, this one limps badly and has its limitations. For example, our experiments show that periodic stress does not always bring on ulcers, and Polish's findings are consistent with this. His measurements indicate that the greatest increase in acidity occurs after a six-hour avoidance session. After a three-hour session acidity rises, but less sharply; after a one-hour session it does not rise at all. Periodic emotional stress apparently causes ulcers only if its period coincides with that of some natural rhythm of the gastrointestinal system.

Obviously our knowledge of the physiological and psychological processes which produce ulcers is far from complete. Our understanding of even the relatively well-controlled experiments I have described is just beginning to progress beyond the primitive level. We have yet to discover why emotional stress steps up the stomach's acidity later rather than immediately. We are still looking for a method of producing ulcers at will, in days rather than weeks. Eventually we hope to learn to detect an incipient ulcer before the animal collapses, by examining the subject's blood, urine and other secretions, thus making post-mortem examinations unnecessary.

There are many other questions about the effects of emotional stress which we have not yet begun to investigate. Really thorough examination of the experimental animals might well show other types of damage of which we are at present unaware. The two monkeys which died of causes unrelated to ulcers, for example, may have succumbed because their resistance had been lowered in some way by psychological stress. It would be surprising to find physical processes wholly unimpaired in monkeys who have been on a 30-minutes-on, 30-minutes-off schedule for several weeks. The opportunity to bring psychosomatic relationships under experimental scrutiny in the laboratory seems to open broad horizons for research into the causes and alleviation of this poorly understood class of ills.

14

The Physiology of
Fear and Anger

DANIEL H. FUNKENSTEIN

Harvard Medical School

Although the connection between emotion and the endocrine system has long been postulated, research on the suspected connection is relatively recent. Walter Cannon's work emphasized the relationship and culminated in what came to be known as the Cannon-Bard theory of emotion (see Part IV for references). Recently, several investigators have continued with this approach.

The following selection discusses Cannon's work and that of other investigators. In addition, the author describes his work on establishing the relationship between the endocrine system and two classic emotions, fear and anger.

The article is reprinted from Scientific American, *1955,* **192,** *74-80, with the permission of the author and publisher.*

When the late Walter B. Cannon, by his historic experiments nearly half a century ago, showed a connection between emotions and certain physiological changes in the body, he opened a new frontier for psychology and medicine. His work, coupled with that of Sigmund Freud, led to psychosomatic medicine. It also made the emotions accessible to laboratory measurement and analysis. Within the last few years there has been a keen revival of interest in this research, because of some important new discoveries which have sharpened our understanding of specific emotions and their bodily expressions. It has been learned, for instance, that anger and fear produce different physiological reactions and can be distinguished from each other. The findings have given us a fresh outlook from which to study mental illnesses.

The best way to begin the account of this recent work is to start with Cannon's own summary of what he learned. Cannon found that when an animal was confronted with a situation which evoked pain, rage or fear, it responded with a set of physiological reactions which prepared it to meet the threat with "fight" or "flight." These reactions, said Cannon, were mobilized by the secretion of adrenalin: when the cortex of the brain perceived the threat, it sent a stimulus down the sympathetic branch of the autonomic nervous system to the adrenal glands and they secreted the hormone. Cannon graphically described the results as follows:

"Respiration deepens; the heart beats more rapidly; the arterial pressure rises; the blood is shifted away from the stomach and intestines to the heart and central nervous system and the muscles; the processes in the alimentary canal cease; sugar is freed from the reserves in the liver; the spleen contracts and discharges its content of concentrated corpuscles, and adrenin is secreted from the adrenal medulla. The key to these marvelous transformations in the body is found in relating them to the natural accompaniments of fear and rage—running away in order to escape from danger, and attacking in order to be dominant. Whichever the action, a life-or-death struggle may ensue.

"The emotional responses just listed may reasonably be regarded as preparatory for struggle. They are adjustments which, so far as possible, put the organism in readiness for meeting the demands which will be made upon it. The secreted adrenin* cooperates with sympathetic nerve impulses in calling forth stored glycogen from the liver, thus flooding the blood with sugar for the use of laboring muscles; it helps in distributing the blood in abundance to the heart, the brain, and the limbs (i.e., to the parts essential for intense physical effort) while taking it away from the inhibited organs in the abdomen; it quickly abolishes the effects of muscular fatigue so that the

[* I.e., adrenalin.]

organism which can muster adrenin in the blood can restore to its tired muscles the same readiness to act which they had when fresh; and it renders the blood more rapidly coagulable. The increased respiration, the redistributed blood running at high pressure, and the more numerous red corpuscles set free from the spleen provide for essential oxygen and for riddance of acid waste, and make a setting for instantaneous and supreme action. In short, all these changes are directly serviceable in rendering the organism more effective in the violent display of energy which fear or rage may involve."

Cannon recognized that among all these physiological changes there were a few which could not be ascribed directly to the action of adrenalin. He therefore postulated that the hormone was supplemented by two additional substances from the sympathetic nerves. An active agent, distinguishable from adrenalin, was eventually identified in 1948, when B. F. Tullar and M. L. Tainter at length succeeded in preparing the optically active form of the substance. It proved to be a second hormone secreted by the adrenal medulla. Called nor-adrenalin, it differs markedly from adrenalin in its physiological effects. Whereas adrenalin elicits profound physiological changes in almost every system in the body, nor-adrenalin apparently has only one important primary effect: namely, it stimulates the contraction of small blood vessels and increases the resistance to the flow of blood.

An animal exhibits only two major emotions in response to a threatening situation: namely, rage and fear. A man, however, may experience three: anger directed outward (the counterpart of rage), anger directed toward himself (depression) and anxiety, or fear. In studies of physiological changes accompanying various emotional states among patients at the New York Hospital, H. G. Wolff and his co-workers noticed that anger produced effects quite different from those of depression or fear. For example, when a subject was angry, the stomach lining became red and there was an increase in its rhythmic contractions and in the secretion of hydrochloric acid. When the same subject was depressed or frightened, the stomach lining was pale in color and there was a decrease in peristaltic movements and in the hydrochloric acid secretion. ✗

The experiments of Wolff, the evidence that the adrenal medulla secreted two substances rather than one, and certain clinical observations led our group at the Harvard Medical School to investigate whether adrenalin and nor-adrenalin might be specific indicators which distinguished one emotion from another. The clinical observations had to do with the effects of a drug, mecholyl, on psychotic patients. We had been studying their blood-pressure responses to injections of adrenalin, which acts on the sympathetic nervous system, and mecholyl, which stimulates the parasympathetic system. On the basis of their bloodpressure reactions, psychotic patients could be classified into seven groups. This test had proved of value in predicting patients' responses to psychiatric treatments, such as electric shock and insulin: certain groups responded better to the treatments than others. But more interesting was the fact that psychotic patients with high blood pressure reacted to the injection of mecholyl in two distinctly different ways. In one group there was only a small drop in the blood pressure after the injection, and the pressure returned to the usually high level within three to eight minutes. In the other group the blood pressure dropped markedly after the injection and remained below the pre-injection level even after 25 minutes. Not only were the physiological reactions quite different, but the two groups of patients also differed in personality and in response to treatment. Thirty-nine of 42 patients whose blood pressure was sharply lowered by mecholyl improved with electric shock treatment, whereas only three of 21 in the other group improved with the same treatment. Further, the two groups showed distinctly different results in projective psychological tests such as the Rorschach.

All this suggested that the two groups of patients might be differentiated on the basis of emotions. Most psychotic patients in emotional turmoil express the same emotion constantly over a period of days, weeks or months. Psychiatrists determined the predominant emotion ex-

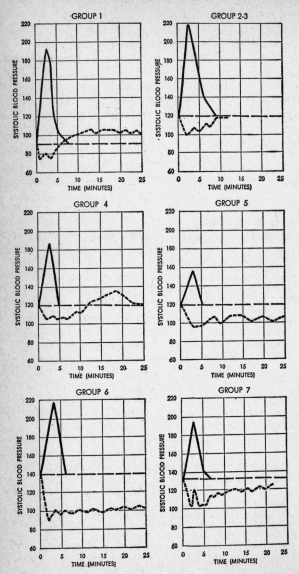

pressed by each of 63 patients who had been tested with mecholyl, without knowing in which physiological group they had been classified. When the subjects' emotional and physiological ratings were compared, it turned out that almost all of the patients who were generally angry at other people fell in Group N (a small, temporary reduction of blood pressure by mecholyl), while almost all those who were usually depressed or frightened were in Group E (sharp response to mecholyl). In other words, the physiological reactions were significantly related to the emotional content of the patients' psychoses.

The next step was to find out whether the same test could distinguish emotions in normal, healthy people, using medical students as subjects. They were studied at a time when they were under stress—while they were awaiting the decisions of hospitals on their applications for internships. As the competition among the students for the hospitals of their choice is keen, the period just prior to such announcements is a time of emotional turmoil for the men. A group of students who responded to this situation with elevated blood pressure was given the standard dose of mecholyl. The results were the same as for the psychotic patients: students who were angry at others for the situation in which they found themselves had a Type N physiological reaction; those who felt depressed (angry at themselves) or anxious showed a Type E physiological reaction. The reaction was related only to their temporary emotional state; after the internships were settled and their blood pressures had returned to pre-stress levels, all the students reacted the same way to the injection of mecholyl.

It was at this point that we undertook to investigate the comparative effects of adrenalin and nor-adrenalin. A group of workers at the Presbyterian Hospital in New

Fig. 1. Seven groups of psychotic patients were distinguished on the basis of their blood pressure after injection with adrenalin or mecholyl. In these six charts the basal systolic blood pressure of the patients is indicated by the broken horizontal line. The solid curve shows their response to adrenalin; the broken curve, their response to mecholyl. Groups 2 and 3 are combined because the difference between them is too slight to show in the graph. The mecholyl response for Group 7 is incomplete because of experimental difficulties.

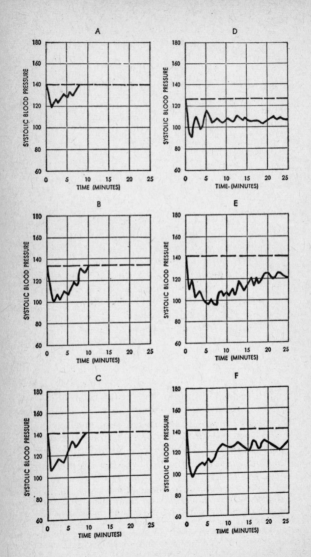

York had shown that injections of nor-adrenalin and adrenalin produced two different types of rise in blood pressure, one due to contraction of blood vessels and the other to faster pumping by the heart. Upon learning of this work, we designed experiments to test the hypothesis that the two types of elevated blood pressure, differentiated by us on the basis of mecholyl tests, indicated in one instance excessive secretion of nor-adrenalin and in the other excessive secretion of adrenalin. Healthy college students were first given a series of intravenous injections of salt water to accustom them to the procedure so that it would not disturb them. Then each subject was tested in the following way. He was given an injection of nor-adrenalin sufficient to raise his blood pressure by 25 per cent. Then, while his blood pressure was elevated, he received the standard dose of mecholyl, and its effects on the blood pressure were noted. The next day the subject was put through the same procedure except that adrenalin was given instead of nor-adrenalin to raise the blood pressure.

Ten students were studied in this way, and in every instance the effect of nor-adrenalin was different from that of adrenalin. When the blood pressure was elevated by nor-adrenalin, mecholyl produced only a small drop in pressure, with a return to the previous level in seven to 10 minutes. This reaction was similar to the Type N response in psychotic patients and healthy students under stress. In contrast, when the blood pressure was elevated by adrenalin, mecholyl produced the Type E response: the

Fig. 2. *Type N response to the injection of mecholyl is traced by the heavy line. The broken line represents the basal blood pressure. The response is shown for three kinds of subject: (A) healthy individuals under stress who respond with anger toward others, (B) healthy individuals whose blood pressure has been elevated with nor-adrenalin and (C) psychotic individuals with elevated blood pressure and anger toward others. Type E response to the injection of mecholyl is similarly traced by the heavy line. In these charts the response is shown for three different kinds of subject: (D) healthy individuals under stress who respond with anger directed inward, or depression, (E) healthy individuals whose blood pressure has been elevated with adrenalin and (F) psychotic individuals with elevated blood pressure and depression.*

pressure dropped markedly and did not return to the previous level during the 25-minute observation period.

These results suggested, in the light of the earlier experiments, that anger directed outward was associated with secretion of nor-adrenalin, while depression and anxiety were associated with secretion of adrenalin. To check this hypothesis, another series of experiments was carried out.

A group of 125 college students were subjected to stress-inducing situations in the laboratory. The situations, involving frustration, were contrived to bring out each student's habitual reaction to stresses in real life; that the reactions actually were characteristic of the subjects' usual responses was confirmed by interviews with their college roommates. While the subjects were under stress, observers recorded their emotional reactions and certain physiological changes—in the blood pressure, the pulse and the so-called IJ waves stemming from the action of the heart. This test showed that students who responded to the stress with anger directed outward had physiological reactions similar to those produced by injection of nor-adrenalin, while students who responded with depression or anxiety had physiological reactions like those to adrenalin.

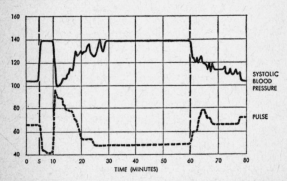

Fig. 3. Effect of nor-adrenalin was observed by administering an infusion of the hormone for 60 minutes. After 5 minutes the blood pressure of the subject rose. After 10 minutes mecholyl was injected and the blood pressure fell. Then it rose in a Type N response.

There remained the question: Does the same individual secrete unusual amounts of nor-adrenalin when angry and of adrenalin when frightened? Albert F. Ax, working in another laboratory in our hospital, designed experiments to study this question. He contrived laboratory stressful situations which were successful in producing on one occasion anger and on another occasion fear in the same subjects. His results showed that when a subject was angry at others, the physiological reactions were like those induced by the injection of nor-adrenalin; when the same subject was frightened, the reactions were like those to

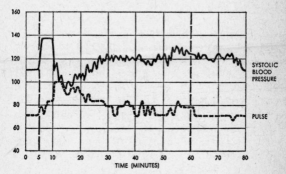

Fig. 4. *Effect of adrenalin was observed by the same procedure. After the injection of mecholyl the systolic blood pressure of the subject remained depressed in a Type E response.*

adrenalin. This indicated that the physiology was specific for the emotion rather than for the person.

In all these experiments the evidence for excessive secretion of nor-adrenalin and adrenalin was based on the physiological changes being similar to those which can be produced by the intravenous injection of nor-adrenalin and adrenalin. Since the substances involved have not been identified chemically, and the evidence is entirely physiological, at the present time we prefer to limit ourselves to the statement that the reactions are *like* those to the two hormones. However, nothing in our experiments would contradict the hypothesis that these substances are actually adrenalin and nor-adrenalin.

What is the neurophysiological mechanism whereby different emotions evoke different adrenal secretions? Although no conclusive work in this area is yet available, some recent investigations suggest a possible answer. U. S. von Euler in Sweden found that stimulation of certain areas of the hypothalamus caused the adrenal gland to secrete nor-adrenalin, whereas stimulation of other areas caused it to secrete adrenalin. These areas may correspond to those which the Nobel prize winner W. R. Hess of Zurich stimulated to produce aggressive behavior and flight, respectively, in animals. The experiments suggest that anger and fear may activate different areas in the hypothalamus, leading to production of nor-adrenalin in the first case and adrenalin in the second. Until more experiments are made, these possibilities must remain suppositions.

Some of the most intriguing work in this field was recently reported by von Euler. He compared adrenal secretions found in a number of different animals. The research material was supplied by a friend who flew to Africa to obtain the adrenal medullae of wild animals. Interpreting his findings, J. Ruesch pointed out that aggressive animals such as the lion had a relatively high amount of nor-adrenalin, while in animals such as the rabbit, which depend for survival primarily on flight, adrenalin predominated. Domestic animals, and wild animals that live very social lives (e.g., the baboon), also have a high ratio of adrenalin to nor-adrenalin.

These provocative findings suggest the theory that man is born with the capacity to react with a variety of emotions (has within him the lion and the rabbit), and that his early childhood experiences largely determine in which of these ways he will react under stress. Stated in another way, the evolutional process of man's emotional development is completed in the bosom of the family. We have found in other studies that individuals' habitual emotional reactions have a high correlation with their perceptions of psychological factors in their families.

This entire series of experiments yielded data which can be understood in the frame of reference of psychoanalytical observations. According to theory, anger directed outward is characteristic of an earlier stage of childhood than is anger directed toward the self or anxiety (conflicts over hostility). The latter two emotions are the result of the acculturation of the child. If the physiological development of the child parallels its psychological development, then we should expect to find that the ratio of nor-adrenalin to adrenalin is higher in infants than in older children. Bernt Hokfelt and G. B. West established that this is indeed the case: at an early age the adrenal medulla has more nor-adrenalin, but later adrenalin becomes dominant.

Paranoid patients show a greater degree of regression to infantile behavior than do patients with depression or anxiety neurosis. And it will be recalled that in our tests paranoid patients showed signs of excessive secretion of nor-adrenalin, while depressed and anxious patients exhibited symptoms of adrenalin secretion.

These parallels between psychological and physiological development suggest further studies and some theories for testing. Standing on the shoulders of Cannon and Freud, we have extended our view of human behavior and discovered fertile new fields for exploration.

15

The Description of Facial Expressions in Terms of Two Dimensions

HAROLD SCHLOSBERG

Brown University

Facial expressions represent one of the more obvious observable behaviors associated with emotion, for one of the most common methods for assessing the emotional status of an individual is by evaluation of the facial expression. Perhaps, it is for this reason that the study of the relationship between emotion and facial expressions has a long history in psychology. While some investigators have argued that judgments of facial expressions are unreliable, other investigators have indicated that facial expressions are interpretable and may be scaled along meaningful continua. Articles concerned with facial expression, and with some of the arguments that have raged between investigators, are included in Part IV.

The following article indicates the results of a study which attempted to scale facial expressions along established dimensions. The report is reprinted from the Journal of Experimental Psychology, 1952, **44**, 229-237, *with the permission of the author and the American Psychological Association.*

Early studies on facial expression stressed the inaccuracy of judgments. In 1938 Woodworth suggested that the inaccuracy was more apparent than real, in that it resulted from scoring judgments on a simple *right-wrong* basis. Through an analysis of published results from earlier studies, he developed a scale, consisting of the following six steps: (1) Love, Happiness, Mirth; (2) Surprise; (3) Fear, Suffering; (4) Anger, Determination; (5) Disgust; (6) Contempt. There was also a seventh category, Scattering, for pictures which didn't fit into the other six. The use of such a scale showed clearly that Ss made many minor errors, but few major ones. That is, they would frequently transpose a picture from Step 3 to Step 4, but they were less apt to misplace it in more remote steps, as 1 or 6.

Schlosberg (6) tested this scale on a new series of pictures, those of Frois-Wittmann (1), published by Hulin and Katz (3). The pictures were sorted into a linear series of bins, labeled in terms of the Woodworth categories. It was immediately obvious that pictures whose modes fell in Step 6 were as apt to spread over into Step 1 as into Step 5. This could only mean that the scale was recurrent, rather than linear. Hence, the computations of mean scale positions and average deviations were based on the assumption that the scale was circular; that is, a picture which was evenly split into Steps 6 and 1 was assigned a mean of 6½, rather than of 3½, which would have put it on the opposite side of the circle.

To check on the possibility that these results were peculiar to one set of pictures, the method was applied to two other series. In an unpublished Honors project in 1943, Miss Marjory L. Brown found that the Ruckmick (5) series showed clear evidence of conforming to a circular scale, with five of the 32 pictures having some overlap between Steps 6 and 1. Another series was also tried, made up of supposedly unposed pictures. Fifteen were from the Munn (4) series, and 17 additional ones were selected from *Life* magazine. Only one of this series spread across the "ends" of the scale, but this partial failure to show circularity may have been due to the selection of pictures. There was only one with a mode in Step 6 (Contempt) and the only four pictures in Step 1 showed very little spread to any other categories. Hanawalt (2) has also reported a failure to find evidence of a circular scale in facial expressions, but this finding was only an incidental one in an experiment designed for other purposes.

The question as to whether or not the Woodworth

scale of facial expressions constitutes a circular or recurrent series is really only a preliminary one. Let us assume for the moment that the scale describes the periphery of a roughly circular surface on which all facial expressions can be located, and examine the consequences. The circular surface may be compared with the color circle, with the six scale steps corresponding to the major hues. This comparison brings out the fact that the facial expression surface should have a neutral point ("gray") in the center; the strength of an expression would correspond roughly to the saturation of a color. Still more important, one should be able to describe the surface in terms of two axes, just as the color surface can be described in terms of blue-yellow and red-green axes. Examination of the results of the 1941 experiment (6) led the writer to suggest that these two axes were pleasantness-unpleasantness and attention-rejection. The first axis needs no further explanation, but the second one does. Attention is exemplified by surprise, in which all receptors are maximally open to stimulation. Rejection is the best term we have found for the other end of this axis; it is shown most clearly in contempt and disgust, in which eyes and nostrils appear to be actively shutting out stimulation (Fig. 2).

This brings us to the really important question—can typical series of facial expressions be adequately described in terms of two axes? If we can answer the question in the affirmative, a very complex field will have been reduced to relatively simple dimensions. One way to test this hypothesis is to obtain ratings of the locations of each of a series of pictures on the P-U and A-R axes, and then to use this joint position to predict the Woodworth scale value of each picture. The present paper reports four separate studies. We may anticipate the results by pointing out that three of the studies, using two different series of pictures, yielded correlations above .90 between obtained scale values and those predicted from independent ratings of P-U and A-R.

PROCEDURE

All four experiments employed the same basic method. The S sorted a set of pictures along a 9-point rating scale ranging

from maximum unpleasantness (1) to pleasantness (9). While
E was tabulating these ratings, S was given duplicate prints of
the same pictures to sort on a scale rejection (1) to attention
(9). Ratings from all Ss were combined by simple averaging to
give a single pair of values for each picture. The pictures were
then plotted on a sheet of graph paper, using P-U values on
the ordinate and A-R values on the base line. This scatter plot
was then mounted on a large 360° protractor, with the center
of the circle at the mid-point (5-5) of the axes, and the P-U
axis oriented at 60° and 240°, corresponding to scale positions
1.00 and 4.00, as we will see in a moment. A thread stretched
from the center, across a plotted point and out to the periphery,
permitted a reading for that picture in degrees, referred to the
circumference of the circular surface. The degree reading could
be converted to predicted positions on the Woodworth circular
scale by dividing by 60, since there were six steps on the Woodworth scale. These predicted values were then compared with
those actually obtained by independent sorting made in the
Woodworth bins.[1]

In Exp. I, the Frois-Wittmann pictures were used. The P-U
and A-R sorting was done in piles on a series of nine numbered
cards. Little trouble was found in getting S to understand the
P-U axis; it was merely necessary to stress the fact that he was
to judge whether "The man felt pleasantness or unpleasantness." The A-R axis caused more trouble. An effort was made
to describe attention as *openness to stimulation* and to point
out that the eyes, nostrils, and mouth tended to be constricted
in rejection.

In Exp. II, a more effective way was found for describing
the rating scales. After the usual explanation of A-R, picture
No. 23 of the Ruckmick series was shown as a typical example
of attention, and No. 13 as rejection. After S had placed these
pictures at the appropriate positions on the scale, these "anchors" were reclaimed, and he was given the pack of Frois-
Wittmann pictures to sort. The S was allowed to review the
anchors if he wished to do so.

The results of Exp. II were so encouraging that it seemed desirable to duplicate this experiment as a check. Experiment III

[1] If the method of predicting Woodworth scale position from
rating data is not clear from this brief description, turn to Fig.
1, under *Results*. In the Discussion, it will be shown that this
method unavoidably discards some information. The location of
a picture on a surface described by two axes can give (*a*) the
distance the picture lies from an arbitrary center, and (*b*) the
radius on which it falls. Since the Woodworth scale is simply
the circumference of the circular surface, we can ultilize only
(*b*), above, in making the predictions.

was run a year later, with only minor changes over II. Two wooden racks of bins were used to facilitate handling and tabulating the pictures, and fresh prints of the pictures were used.

Experiment IV was planned to check the results of II and III on another series, that of Ruckmick, which consisted of 32 pictures of a female face. Both the P-U and A-R scales were anchored by showing pictures from the Frois-Wittmann series,

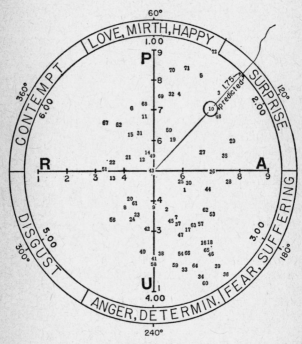

Fig. 1. *The location of each of the 72 Frois-Wittmann pictures on an oval surface. Picture No. 10 (encircled) serves as an example of the method used. It is plotted at axis values of P–U = 7, A–R = 7, as determined by the rating scales. A thread is then stretched from the intersection of the axes (5–5) across the plotted point, and its position read off in degrees. Dividing by 60 yields the predicted Woodworth scale value (1.75), which is compared with that obtained earlier by direct sorting on the Woodworth scale (1.65). This picture might be called "Pleased Surprise," and both predicted and obtained values place it in the appropriate step of the Woodworth scale.*

each end being exemplified by six pictures. In this experiment, Ss sorted the pictures into the Woodworth scale bins both before and after the rating, using the same rack and method employed earlier (6). This was done largely to build up a new set of scale values for this series, which could be compared with those obtained approximately a decade earlier.

All experiments were conducted by undergraduates as special projects in the writer's laboratory course.[2] The students made their own analyses of the data, but the writer has verified and extended all computations in Exp. III and IV. All Ss in the first three experiments were members of the same course, and were approximately equally divided as to sex. There were eight Ss in Exp. I and nine in II. In Exp. III, there were 18, but two Ss repeated the experiment, giving 20 sets of data. Of the 20 Ss in Exp. IV, 8 were from the laboratory course, and the remaining 12 were nonstudents, ranging in age from 20 to 55 yr. No S participated in more than one experiment.

RESULTS

Table 1 presents the detailed results from the Ruckmick series in Exp. IV.[3] For comparison with the present data, the unpublished results obtained in 1943 by Miss Brown are also presented. The older scale positions were based on three sortings by each of 23 Ss. The method of deriving the predicted scale position from P-U and A-R ratings is given in the Procedure, and is illustrated in Fig. 1.

Table 2 summarizes the results of all four experiments together with key words to identify the methods. Notice that all three experiments which employed anchors yielded predictions which correlated above .90 with the scale positions obtained by sorting the pictures into the Woodworth scale. One may question the precise significance of these correlations, for the scale values are

[2] I wish to express my thanks to the students who served as Es in the following experiments: I—Robert F. Shepard, Jr.; II —Mark T. Sheehan; III—Louise Anthony, Jean M. Coraci, Sheila K. Hart, Ann M. Thomas; IV—Shirley A. Juskalian, John J. Kennedy. Dr. W. S. Hulin kindly supplied several sets of the Frois-Wittmann pictures, which speeded up the collection of data.

[3] The data on individual pictures of Exp. III will not be tabulated, since the ratings and predicted scale positions can be determined from Fig. 1 and the obtained scale positions are in print (6).

TABLE 1

Predicted and obtained scale values for the Ruckmick pictures

Description[a]	Picture Number (1)	P-U (2)	A-R (3)	6-Step Scale Position				1943 Scale Data	
				Predicted (4)	Obtained (5)	Error (6)		Position (7)	Av. Dev. (8)
Reconciliation	28	8.05	7.15	1.60	0.90	0.70		0.92	0.19
Interested inquiry	30	7.90	7.10	1.62	0.92	.70		1.01	.05
Amusement	29	8.20	7.25	1.60	1.00	.60		1.00	.00
Mirth	31	8.80	8.15	1.67	1.00	.67		1.00	.00
Joy	32	8.80	8.25	1.68	1.00	.68		1.00	.00
Adoration	17	6.60	6.25	1.65	1.05	.60		1.20	.29
Wistful appeal	26	6.95	6.75	1.70	1.22	.48		1.10	.20
Cynical interest	19	6.70	6.40	1.65	1.23	.42		1.41	.41
Interested observation	27	7.20	6.85	1.67	1.27	.40		1.28	.45
Astonishment	23	4.60	5.95	2.87	2.05	.82		2.10	.28
Consternation	24	3.85	7.10	2.98	2.05	.93		2.10	.30
Pleading	20	5.25	5.70	2.17	2.08	.09		2.50	.87
Apprehension	2	2.25	6.10	3.65	2.70	.95		2.77	.59
Startled fear	3	1.75	5.30	3.92	2.72	1.20		2.67	.50
Dread	7	2.05	5.75	3.77	2.85	.92		3.00	.30
Anguish	8	2.05	5.10	3.97	2.97	1.00		3.00	.08
Resentment	14	3.30	4.90	4.09	3.13	.96		3.45	.75
Interested attention	18	3.25	6.45	3.35	3.15	.20		2.59	1.06
Sorrow	5	4.65	5.50	3.12	3.19	-.07		2.85	.40
Exhausting pain	6	2.40	3.15	4.60	3.47	1.13		3.75	1.13

TABLE 1 (continued)

Anxiety	21	3.40	4.95	4.05	3.63	.42	3.28	.52
Fear	4	1.45	5.90	3.77	4.00	−.23	3.93	.54
Anger	1	2.00	4.60	4.13	4.17	−.04	4.13	.38
Distrust	12	2.65	4.20	4.32	4.37	−.05	4.65	.69
Haughtiness	15	4.35	3.75	5.05	4.52	.53	4.72	.85
Contemplation	10	3.70	3.75	4.75	4.62	.13	4.36	.51
Defiance	16	3.10	3.80	4.55	4.73	−.18	4.50	.77
Critical distrust	11	3.50	3.45	4.79	4.87	−.08	5.14	.79
Rueful meditation	22	4.55	3.70	5.19	5.27	−.08	4.74	.91
Scorn	13	3.60	2.25	5.05	5.58	−.53	5.68	.51
Sulkiness	9	4.00	2.60	5.13	5.68	−.55	3.50	.80
Contempt	25	6.00	5.55	7.47	6.40	1.07	6.10	.33
Mean		4.59	5.42	(r = .96)		.54		

[a] The descriptions are slightly condensed from the "Adopted Description" column of Ruckmick's leaflet which is furnished with the set of photographs by C. H. Stoelting Co., Chicago, Ill. The numbers used in this study are those printed on the backs of the photographs; they do not correspond to those given in Ruckmick's original paper (5). The pictures are listed in order of Woodworth's scale position (Col. 5), with breaks to separate the six steps.

TABLE 2

Correlations and average errors between predicted and obtained scale values

Exp.	Pictures Used	Type of Anchor	S_S	r	Average/Error
I	Frois-Wittmann	Verbal	8	.76	not avail.
II	Frois-Wittmann	Samples	9	.94	not avail.
III	Frois-Wittmann	Samples	18	.92	.52, .46[a]
IV	Ruckmick	Samples	20	.96	.54, .33[a]

[a] These average errors were obtained against an adjusted scale. (Experiments I-III used the Schlosberg scale values for the Frois-Wittmann pictures.)

not normally distributed. Further, the coefficient does not yield all the information that might be desired.

A more revealing analysis can be made by examining the errors in prediction. Mean errors were computed for Exp. III and IV, and are included in Table 2. In both experiments, the average error of the prediction was about half a scale step; chance would give three times this error, for in a circular scale of six steps the maximum error is three steps, and the average error would be one and one-half steps.

DISCUSSION

The correlations and the relatively small errors show that reasonably good predictions of Woodworth scale positions can be made from ratings on two axes, pleasantness-unpleasantness and attention-rejection. There is reason to believe that a large portion of what errors there are may be attributed to the scale itself, and to certain working assumptions made in relating the scale to the axes. These assumptions were (*a*) that the center of the circular scale was at axis position 5-5, the midpoints of the two 9-point rating scales, (*b*) that axis ends P, A, U, and R fell at circular scale positions 1.0, 2.5, 4.0, and 5.5, respectively, and (*c*) that the six steps on the circular scale were equal. The results should en-able us to refine these assumptions, and to improve the prediction.

Examination of Table 1 will show that the second assumption is markedly in need of correction for the Ruckmick series. Column 6 shows a marked preponderance of positive errors, in which the axis positions predicted scale values that were too high. The constant error is approximately .43 scale steps; when most of this is removed by rotating the plotted surface counter-clockwise, putting P at .60 scale position, the average error drops from .54 to .42 scale steps. Simple rotation was not tried on the Frois-Wittmann results (Exp. III) for there was little indication of a constant error throughout the scale.

Assumption (a), the locus of the mid-point of the circular scale, does not seem to be critical. Recalculations were made on both series of pictures after shifting the center to axis positions 5-5½; 4-5; and on the Ruckmick series, 4½-4½. These shifts increased the average error slightly, but never beyond one of .55 scale points.

Assumption (c), that the units are equal throughout the scale, is obviously only a gross approximation. In the Ruckmick series the variability of judgment, as shown by the average deviation, is about one-third as large in Step 1 as in the other five steps. This suggests that Step 1 is three times as big as any of the other steps. As a way of testing the effects of a rough adjustment of the circular scale, a base line was marked off with the first step doubled in width, and the others cut to .8 units. Using predicted scale positions on the ordinate, the Ruckmick circular scale positions were plotted on this base line, and a line with a slope of one was fitted to the points by inspection. The deviations of the predictions from this line were then measured and averaged, yielding a mean error of .33 scale steps. This was by far the smallest average error of prediction obtained. A similar treatment of the Frois-Wittmann data, using a scale adjusted to conform to the average deviations of this series (6), gave an average error of .49 scale steps. Omitting one picture which cannot be adequately located on the circular scale (No. 43, see below), the average error becomes .46.

An average error of prediction of .33 scale steps is probably close to the minimum. One limiting factor is the stability of the circular-scale positions we are trying to predict. In Table 1, two sets of such positions are given for the Ruckmick series, the set obtained in Exp. IV, and that obtained a decade earlier. The average difference between these two sets of values is .23. The reason for this difference is not hard to find; the scale forces all pictures out to the circumference, when some of them belong near the center of a circular surface. This is particularly clear in the case of picture No. 43, which appears at the center of both Fig. 1 and 2. It received an axis rating of 5.0 and 4.9, leading to a predicted position of 5.50 on the circular scale. But if 4 of the 20 Ss had increased their rating by one step on the A-R scale, thereby changing the picture's mean rating to 5.1 on the other side of the center, the prediction would have been 2.50. Thus the circular-scale position of this picture is largely a matter of chance. This showed clearly in the results of the 1941 experiment, for about one-third of the Ss put this picture in the "Scattering" bin, and the rest distributed it almost randomly in five of the six main categories. This picture is an extreme case, but there were others that showed large spread; for example, 8 of the 32 Ruckmick pictures showed average deviations (Table 1, col. 8) greater than .75 scale steps. For such pictures it seems probable that the axis positions give a better description than do the circular-scale values. That is, a relatively neutral picture like No. 43 belongs not at the circumference of the circular surface, but near its center.

Now that we know we are dealing with the whole surface rather than with its circumference, we can ask for a description of the surface. Like the "color circle," it is only roughly circular. Figure 2 probably gives a reasonable first approximation to its outline, for it includes all the extreme pictures. It was not practical to mount all the pictures in the more crowded areas, but their location is indicated by the scatter diagram reproduced in Fig. 1. The surface seems to be roughly oval in form, with the P-U axis longer than the A-R axis. This agrees with the conclusion drawn in the writer's 1941 paper, based on the distribution and average deviations of the pictures on the circular scale. It is difficult to determine the exact form of the surface, for there is no reason to believe that the distances are equal on the two axes. The present rating data are not extensive enough to warrant any elaborate scaling attempts. There is also the question as to whether or not the two axes are perpendicular; the difficulty some Ss experienced in distinguishing between rejection and unpleasantness suggests that the included angle is somewhat less than 90°. Perhaps some of these relations might be worked out by comparison with the Hulin and Katz (3) data. They had their Ss sort the Frois-Wittmann pictures into piles, putting together any pictures that seemed similar. If our description of the circular surface is correct, the distance between any two pictures should vary inversely with the number of times the two pictures were put in the same pile. But before this comparison is attempted, it would probably be advisable to obtain more precise ratings on P-U and A-R than our 20 Ss have furnished.

One final point may be added—the writer is still not satisfied with the present method of obtaining ratings on the A-R axis. Inspection of the individual ratings assigned to the same picture shows that they occasionally range from 1 to 9. The fact that the final predictions work as well as they do shows that these errors average out; there seems to be a genuine dimension that shows up in spite of the difficulty with which it is described and judged. Perhaps the difficulty is due to the fact that our language has no good word for the "rejection" end of the axis; attention and inattention describe only half the axis. But certainly the fact that common speech is not cognizant of the whole range of a dimension proves little about the utility of that dimension in analyzing facial expression, except only that the dimension may be difficult to handle experimentally or to describe in any but operational terms.

The question was raised earlier as to whether or not the Woodworth scale was recurrent. The results of the foregoing analysis show clearly that the scale represents the circumference of an oval surface into which some pictures are forced by lack of a better place to put them. If a given series contains one or more pictures that lie somewhat above and slightly to the left of the center of the surface, as at axis position P-U 6, A-R 4.5, they will be projected to a circular-scale position of 6.5. This means that they will be judged in Step 6 (Contempt) half the time, and in Step 1 (Love, Mirth, Happiness) the other half of the time. This spread across the ends of the scale happened in both the Frois-Wittmann and Ruckmick series, and furnished the original evidence for circularity. For example, the Frois-Wittmann picture No. 15 fell at 6.2-4.2, resulting in a predicted value of 6.21, compared with an obtained value of 6.27. But the obtained value represents a mode of 54 judgments in Step 6 with most of the spread, 50 judgments, to Step 1. The Frois-Wittmann series happens to be rich in pictures that fall in this area, which probably accounts for the fact that the circularity is so apparent. On the other hand, there happened to be no picture in Miss Brown's supposedly unposed series that could have been

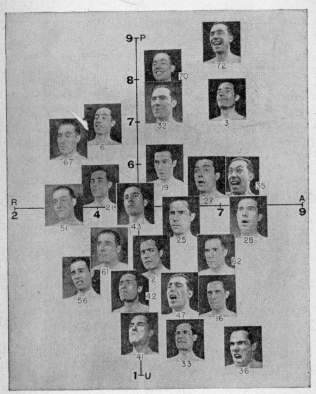

Fig. 2. *The location of typical pictures of the Frois-Wittmann series. This display includes those pictures which are shown around the margin of the surface in Fig. 1, and as many of the more centrally located ones as could be mounted. The average error of prediction for these 25 pictures is a half-scale step, just as it is for the whole series of 72 pictures. The picture with the worst prediction of the whole series is No. 43, at the intersection of the axes (see text).*

expected to spread across Steps 6 and 1. The pictures of Mirth showed no spread at all, and the only picture in Contempt was very close to Disgust, leaving a gap of a whole step at the crucial point. Parenthetically, it may be added that Contempt is a sophisticated expression, and is rather hard to judge. It is interesting that the oval surface has a place on which it fits so nicely.

But to return to the circularity of the Woodworth scale. It was a fortunate choice of pictures that led to the original detection of the circularity, for there is no assurance that a given set of pictures will show the overlapping spread across the two supposed ends of the Woodworth scale. Failure to find such spread does not alter the more fundamental fact that all pictures of two different series, 72 posed by a man and 32 by a woman, can be placed rather well on an oval surface described in terms of two axes.[4] These axes are proposed as the basic dimensions in which facial expressions may vary. The fine shades that are familiar in literary usage may well involve additional factors, as knowledge of the situation and of the past history of the individual.

REFERENCES

1. FROIS-WITTMANN, J., The judgment of facial expression, *J. exp. Psychol.*, 1930, **13**, 113-151.
2. HANAWALT, N. G., The role of the upper and lower parts of the face as a basis for judging facial expressions: II. In posed and "candid-camera" pictures, *J. gen. Psychol.*, 1944, **31**, 23-36.
3. HULIN, W. S., and KATZ, D., The Frois-Wittmann pictures of facial expression, *J. exp. Psychol.*, 1935, **18**, 482-498.
4. MUNN, N. L., The effect of knowledge of the situation upon judgment of emotion from facial expressions, *J. abnorm. soc. Psychol.*, 1940, **35**, 324-338.

[4] Many of our Ss reported that they tended to judge P-U on the basis of the mouth, and A-R from the eyes. This is consistent with Hanawalt's (2) report that happiness is often confused with pain-suffering when judgments are based on only the upper half of unposed pictures. If the mouth is blotted out, S should have difficulty in distinguishing between P and U, the dimension which differentiates happiness from pain-suffering. Careful study of confusions in half-face judgments might throw further light on the determiners of our two axes.

5. RUCKMICK, C. A., A preliminary study of the emotions, *Psychol. Monogr.*, 1921, **30**, No. 3 (Whole No. 136), 30-35.

6. SCHLOSBERG, H., A scale for the judgment of facial expressions, *J. exp. Psychol.*, 1941, **29**, 497-510.

7. WOODWORTH, R. S. *Experimental psychology*. New York: Holt, 1938.

16

An Experimental Approach to the Analysis of Emotional Behavior

JOSEPH V. BRADY[1] AND HOWARD F. HUNT

Walter Reed Army Institute of Research and University of Chicago

Emotional behavior has been the subject of two relatively new approaches of psychology. The first is the technique of conditioning which was used by Lacey, Smith and Green in an article which appeared earlier in this book. The second method is represented by studies concerned with ablation and stimulation of portions of the brain and the search for a "seat of emotion" in the brain. These investigations support the idea that certain areas of the brain are directly related to behavior which we commonly call "emotional."

The following paper reviews studies of both types. More recent reports on work of this type are included in Section IV of this book. The paper is from The Journal of Psychology, 1955, 40, 313-324, and is reprinted with the permission of the authors and publisher.

Both clinical and experimental observation indicates that emotional disturbance can, as one of several possible effects, disrupt or interfere with an organism's ongoing behavior. Of course, emotion, broadly defined, is but one of several classes of events which have this property. But with proper experimental controls, it is possible to

---

[1] The substance of this report was presented by the senior author as an invited paper in a symposium on "Mechanisms of Motivated Behavior" at the XIV International Congress of Psychology, Montreal, Canada, June 9, 1954.

produce such emotional disruption dependably and to isolate important variables of which it is a function. The present paper describes some applications of a method derived from this observation to the experimental analysis of emotional behavior.

A. GENERAL METHODOLOGICAL CONSIDERATIONS

The suppression of some stable aspects of an animal's ongoing behavior under conditions of emotional disturbance provides the fundamental empirical fact upon which the present approach to this problem depends. Specifically, these studies have focused primarily upon the suppressing effect of anticipated pain upon a stable lever pressing habit in trained experimental animals.

Estes and Skinner first reported the technique involved in superimposing such a conditioned emotional response upon the lever pressing behavior of albino rats (22). In the present modification of this technique, thirsty animals—in this case albino rats—initially are trained in lever pressing first for a continuous, and then for an aperiodic water reward. Then when their lever pressing output has stabilized, they receive a series of conditioning trials, each consisting of a clicking noise as the conditioned stimulus, followed by a pain-shock to the feet as the unconditioned stimulus. The clicking noise continues for three minutes and is terminated contiguously with the shock. Within a few trials the anticipatory response to the clicker begins to appear as a perturbation in the lever pressing curve, accompanied by crouching, immobility, and usually defecation. This has been referred to as "conditioned anxiety" (22) or by the neutral but inclusive term, "conditoned emotional response" (CER) (12, 29). The phenomena are referred to as a "response" because overt reactions are used as indicators; it is referred to as "emotional" because these overt reactions develop as a consequence of reinforcement with a mildly painful electric shock and because of the character of the reaction; and it is called "conditioned" because the experimental procedure brings these reactions under the control of an ordinarily neutral stimulus. Of course, experimental extinction of this response (with progressive recovery of the lever pressing rate in the presence of the conditioned stimulus) follows successive unreinforced presentations of the clicker alone during daily lever pressing trials (8).

This emphasis upon a rather primitive and in some respects, at least, unlearned reaction pattern as the indicator of conditioning departs somewhat from the more common custom of studying some specific instrumental response, the performance of which avoids or terminates the conditioned emotional stimulus. The present method provides for a more direct assessment of the conditioned "anxiety" response as such, from which, as Schoenfeld has recently shown (46), virtually all systematic treatments of punishment, escape, and avoidance behavior can be derived.

Several clear cut advantages appear to derive from the utilization of this unlearned indicator response as the starting point for the experimental analysis of emotional behavior. First, insofar as the conditioned emotional response used in these studies can be said to underlie escape and avoidance reactions, focus upon the "anxiety" response as such eliminates a major source of error attributable to variables that affect the instrumental behavior commonly used in such conventional learning experiments. Secondly, this simple, relatively uncomplicated response is elicitable under a wide range of conditions and appears in quite consistent form or topography in all animals. Thirdly, this response appears to be remarkably stable over time, surviving without apparent dimunition in the absence of exercise or further reinforcement for intervals as long as one year and probably even longer. Finally, this technique of superimposing the emotional response upon a well-established lever pressing habit makes it possible to approximate a quantification of the strength or magnitude of the response in terms of changes in output during various segments of the lever pressing curve.

The study of the vicissitudes of such a stable response—its increases and decreases in strength—clearly provides an opportunity for the experimental analysis of the differential effects of various physiological and psychological conditions upon which the organization of emotional behavior depends. In addition, the use of this quantifiable indicator of an acquired emotional reaction superimposed upon a simple repetitive act, while complicating the interpretation of experimental findings somewhat, makes it possible to study the specific behavioral effects of such variables as electro-convulsive shock, central nervous system damage, pharmacologic agents and the like, by separating the more specific emotional changes from the general behavioral and motor disturbances, debilitation, and the like that often appear as temporary and nonspecific residuals of such treatments. A demonstration that animals are able to work in the lever pressing situation, emitting a fairly regular output of lever pressing activity, indicates that they are functioning adequately enough to allow a reasonably reliable and clear-cut test for retention of this simple discrimination.

B. EXPERIMENTS ON ELECTRO-CONVULSIVE SHOCK

The initial experimental application of this technique explored the effects of electro-convulsive shock (ECS) upon both the conditioned emotional response (CER) and lever pressing behavior. For some time, numerous investigators have concerned themselves with the effects of ECS upon various aspects of animal behavior. For the most part, these studies have dealt primarily with behaviors such as maze running, discrimination, conditioned avoidance, or escape responses, and the like (23, 52). The differential effects of ECS on acquired emotional sensitivities and responses similar to the "anxiety" paradigm described above have received surprisingly little attention. Early findings (29), however, indicated quite clearly that a series of 21 ECS treatments administered three times per day for seven days, could attenuate this CER without any apparent adverse effects upon retention of lever pressing behavior. That this differential effect of ECS upon the CER and upon bar-pressing behavior is not a function of the temporal order in which the lever pressing and the CER were conditioned, has been demonstrated in a recent control experiment (24). Furthermore, it has been shown that this attenuating effect of ECS is not attributable to any impairment in auditory function produced by the treatment (10), nor does it appear to be attributable to the painful characteristics the ECS stimulus or the convulsions might have (unpublished data).

Several experiments have indicated that this effect of ECS upon the CER has some interesting quantitative characteristics. By way of identifying the parameters on which it depends, Goy (26) found that the intensity of the unconditioned shock stimulus is a more important variable than the number of conditioning trials in determining the effect of ECS upon the CER, the degree of attenuation by ECS being inversely related to the unconditioned stimulus strength during conditioning. In addition, the effect of ECS upon the "anxiety" response has also been shown to be a function of both the number and temporal distribution of the ECS treatments (13). When the 21 ECS treatments are administered anywhere from one every hour for 21 hours to one every day for 21 days, they have their full attenuating effect upon the emotional response. Fourteen, ten, seven, and three ECS treatments, however, have progressively (and respectively) less effect (unpublished data). But 21 ECS treatments given at intervals as often as one every half-hour or as far apart as one every two or three days have also been shown to be less effective in eliminating the emotional responses (13).

Further exploration has revealed that this attenuating effect of ECS upon the "anxiety" response is transient, the conditioned emotional response reappearing within 30 days following treatment (8). Furthermore, when the ECS treatments are delayed for as long as 30 days after conditioning of the "anxiety" response, they fail to have their usual attenuating effect (9). It is now also clear, however, that "additional" convulsions, given after the intensive series of 21 ECS, can prevent the post-ECS recovery of the CER, while additional convulsions given prior to delayed intensive ECS can make the CER less resistant to attenuation by the delayed intensive treatment (18).

If, on the other hand, a series of experimental extinction trials (clicker alone without shock) follow the 21 intensive ECS treatments immediately, the CER fails to reappear 30 days later even though the "anxiety" response (cessation of lever pressing, crouching, and defecation) does not appear to be present during extinction (31). This finding would seem to indicate that the learning or conditioning involved in the CER is retained and the ECS in some way interferes with the overt expression of the CER. The comparatively durable effect of extinction found here suggests that the unreinforced presentation of the conditioned stimulus in extinction actually must have had a decremental effect on the conditioning or habit underlying the CER; otherwise, the CER would have reappeared in those animals given extinction. For this to have occurred, some psychological representation of the CER (the conditioning or the habit) must have survived ECS to be present contiguously with the unreinforced presentation of the conditioned stimulus.

Finally, it is now quite clear that the convulsion or some concomitant of it (as distinguised from the convulsive stimulus) appears to play a critical role in attenuating the emotional response. The demonstrated attenuating effect on the CER of both ECS and carbon disulphide convulsions (33) is blocked when the appearance of convulsions during such treatment is prevented by administration of ether anesthesia (32). Furthermore, of a group of animals receiving audiogenic stimulation, only those sustaining convulsions as a result of such stimulation show any degree of attenuation of the previously conditioned "anxiety" response, and this degree of attenuation is highly correlated with the frequency of convulsions (17).

This rather provocative series of findings concerned with the effects of ECS and similar variables upon the conditioned "anxiety" response obviously suggests the value of a somewhat more direct attack upon the problem of neural correlates for such emotional behavior. The following experiments undertaken in this area were intended to provide some elaboration of the rôle of specific neuroanatomic structures in mediating such affective responses.

C. ABLATION STUDIES

During the past two decades, numerous investigators have reported affective behavioral changes associated with a wide variety of experimental brain lesions in laboratory animals. Such changes have been found in preparations following transection of the brain stem at the intercollicular level (Sherringtonian decerebration) (7, 25, 35, 44, 45, 54), neocortical ablation (20, 21), lesions of the hypothalamus (1, 2, 3, 4, 6, 34, 43, 53), lesions of the septal region (51, 38), lesions of the amygdaloid complex (5, 19, 36, 37, 51), and lesions of the various parts of the thalamus (48). These findings, along with the more systematic treatments by Papez (42) and MacLean (39) of the "visceral brain" as the anatomic substrata of emotion raise provocative questions concerning the mediating rôle of this fornix circuit (hippocampus-fornix-septum-hypothalamus-anterior thalamus-cingulate-presubiculum-hippocampus) in conditioned emotional behavior, and have provided the setting for a series of ablation studies using the CER response and a closely related avoidance technique.

Early exploratory findings revealed little if any effect upon either the acquisition, retention, or extinction of the conditioned "anxiety" response in a group of albino rats with rather extensive lesions of the neocortex and/or cingulate gyrus. Nor were any gross behavioral changes apparent in such animals with involvement only of cortical and cingulate structures. When, however, the experimental lesions intrude upon more paleocortical and brain stem structures, durable changes in the animal's affective behavior as a whole, and in the more specifically conditioned emotional aspects of the animal's behavioral repertoire do indeed appear.

Lesions in the septal forebrain region of the rat, for example, in addition to producing rather gross increases in emotional reactivity (wildness, savageness, hypersensitivity) also produce a significant reduction in the strength of this previously conditioned "anxiety" response (14). Moving more caudally to the habenular complex of the thalamus—one of the more direct and prominent end points of the septal outflow—lesions fail to produce any of the gross increases in emotional reactivity found in septal animals but at least some minimal changes in the strength of the "anxiety" response can be demonstrated. Animals with rather extensive involvement of this nuclear complex show significantly more rapid extinction of the previously conditioned "anxiety" response when compared with both operated and unoperated controls (15).

Most recently, tests conducted with rats following both bilateral and unilateral extirpation of the hippocampus just posterior to its main outflow through the fornix column, have revealed similar involvement of this paleocortical structure in the mediation of such conditioned emotional behavior. Although the animals showed little apparent effect of the unilateral lesion, bilateral injury of the hippocampus attenuated the "anxiety" response in several animals and apparently made it impossible or unusually difficult to recondition. In addition, these same bilateral animals showed a rather striking deficit in their ability to localize and attack the source of a noxious stimulus (forceps applied to the tail), even though normal affective expression in these animals seemed unimpaired and no gross increases in emotional reactivity were apparent (unpublished data). Of course, the results of these recent experiments must be interpreted with caution since the number of animals so far is small and some degree of cortical damage is also involved in such hippocampal extirpation. The cortical lesions alone certainly do not produce this decrement, however, and it is quite clear from some earlier studies that involvement of the fornix column anterior to the hippocampal outflow does not have this effect. Of course, isolation of the hippocampus without involving the cortex would provide the critical experiment which will have to await the development of more refined lesion-making techniques (ultra-sound, etc.).

In an additional series of experiments concerned with a closely related component of this rhinencephalic system, the effects of rather restricted lesions in the amygdaloid nuclei upon both conditioned and unconditioned emotional behavior in cats has been explored. Following such lesions, gross behavioral modifications include increased motor activity in response to visual stimuli, exaggerated oral and vocal activity, relative docility, and marked hypersexuality (47). Furthermore, in a series of 28 such cats, we found that animals with amygdala lesions had considerably more difficulty and indeed took significantly more trials to acquire an avoidance response (conditioned in a conventional double grill box) than either unoperated cats or cats with control lesions of the cingulate gyrus. Interestingly enough, however, animals which had acquired the avoidance response to criterion before amygdalectomy showed no decrement in retention of the response post-operatively. A group of control animals, however, with large frontal lesions showed complete post-operative loss of the pre-operatively conditioned avoidance response, and have as yet been unable to relearn the response to criterion (16).

These experiments indicate that the selective ablation of different parts of this rhinencephalic complex produces somewhat different effects upon an animal's repertoire of emotional behavior. Such findings suggest that further correlational studies of this sort may hold considerable promise for providing a foundation from which systematic analyses of both the physiological and psychological determinants of emotional behavior may proceed. In the light of these results, for example, Nauta's recent elaboration of the intimate anatomy of the fornix and related systems (41) acquires new significance for the understanding of behavior. Furthermore, insofar as these anatomical structures can be regarded as playing a central rôle in the mediation of emotional behavior, the results of these experiments would appear to have important implications for theoretical arguments which refer to the concept of "anxiety," "fear reduction," or other emotional states for the interpretation of affective behavior (40).

D. SOME FUNCTIONAL PROPERTIES OF THE CER

Empirically, then, numerous observations establish the reality of this phenomenon we call conditioned "anxiety," and elaborate somewhat the conditions under which durable changes as a function of electro-convulsive shock, neural ablation, and other experimental operations, can be effected in such emotional behavior. Only recently, however, has any attempt been made, through systematic experimental observation, to determine the exact nature of the functional relationship between this phenomenon and other behavior. In one rather tedious experiment, for example, it has been possible to show that both the rate of acquisition and resistance to extinction of the conditioned emotional response are a function of the intensity of the unconditioned shock stimulus and the number of conditioning trials. Acquisition of the CER was found to be significantly faster and extinction significantly slower as the intensity of the shock and the number of conditioning trials increased (unpublished data). Furthermore, the critical rôle of the reinforcement contingencies in determining the character of the emotional response has been amply demonstrated in a recent series of studies (30, and unpublished data). These studies have compared the effects of CER or "anxiety" conditioning (in which the shock inevitably follows presentation of the clicker), with a "punishment" conditioning procedure in which the shock follows every lever response in the presence of the clicker. Although both procedures suppress lever pressing during presentation of the clicker, the specific behavioral response expressions which occur in conjunction with this suppression of lever pressing differ quite markedly in the two situations. As indicated above, the "anxiety" procedure produces a characteristic crouching, immobility, and is usually accompanied by defecation. In contrast, animals conditioned using the "punishment" procedure, commonly move about freely during presentation of the clicker, make abortive lever pressing responses, and appear relatively free of autonomic disturbance as indicated by the absence of defecation, pilo erection and similar indicators of such involvement. Furthermore, the "anxiety" response and the discrimination based on "punishment," appear to differ somewhat in their responsiveness to similar experimental operations. Although the "anxiety" response can be attenuated quite readily by electroconvulsive shock, for example, whether it has been established by a small or large number of conditioning trials, the "punishment" response appears attenuable by such treatments following a relatively small number of conditioning trials. But, the power of ECS to attenuate the "punishment" discrimination when it has been conditioned using a large number of trials is clearly questionable, at least from unpublished evidence presently available. This is a rather curious finding requiring further study. Heistad (28) has found that ECS can attenuate a conditioned avoidance response and other unpublished data indicate that the convulsions ultimately attenuate the expression of experimental "conflict" established in an alley runway in which thirsty animals receive a shock while running to obtain a water reward.

In a further analysis of some of the functional properties of the conditioned "anxiety" response, consideration of the definition of this emotional reaction in terms of changes in the probability of the lever pressing response suggested that the appearance of the "anxiety" behavior may well be a function of variables affecting the maintenance of the lever pressing habit. And indeed, it has now been possible to show that the rate of acquisition and the rate of extinction of the CER depends rather clearly upon the schedule of positive reinforcement used to maintain the lever pressing behavior upon which the "anxiety" response is superimposed. Specifically, if the lever pressing behavior is maintained by continuous reinforcement or by ratio reinforcement, the CER is more difficult to condition than if the lever pressing behavior is maintained on an interval schedule for primary reinforcement (27 and unpublished data). Similarly, the CER is extinguished more rapidly if lever pressing is maintained on continuous or ratio reinforcement than when any of the variable interval or aperiodic schedules are used (11). The significance of these results become even more interesting in view of the finding that essentially no correlation exists between the rate of acquisition or extinction of the CER and the rate of lever pressing, as such (26).

A related analysis of such interacting response systems has recently been undertaken in a series of experiments extending Sidman's work on the aversive control of behavior (49, 50). In these experiments, it has been possible to show that the conditioned "anxiety" response can be superimposed upon lever pressing which is itself maintained by painful shock of the same intensity employed in conditioning the CER. In a situation, for example, where an animal is shocked at regular intervals, say every 20 seconds, unless a lever response is made during that interval, it is possible to generate an extremely stable lever pressing curve based upon avoidance of the noxious stimulus, without any exteroceptive warning signal of any kind. Now using this ongoing behavior baseline, these studies have shown that the same depression in lever pressing develops to the presentation of an exteroceptive conditioned stimulus,—say a light or a tone—which is followed by an unavoidable shock of the same magnitude used to maintain lever pressing behavior (unpublished data).

In general, these research studies reported in this section may be said to share a common emphasis upon the detailed experimental analysis, comparison, and contrast of a broad class of behavior based upon strikingly similar fundamental variables—various combinations of stimuli which serve as cues in one form or another, and an aversive or unpleasant event of some kind. It is clear, however, that minor variations in the contingencies which determine the relationship between these stimuli can produce major variations in both the topography and dynamic functional properties of the observed behavior. Many attempts have been made to order these diversities in behavior to a single broad principle—i.e., emphasis on the rôle of conditioned "fear" as a motivational construct mediating the establishment of instrumental behavior in such experimental situations (40). The general orientation of the experiments summarized in this paper appear in rather clear contrast to this contemporary emphasis upon acquired drives and similar constructs. This more empirical approach, however, may clearly be seen to reflect some concern that such monolithic ordering, prematurely embraced, might serve to obscure important differences as well as significant similarities and relationships among behaviors which have in common some crucial dependence on what we conventionally regard as emotion.

REFERENCES

1. Bard, P., Central nervous mechanisms for emotional behavior patterns in animals, *Res. Publ. Assn. Nerv. Ment. Dis.*, 1939, **19**, 190-218.

2. ———, A diencephalic mechanism for the expression of rage with special reference to the sympathetic nervous system, *Amer. J. Physiol.*, 1928, **84**, 490-515.

3. ———, Emotion: I. The neuro-humoral basis of emotional reactions. In C. Murchison (*Ed.*), *Handbook of General Experimental Psychology*, Worcester: Clark Univ. Press, 1934.

4. ———, On emotional expression after decortication, with some remarks on certan theoretical views. Parts I and II, *Psychol. Rev.*, 1934, **41**, 309-329; 424-449.

5. Bard, P., and Mountcastle, V. B., Some forebrain mechanisms involved in expression of rage with special reference to suppression of angry behavior, *Res. Publ. Assn. Nerv. Ment. Dis.*, 1947, **27**, 362-404.

6. Bard, P., and Rioch, D. McK., A study of four cats deprived of neocortex and additional portions of the forebrain, *Johns Hopk. Hosp. Bull.*, 1937, **60**, 73-147.

7. Bazett, H. C., and Penfield, W. G., A study of the Sherrington Decerebrate animal in the chronic as well as the acute condition, *Brain*, 1922, **45**, 185-265.

8. Brady, J. V., The effect of electro-convulsive shock on a conditioned emotional response: The permanence of the effect, *J. Comp. and Physiol. Psychol.*, 1951, **44**, 507-511.

9. ———, The effect of electro-convlusive shock on a conditioned emotional response: the significance of the interval between the emotional conditioning and the electro-convulsive shock, *J. Comp. and Physiol. Psychol.*, 1952, **45**, 9-13.

10. Brady, J. V., and Hunt, H. F., The effect of electroconvulsive shock on conditioned emotional response: A control for impaired hearing, *J. Comp. and Physiol. Psychol.*, 1952, **45**, 180-182.

11. Brady, J. V., Extinction of a conditioned "fear" response as a function of reinforcement schedules for competing behavior, *J. of Psychol.*, 1955, **40**, 25-34.

12. Brady, J. V., and Hunt, H. F., A further demonstration of the effects of electro-convulsive shock on a conditioned emotional response, *J. Comp. and Physiol. Psychol.*, 1951, **44**, 204-209.

13. Brady, J. V., Hunt, H. F., and Geller, I., The effect of electroconvulsive shock on a conditioned emotional response as a function of the temporal distribution of the

treatments, *J. Comp. and Physiol. Psychol.*, 1954, **47**, 454-457.

14. BRADY, J. V., and NAUTA, W. J. H., Subcortical mechanisms in emotional behavior: Affective changes following septal forebrain lesions in the albino rat, *J. Comp. and Physiol. Psychol.*, 1953, **46**, 339-346.

15. ———, Subcortical mechanisms in emotional behavior: The duration of affective changes following septal and habenular lesions in the albino rat, *J. Comp. and Physiol. Psychol.*, 1955, **48**, 412-420.

16. BRADY, J. V., SCHREINER, L., GELLER, I., and KLING, A., Subcortical mechanisms in emotional behavior: The effect of rhinencephalic injury upon the acquisition and retention of a conditioned avoidance response in cats, *J. Comp. and Physiol. Psychol.*, 1954, **47**, 179-186.

17. BRADY, J. V., STEBBINS, W. C., and GALAMBOS, R., The effect of audiogenic convulsions on a conditioned emotional response, *J. Comp. and Physiol. Psychol.*, 1953, **46**, 363-367.

18. BRADY, J. V., STEBBINS, W. C., and HUNT, H. F., The effect of electro-convulsive shock (ECS) on a conditioned emotional response: The effect of additional ECS convulsions, *J. Comp. and Physiol. Psychol.*, 1953, **46**, 368-372.

19. BUCY, P. C., and KLÜVER, H., Anatomic changes secondary to temporal lobectomy, *Arch. Neurol. and Psychiat.*, 1940, **44**, 1142-1146.

20. CANNON, W. B. and BRITTON, S. W., Studies on the conditions of activity in endocrine glands: XV. Pseudoaffective medulliadrenal secretion, *Amer. J. Physiol.*, 1925, **72**, 285-294.

21. DUSSER DE BARRENNE, J. G., Recherches experimentales sur les functions du systeme nerveux central, faites en particulier sur deux chat dont le neopallium avait été enleve, *Arch. Neerl. Physiol.*, 1920, **4**, 31-123.

22. ESTES, W. K., and SKINNER, B. F., Some quantitative properties of anxiety, *J. Exp. Psychol.*, 1941, **29**, 390-400.

23. FINGER, F., Convulsive behavior in the rat, *Psychol. Bull.*, 1947, **44**, 201-248.

24. GELLER, I., SIDMAN, M., and BRADY, J. V., The effect of electro-convulsive shock on a conditioned emotional response: A control for acquisition recency, *J. Comp. and Physiol. Psychol.*, 1955, **48**, 130-131.

25. GOLZ, F., Der Hund ohne Grosshirn, *Arch. ges. Physiol.*, 1892, **51**, 570-614.

26. GOY, R. W., The effect of electro-convulsive shock on conditioned emotional response: The relation between the amount of attenuation and the strength of the condi-

tioned emotional response. Unpublished Ph.D. dissertation, Univ. Chicago, 1953.

27. Goy, R. W., and Hunt, H. F., The resistance of an instrumental response to suppression by conditioned fear, *Amer. Psychol.*, 1953, **8**, 509.

28. Heistad, G. T., Some effects of electroconvulsive shock on a conditioned avoidance response. Unpublished Ph.D. dissertation, Univ. Chicago, 1954.

29. Hunt, H. F., and Brady, J. V., Some effects of electroconvulsive shock on a conditioned emotional response ("Anxiety"), *J. Comp. and Physiol. Psychol.*, 1951, **44**, 88-98.

30. ———, Some quantitative differences between "anxiety" and "punishment" conditioning, *Amer. Psychol.*, 1951, **6**, 276-277.

31. Hunt, H. F., Jernberg, P., and Brady, J. V., The effect of electro-convulsive shock (ECS) on a conditioned emotional response: The effect of post-ECS extinction on the reappearance of the response, *J. Comp. and Physiol. Psychol.*, 1952, **45**, 589-599.

32. Hunt, H. F., Jernberg, P., and Lawlor, W. G., The effect of electro-convulsive shock on a conditioned emotional response: The effect of electro-convulsive shock under ether anesthesia., *J. Comp. and Physiol. Psychol.*, 1953, **46**, 64-68.

33. Hunt, H. F., Jernberg, P., and Otis, L., The effect of carbon disulphide convulsions on a conditioned emotional response, *J. Comp. and Physiol. Psychol.*, 1953, **46**, 465-469.

34. Ingram, W. R., Barris, R. W., and Ranson, S. W., Catalepsy: An experimental study, *Arch. Neurol. and Psychiat.*, 1936, **35**, 1175-1197.

35. Keller, A. D., Autonomic discharges elicited by physiological stimuli in midbrain preparations, *Amer. J. Physiol.*, 1932, **100**, 576-586.

36. Klüver, H., and Bucy, P. C., An analysis of certain effects of bilateral temporal lobectomy in the Rhesus monkey, with special reference to "psychic blindness," *J. of Psychol.*, 1938, **5**, 33-54.

37. ———, Preliminary analysis of functions of the temporal lobes in monkeys, *Arch. Neuro. and Psychiat.*, 1939, **42**, 979-1000.

38. Krieg, W. J. S., Personal communication to W. E. Le Gros Clark. In *The Hypothalamus*. London: Oliver & Boyd, 1938.

39. MacLean, P. D., Psychosomatic disease and the "visceral brain," *Psychosom. Med.*, 1949, **11**, 338-353.

40. MILLER, N. E., Learnable drives and rewards. In S. S. Stevens (Ed.), Handbook of Experimental Psychology. New York: Wiley, 1951.

41. NAUTA, W. J. H., An experimental study of the fornix system in the rat, J. Comp. Neurol. 1956, 104, 247-271.

42. PAPEZ, J. W. A., A proposed mechanism of emotion, Arch. Neurol. and Psychiat., 1937, 38, 725-743.

43. RIOCH, D. McK., Certain aspects of the behavior of decorticate cats, Psychiatry, 1938, 1, 339-345.

44. ROTHMANN, H., Zusammenfassender Bericht uber den Rothmannschen grosshirnlosen Hund nach klinischer und anatonischer Untersuchung. J. ges. Neurol. Psychiat., 1923, 87, 247-313.

45. SCHALTENBRAND, G., and COBB, S., Clinical and anatomical studies on two cats without neocortex, Brain, 1930, 53, 449-488.

46. SCHOENFELD, W. N., An experimental approach to anxiety, escape, and avoidance behavior. In P. H. Hoch and J. Zubin (Eds.). Anxiety. New York: Grune & Stratton, 1950.

47. SCHREINER, L., and KLING, A., Behavioral changes following rhinencephalic injury in the cat, J. Neurophysiol., 1953, 16, 643-659.

48. SCHREINER, L., RIOCH, D. McK., MASSERMAN, J., and PECHTEL, C., Behavioral changes following thalamic injury in the cat, J. Neurophysiol., 1953, 16, 234-246.

49. SIDMAN, M., Avoidance conditioning with brief shock and no extereoceptive "warning signal," Science, 1953, 118, 157-158.

50. ———, Two temporal parameters of the maintenance of avoidance behavior by the white rat, J. Comp. and Physiol. Psychol., 1953, 46, 253-261.

51. SPEIGEL, E. A., MILLER, H. R., and OPPENHEIMER, M. J., Forebrain and rage reactions, J. Neurophysiol., 1940, 3, 538-548.

52. STAINBROOK, E., The effect of electrically induced convulsions on animal behavior, J. Person., 1948, 17, 2-8.

53. WHEATLEY, M. D., The hypothalamus and affective behavior in cats: A study of the effects of experimental lesions, with anatomic correlations. Arch. Neurol. and Psychiat., 1944, 52, 296-316.

54. WOODWORTH, R. S., and SHERRINGTON, C. S., A pseudo-affective reflex and its spinal path, J. Physiol., 1904, 31, 234-243.

Part IV
Additional Readings

Additional Readings

The following sources have been chosen from those not necessarily included among the references to the papers in this book of readings in order to guide the reader further in the study of emotion. The references have been chosen for their relevance, recency and accessibility. No attempt has been made to provide the reader with a complete list of sources. The articles are listed under the section titles of this book and a "general" category has been included.

I. PROBLEMS AND THEORY

BARD, P., The neurohumoral basis of emotional reactions. In C. A. Murchison (Ed.). *Handbook of General Experimental Psychology.* Worcester: Clark Press, 1934.

————, On emotional expression after decortication with some remarks on certain theoretical views, Parts I and II, *Psychol. Rev.,* 1934, **41**, 309-329, 424-449.

————, Central nervous mechanisms for the expression of anger. In M. L. Reymert (Ed.). *The Second International Symposium on Feelings and Emotions.* New York: McGraw-Hill, 1950.

BRIDGES, K. M. B., A genetic theory of emotions, *Ped. Sem. and J. genet. Psychol.,* 1930, **37**, 514-527.

BROWN, J. F., The methods of Kurt Lewin in the psychology of action and affection, *Psychol. Rev.,* 1929, **36**, 200-221.

BULL, NINA, The attitude theory of emotion, *Nerv. and Ment. Dis. Mono.* New York, 1951.

CANNON, W. B., The James-Lange theory of emotions: A critical examination and an alternative theory, *Amer. J. Psychol.,* 1927, **39**, 106-124.

————. *Bodily Changes in Pain, Hunger, Fear and Rage.* New York: Appleton, 1929.

————, Again the James-Lange and the thalamic theories of emotion, *Psychol. Rev.,* 1931, **38**, 281-295.

DARWIN, C. *The Expression of the Emotions in Man and Animals.* London: Murray, 1904.

DUFFY, ELIZABETH, Emotion: An example of the need for reorientation in psychology, *Psychol. Rev.,* 1934, **41**, 184-198.

————, Leeper's "motivational theory of emotions." *Psychol. Rev.*, 1948, **55**, 324-328.

————, The psychological significance of the concept of "arousal" or "activation," *Psychol. Rev.*, 1957, **64**, 265-275.

DUNBAR, HELEN F. *Emotions and Bodily Changes* (4th ed.). New York: Columbia Univ. Press, 1954.

GARDINER, H. N., METCALF, R. C., and BEEBE-CENTER, J. G. *Feelings and Emotion: a History of Theories.* New York: American, 1937.

GOLDSTEIN, K., On emotions: considerations from the organismic point of view, *J. of Psychol.*, 1951, **31**, 37-49.

HEBB, D. O., Emotion in man and animal: an analysis of the intuitive processes of recognition, *Psychol. Rev.*, 1946, **53**, 88-106.

LEEPER, R. W., A motivational theory of emotion to replace "emotion as disorganized response," *Psychol. Rev.*, 1948, **55**, 5-21.

LURIA, A. R. *The Nature of Human Conflict or Emotion, Conflict and Will* (W. H. Gannt, trans.). New York: Liveright, 1932.

MACLEAN, P. D., Psychosomatic disease and the "visceral brain:" Recent developments bearing on the Papez' theory of emotion, *Psychosom. Med.*, 1949, **11**, 338-353.

NEWMAN, E. B., PERKINS, F. T., and WHEELER, R. H., Cannon's theory of emotion: a critique, *Psychol. Rev.*, 1930, **37**, 305-326.

PAPEZ, J. W., The brain considered as an organ: neural systems and central levels of organization, *Amer. J. Psychol.*, 1937, **49**, 217-232.

————, A proposed mechanism of emotion, *Arch. Neurol. Psychiat.*, Chicago, 1937, **38**, 725-743.

RAPAPORT, D. *Emotions and Memory.* New York: International Universities Press, 1950.

SCHLOSBERG, H., Three dimensions of emotion, *Psychol. Rev.*, 1954, **61**, 81-88.

TOLMAN, E. C., A behavioristic account of the emotions, *Psychol. Rev.*, 1923, **30**, 217-227.

WEBB, W. B., A motivational theory of emotions . . . *Psychol. Rev.*, 1948, **55**, 329-335.

WENGER, M. A., Emotion as visceral action: an extension of Lange's theory. In Reymert (Ed.). *The Second International Symposium on Feelings and Emotions.* New York: McGraw-Hill, 1950.

YOUNG, P. T. *Emotion in Man and Animal.* New York: Wiley, 1943.

————, Emotion as disorganized response—a reply to Professor Leeper, *Psychol. Rev.*, 1949, **56**, 184-191.

————, The role of hedonic processes in the organization of behavior, *Psychol. Rev.*, 1952, **59**, 249-262.

————. *Motivation and Emotion: a Survey of Determinants of Human and Animal Activity*. New York: Wiley, 1961.

II. METHODS AND TECHNIQUES

DAVIS, R. C., Methods of measuring and recording action. In T. G. Andrews (Ed.). *Methods of Psychology*. New York: Wiley, 1948.

LINDSLEY, D. B., Emotion. In S. S. Stevens (Ed.). *Handbook of Experimental Psychology*. New York: Wiley, 1951.

The "Apparatus" section of the *American Journal of Psychology* has contained descriptions of apparatus for use in studies of emotion for the past several decades.

III. EXPERIMENTAL FINDINGS AND OBSERVATIONS

ADER, R., TATUM, R., and BEELS, C. C., Social factors affecting emotionality and resistance to disease in animals. I. Age of separation from the mother and susceptibility to gastric ulcers in the rat, *J. comp. physiol. Psychol.*, 1960, **53**, 446-454.

ADER, R., BEELS, C. C., and TATUM, R., Social factors affecting emotionality and resistance to disease in animals. II. Susceptibility to gastric ulceration as a function of interruptions of social interactions and the time at which they occur, *J. comp. physiol. Psychol.*, 1960, **53**, 455-458.

BARD, P., and MONTCASTLE, V. B., Some forebrain mechanisms involved in expression of rage with special reference to suppression of angry behavior, *Res. Publ. Ass. Nerv. Ment. Dis.*, 1947, **27**, 362-404.

BARON, M. R., and CONNER, J. P., Eyelid conditioned responses with various levels of anxiety, *J. exp. Psychol.*, 1960, **60**, 310-313.

BEEBE-CENTER, J. G., and STEVENS, S. S., Cardiac acceleration in emotional situations, *J. exp. Psychol.*, 1937, **21**, 72-87.

BINDRA, D., and THOMPSON, W. R., An evaluation of defecation and urination as measures of fearfulness, *J. comp. physiol. Psychol.*, 1953, **46**, 43-45.

BRADY, J. V., Assessment of drug effects on emotional behavior, *Science*, 1956, **123**, 1033.

BRADY, J. V., and CONRAD, D. G., Some effects of limbic system self-stimulation upon conditioned emotional behavior, *J. comp. physiol. Psychol.*, 1960, **53**, 128-37.

BRADY, J. V., and NAUTA, W. J. H., Subcortical mechanisms

in emotional behavior: affective changes following septal forebrain lesions in the albino rat, *J. comp. physiol. Psychol.*, 1953, **46**, 339-346.

BROADHURST, P. L., Determinants of emotionality in the rat. I. Situational factors. *Brit. J. Psychol.*, 1957, **48**, 1-12.

———, Determinants of emotionality in the rat. II. Antecedent factors, *Brit. J. Psychol.*, 1958, **49**, 12-20.

———, Determinants of emotionality in the rat. III. Strain differences, *J. comp. physiol. Psychol.*, 1958, **51**, 55-59.

———, A "Crespi effect" in the analysis of emotionality as a drive in rats, *Brit. J. Psychol.*, 1958, **49**, 56-58.

CAMPBELL, B. A. and CANDLAND, D. K. Effect of prior shock on the emotionality of young rats in an open field. Canad. J. Psychol., 1961, **15**, 1-5.

CHURCH, R. M., Emotional reactions of rats to the pain of others, *J. comp. physiol. Psychol.*, 1959, **52**, 132-134.

COLEMAN, J. C., Facial expressions of emotions, *Psychol. Mono.*, 1949, **63**, No. 1 (Whole no. 296).

DELGADO, J. M. R., ROBERTS, W. W., and MILLER, N. E., Learning motivated by electrical stimulation of the brain, *Amer. J. Physiol.*, 1954, **179**, 587-593.

DELGADO, J. M. R., ROSVOLD, H. E., and LOONEY, E., Evoking conditioned fear by electrical stimulation of subcortical structures in the monkey brain, *J. comp. physiol. Psychol.*, 1956, **49**, 373-380.

GOODENOUGH, FLORENCE L., The expression of the emotions in infancy, *Child Develop.*, 1931, **2**, 96-101.

———, Expression of the emotions in a blind-deaf child, *J. abn. soc. Psychol.*, 1932, **27**, 328-333.

HALL, C. S., Drive and emotion: factors associated with adjustment in the rat, *J. comp. Psychol.*, 1934, **17**, 89-108.

———, Emotional behavior in the rat. I. Defecation and urination as measures of individual differences in emotionality, *J. comp. Psychol.*, 1934, **18**, 385-403.

HUNT, H. F., and OTIS, L. S., Conditioned and unconditioned emotional defecation in the rat, *J. comp. physiol. Psychol.*, 1953, **46**, 378-382.

JONES, H. E., The galvanic skin reflex in infancy, *Child Develop.*, 1930, **1**, 106-110.

KAMIN, L. J., Trace conditioning of the conditioned emotional response, *J. comp. physiol. Psychol.*, 1961, **54**, 149-153.

LANDIS, C., and HUNT, W. A. *The Startle Pattern*. New York: Farrar and Rinehart, 1939.

LEVY, N., and SCHLOSBERG, H., Woodworth Scale values of the Lightfoot pictures of facial expression, *J. exp. Psychol.*, 1960, **60**, 121-125.

MAHER, B. A. and McINTIRE, R. W., The extinction of the

CER following frontal ablation, *J. comp. physiol. Psychol.*, 1960, **53**, 549-552.

MELZACK, R., The genesis of emotional behavior: An experimental study of the dog, *J. comp. physiol. Psychol.*, 1954, **47**, 166-168.

————, The perception of pain, *Scientific American*, 1961, **204**, 41-49.

MILLER, N. E., Studies of fear as an acquirable drive: I. Fear as motivation and fear-reduction as reinforcement in the learning of new responses, *J. exp. Psychol.*, 1948, **38**, 89-101.

————, Learning resistance to pain and fear: effects of overlearning, exposure and rewarded exposure in context, *J. exp. Psychol.*, 1960, **60**, 137-145.

MUNN, N. L. The effect of knowledge of the situation upon judgment of emotion from facial expressions, *J. abn. soc. Psychol.*, 1940, **35**, 324-338.

OLDS, M. E., and OLDS, J., Emotional and associative mechanisms in rat brain, *J. comp. physiol. Psychol.*, 1961, **54**, 120-126.

PATRICK, J. R., Studies in rational behavior and emotional excitement: II. The effect of emotional excitement on rational behavior in human subjects, *J. comp. Psychol.*, 1934, **18**, 153-195.

ROSS, L. E., Conditioned fear as a function of CS-UCS and probe stimulus intervals, *J. exp. Psychol.*, 1961, **61**, 265-273.

ROYCE, J. R. A factorial study of emotionality in the dog, *Psychol. Mono.*, 1955, **69**, No. 407.

SHERMAN, M., The differentiation of emotional responses in infants: I. Judgments of emotional responses from motion picture views and from actual observation, *J. comp. Psychol.*, 1927, **7**, 265-284.

————, The differentiation of emotional responses in infants: II. The ability of observers to judge the emotional characteristics of the crying of infants, and of the voice of an adult, *J. comp. Psychol.*, 1927, **7**, 335-351.

————, The differentiation of emotional responses in infants: III. A proposed theory of the development of emotional responses in infants, *J. comp. Psychol.*, 1928, **8**, 385-394.

SILVERMAN, R. E., Eliminating a conditioned GSR by the reduction of experimental anxiety, *J. exp. Psychol.*, 1960, **59**, 122-125.

SINGH, S. D., Conditioned emotional response in the rat: I. Constitutional and situational determinants, *J. comp. physiol. Psychol.*, 1959, **52**, 574-578.

THOMPSON, J., Development of facial expression of emotion in blind and seeing children, *Arch. Psychol. N. Y.*, No. 264, 1941.

WATSON, J. B., and RAYNER, R., Conditioned emotional reactions, *J. exp. Psychol.*, 1920, **3**, 1-14.

WILLINGHAM, W. W., The organization of emotional behavior in mice, *J. comp. physiol. Psychol.*, 1956, **49**, 345-348.

IV. GENERAL

ANDERSON, J. E., Changes in emotional responses with age. In M. L. Reymert (Ed.). *Feelings and Emotions:* the Moosehart symposium in cooperation with the University of Chicago. New York: McGraw-Hill, 1950.

ARNOLD, MAGNA B. *Emotion and Personality*. Vol. I: *Psychological Aspects*. Vol. II: *Neurological and Psychological Aspects*. New York: Columbia Univ. Press, 1960.

BEEBE-CENTER, J. G., Feeling and emotion. In Helson (Ed.). *Theoretical Foundations of Psychology*. New York: Van Nostrand, 1951.

FRANK, L. K. *Feelings and Emotions:* New York: Doubleday, 1954.

JERSILD, A. T., Emotional development. In C. E. Skinner (Ed.). *Educational Psychology* (3rd ed.). New York: Prentice-Hall, 1951.

JERSILD, A. T., Emotional development. In L. Charmichael (Ed.). *Manual of Child Psychology* (2nd ed.). New York: Wiley, 1954.

JONES, MARY COVER, Emotional development. In C. A. Murchison (Ed.). *A Handbook of Child Psychology* (2nd ed. rev.). Worcester: Clark Univ. Press, 1933.

INBAU, F. E. *Lie Detection and Criminal Investigation*. Baltimore: Williams & Wilkins, 1942.

LONDON, I. D., The treatment of emotions in contemporary Soviet psychology, *J. gen. Psychol.*, 1949, **41**, 89-100.

LUND, F. H. *Emotions: Their Psychological, Physiological and Educative Implications*. New York: Ronald, 1939.

McCLEARY, R. A., On the nature of the galvanic skin response, *Psychol. Bull.*, 1950, **47**, 97-117.

McGINNIES, E., Emotionality and perceptual defense, *Psychol. Rev.*, 1949, **56**, 244-251.

MARTIN, B., The assessment of anxiety by physiological behavioral measures, *Psychol. Bull.*, 1961, **58**, 234-255.

MASSERMAN, J. H., Is the hypothalamus a center of emotion? *Psychosom. Med.*, 1941, **3**, 3-25.

REYMERT, M. L. (Ed.). *Feelings and Emotions:* the Moosehart symposium in cooperation with the University of Chicago. New York: McGraw-Hill, 1950.

RUCKMICK, C. A. *The Psychology of Feeling and Emotion.* New York: McGraw-Hill, 1936.

SAUL, L. J., Physiological effects of emotional tension. In J. McV. Hunt (Ed.). *Personality and the Behavior Disorders.* New York: Ronald, 1944, Vol. 1.

SIMON, A., HERBERT, C. C., and STRAUS, RUTH. *The Physiology of Emotions.* Springfield, Ill.: Thomas, 1961.

Index

Ablation, 78-83, 241-243
  and hypothalamus, 78, 80, 241
Adrenalin (*see also* nor-Adrenalin), 31, 189, 209-210, 213, 216-217
Affective, experience, 61
  judgment, 64
Alarm reaction (AR), 189
Albert, case of, 92-93
Allport-Vernon scale, 70
Anxiety, 241, 243-244
  conscious and unconscious, 170-186
  free-floating, 52
  level, 182-183
Apparatus, 61, 63, 68-69, 80-82
Aristotle, 5
Ataximeter, 69
Attention-rejection axis, 222
Attitudes, 70
Automatograph, 70
Autonomic nervous system, 7, 8, 170-186
Avoidance, as conditioned response, 172
  of dead bodies, 148-150
  of electric shock, 170-186, 201-205
  of strangers, 155-156
Ax, A. F., 217
Axes, in facial expressions, 222

Bard, P., 7
Behaviorism, 17-21, 68, 91
Beaumont, W., 205

Cannon, W. B., 7, 25, 71-72, 208, 209, 210, 219
Cannon-Bard theory, 7, 71-72, 208
Carr, H. A., theory of, 64
Cattell, R. B., 70-71
Conditioned emotional response (CER), 17-21, 236-246
  functional properties of, 243-246
Conditioning, 17-21, 80, 91-99, 170-186
  unconscious, 173
Culler, E. A., 78-79

Darwin, C., 45, 78, 83
Decortication (decerebration), 78-79, 151, 159
Delight, in infants, 115-122
Desoxycorticosterone (DCA), 190, 193-195
Distress, in infants, 105-115
Duffy, E., 35
Dynamometer, 69

Electroencephalograph, 69, 75
Electro-convulsive shock (ECS), 238-240
Emotion, biological advantages of, 45-50
  bodily change in, 6-7, 11-16
  recording of, 72-75
  conditioning of, 21, 91-99, 170-186
  in chimpanzees, 139-169
  classification of, 16
  use of concept, 22
  as conscious experience, 6, 29-33
  discriminatory behavior, 33
  disorganized response, 28-29, 53-54
  electro-convulsive shock and, 238-240
  endocrine system and, 208-219
  facial expressions and, 83, 220-234
  in infants, 100-125
  inherited (rats), 128-129

as mental event, 7
and motivation, 6, 27, 32, 39, 44-45
and perceptual processes, 6-7, 11, 50-53
surgical methods in, 78-83
in the rat, 126-137
as reflex pattern, 72
as unconscious conditioning, 173
views of, 5-7
as visceral action, 5-6
Endocrine system, influence of, 208-219
stress and, 187-196
Energy level, 25, 26, 29, 33
Ergograph, 69
Excitement, in infants, 102-105
Expression, in facial expression, 220-234
methods of, 67-69
and social expression, 83-85

Facial expressions, 220-234
Factor analysis, use of, 70-71
Fear, of cats and snakes, by rats, 132-134
in chimpanzees, 139-169
conditioned, 17-21
development of, in children, 19-21
as drive, in rats, 134-136
nature of, 139-169
and rage, 164-165
sensory and central factors in, 164-165
spontaneity of, in chimpanzees, 147-148
of strangers, by chimpanzees, 153
Fechner, G. T., 65
Feedback, negative (reverse), 48
positive, 48
Freud, S., 208, 219

Galvanic Skin Response (GSR), 8, 69, 74
General Adaptation Syndrome (GAS), 192, 195-196

Generalization, 173
conscious and unconscious compared, 177-182
Gestalt, 152
Green, A., 235

Horsley-Clarke apparatus, 80-82
Hunger, compared to emotion, 35-39
Hypothalamus, 6, 7, 79-83, 150-151, 241

Impression, methods of, 65-67
Introspection, 58

James, W., 6, 7, 11, 23
theory of emotion, 11
Jones, Mary Cover, 17, 100

Lacey, J. I., 235
Lange, C., 6, 11, 16
Leeper, R. W., 35, 170
"Lie" Detecting, 72
Likes and dislikes, 59-61

Masserman, J. H., 79-80, 83
Microphone, 69
Mecholyl, 211, 213, 215
Methods, of choice, 65
of expression, 65
of impression, 65
of merit, 65
of paired comparisons, 66
of percentage of pleasantness, 67
of single exposure, 66

Nafe, J. P., 58
Neurosis, 4
nor-Adrenalin, 210, 213, 215-217
in children, 219

Peter, case of, 91-99
Phase, in Hebb's theory, 156-157
Pituitary, 191
Plato, 5
Pleasantness (and unpleasantness), 58-59

as axis in facial expression, 222

in Carr's theory, 64-65

Plethysmograph, 68

Pneumograph, 69, 73, 75

Polish, E., 205, 206

Psychosis, 4

Preference behavior, 61-64

Psychosomatic disorders, 4, 198

Rage, relation to fear, 164-165

Selye, H., 187-189

Shackleton, Sir Ernest, 35, 38

Sham-rage (sham-emotion), 6, 78-79

Smith, R. L., 235

Sphygmograph, 68

Sphygmomanometer, 68-69

Startle pattern, 76-78

Stress, and endocrine system, 191-197

and ulcers, 198-207

students and, 216

Sympathetic nervous system, 9

Temperament (rat), 126-132

Tests, 70-71, 211

Tremograph, 69-73

Ulcer, 4, 198

Voice Key, 69

Watson, J. B., 68, 91-94, 100, 149, 170

theory of, 17-21

Wolff, H. G., 205, 210, 211

Wolf, S. G., 205

Young, P. T., 35, 57